D1152223

*C**hoosing with Care*

THE REPORT OF THE COMMITTEE OF INQUIRY INTO THE SELECTION,
DEVELOPMENT AND MANAGEMENT OF STAFF IN CHILDREN'S HOMES

London : HMSO

1698732

CONTENTS

CHAPTER 1:   OUR APPROACH AND CONCERNS

"Children wish for so much but can arrange so little of their own lives which are so often dominated by adults without sympathy for the children's priorities"

Bruno Bettelheim, Recollections and Reflections, 1990

Our Approach

1.1   The establishment of this inquiry was announced on 29 November 1991 by the then Secretary of State for Health following the trial and conviction of Frank Beck at Leicester Crown Court for numerous sexual and other offences against young people in a local authority children's home. The full membership of the Committee of Inquiry (see Appendix 1) was announced on 31 January 1992 and we started work in early February.

1.2   Our terms of reference were:

"To examine selection and recruitment methods and criteria for staff working in children's homes and recommend practicable improvements; to make such further examination as the Committee may consider justified of management and other issues relevant to the protection of children and young people and to the support and guidance of staff in such homes; and to report with recommendations to the Secretary of State for Health".

1.3   We have concentrated on the recruitment, selection and appointment of staff in children's homes. However, we have paid considerable attention to a closely related issue in our terms of reference - the management of homes, including appraisal, supervision and staff development. Part of our terms of reference was concerned with the support of staff and we have devoted much time to this issue. Our remit was concerned with the protection of children. Because children's homes are often regarded as closed institutions we have examined as part of the management arrangements the overall system of checks and balances that ensure external contact and involvement with homes and the ability of children to make their concerns known outside homes. Lastly we have explored some issues relating to the national framework of policy, standards and planning because these govern the total environment within which individual staff and homes operate. The linkage of all these issues in the protection of children has made it impossible to interpret our terms of reference in a narrow way.

1.4   We have regarded the term "children's home" as meaning homes run by a local authority, voluntary organisation or private individual or organisation that provides residential care (including secure accommodation) for children under the age of 18 -

although our survey suggests that some young people stay in these homes until their twenties. There are over 11,000 children in the homes covered by this inquiry, including about 300 in secure accommodation provided in accordance with section 25 of the Children Act 1989. We have not examined the situation in family centres (which may have a few residential beds); Youth Treatment Centres (which accommodate very few young people, and which have been reviewed recently by the Social Services Inspectorate); youth penal establishments; or boarding schools. We consider that some of our recommendations have implications for such establishments, which often have similarities to children's homes.

1.5   In conducting this inquiry we have obtained information and views by a variety of means:

- We have considered numerous publications, including reports of eight other inquiries.

- We have obtained written evidence from some 52 organisations and individuals and met with a number of other organisations: Their names are shown in Appendix 2.

- We have visited 10 local authority areas in different parts of England for discussions with Chief Executives, Personnel Directors and Directors of Social Services and their staff. During these visits we have visited local authority and independent sector homes and discussed issues separately with staff and children. The local authorities visited are listed in Appendix 2.

- We commissioned Price Waterhouse to conduct the first comprehensive national survey of the characteristics, staffing and employment practices in local authority and independent sector children's homes. Their findings are summarised in Appendix 3.

- We have obtained written and oral evidence from three Government Departments - the Home Office, the Department of Health and the Department for Education, together with written evidence from the Crown Prosecution Service.

- We have visited Scotland, Wales, Northern Ireland and the Netherlands for discussions on the staffing and management of children's homes with Government officials, Social Services managers and staff and voluntary organisations.

- We consulted the European Children's Centre at the National Children's Bureau on children's residential care in Europe.

- We conducted two whole-day seminars with many of those who had submitted written evidence to test out our emerging ideas in terms of viability and acceptability.

We are extremely grateful to those who gave us information, views and time.

1.6   To expedite our work we have operated for part of the time in smaller working groups tackling particular issues. However, all our findings and recommendations have been discussed fully by the Committee as a whole, and all the recommendations are supported unanimously by the members of the Inquiry.

1.7   We are indebted to our Secretary, Mark Davies, whose hard work, analytical skills and good humour have been invaluable in the preparation of this report. Without his efforts we would not have completed our work so quickly.

Other Inquiries

1.8   There have been many reports and inquiries into aspects of residential care for children, some of which go back to the 1950s. We have not attempted to undertake a full-scale historical analysis of all these. Instead we have concentrated on examining eight inquiries from the 1980s and early 1990s. Four of these were of a general nature:

- Residential Care - A Positive Choice. Report of the Independent Review of Residential Care chaired by Lady Wagner, published in 1987.

- Children in the Public Care. A Review of Residential Child Care by Sir William Utting, published in 1991.

- Accommodating Children. A Review of Children's Homes in Wales by the Social Services Inspectorate of the Welsh Office, published in 1992.

- The Quality of Care. A Report of the Residential Staffs Inquiry chaired by Lady Howe, published in 1992.

Three were inquiries into serious misconduct and unsatisfactory events in particular children's homes:

- The Leeways Report. This was an Inquiry set up by the London Borough of Lewisham and chaired by Elizabeth Lawson QC, whose report was published in 1985.

- The Pindown Experience and the Protection of Children. Report of the Staffordshire child care inquiry by Allan Levy QC and Barbara Kahan, published in 1990.

- Ty Mawr Community Home Inquiry. Report of the Inquiry by Gareth Williams QC and Mr John McCreadie, published in 1992.

We considered also the report of the Committee of Inquiry into Children's Homes and Hostels, chaired by His Honour Judge Hughes. This inquiry was a mixture of particular homes and overall concerns, following the exposure of a series of scandals in Kincora Boys Hostel and other boy's hostels and homes in Northern Ireland. The Report was published in December 1985.

1.9   We are aware that Andrew Kirkwood QC will be producing a report on events in Leicestershire following the conviction of Frank Beck and his colleagues but we have not had access to his findings. While we were at work grave concerns about incidents in children's homes in North Wales and elsewhere were the subject of other investigations.

1.10   There are many features of these other inquiries that are directly relevant to our own work and to which we wish to draw attention. They illustrate some deep-seated problems with the management of children's homes that will not be resolved by the simple expedient of establishing a Committee of Inquiry. We will return to the issue of changing the culture and environment of children's residential care in Chapter 10. But first the evidence from other inquiries.

1.11   <u>The Leeways Report</u> related to an officer in charge of a children's home who was convicted of various offences involving indecent photography of young children. The principal conclusions of the report showed that for six years or so the officer in charge's "immediate superiors were aware of unacceptable behaviour in a head of home which had sexual implications" but failed to tackle the officer about the concerns. They also found that "at almost every point at which collectively or individually the people involved had to choose between making the welfare of the child the first consideration, and some conflicting loyalty or priority, they chose the latter". The report's recommendations strike many chords with our own thinking. It wanted people in management positions to be held to account for how they carry out their responsibilities. All employees should be given clear job descriptions. "The progress and performance of staff should be regularly monitored and assessed and they should be confronted with any criticisms". "Management should accept that it has a duty to provide proper opportunities for staff training and development". "Those interviewing for jobs in child care should be permitted to ask questions directed towards a candidate's suitability for such employment". We come back to many of these issues in our own analysis and recommendations.

1.12   <u>The Staffordshire Pindown Inquiry</u> in 1991 revealed unacceptable practices in a local authority's children's homes for exercising control over children by depriving them of their liberty and using a regime of social isolation. The recommendations included unannounced visits to homes by Statutory Visitors; improved procedures with the police for checking on possible sex offenders; Government Departments extending the arrangements for providing employing authorities with information on criminal backgrounds. There were several recommendations on the staffing and management of children's homes. Precise job descriptions should be provided for professional posts; homes should have written statements on their agreed roles; a "systematic monitoring and evaluation system should be introduced"; "more posts should be advertised nationally, and in particular senior and managerial appointments"; "there should be an agreed staff recruitment policy to attract senior and managerial appointments"; communication between homes and senior management should be improved; as a matter of urgency "a system of supervision" should be installed; and a five-year strategy for training staff should be developed. The inquiry report also drew attention to the inadequate support for staff in homes and recommended that "residential homes advisers with appropriate experience and training be appointed to provide professional support to residential care staff". We found many of the concerns expressed in relation to Staffordshire to have a wider application and we return to them later in this report.

1.13   <u>The Hughes Report on the Kincora "scandals"</u> was concerned with homosexual acts and prostitution in nine boys homes and hostels in Northern Ireland. It dealt with altogether more serious and politically controversial issues than the other inquiries we mention, with allegations of an official 'cover-up' and linkage with loyalist para-military organisations. Nevertheless its 56 recommendations included many which are relevant to our own inquiry. "Training profiles should be maintained" for staff and managers; "a staff appraisal scheme should be introduced"; regular staff meetings should be an integral part of homes' management; and each home should have "a statement of aims and objectives". The report made it clear that anti-discrimination legislation should not prevent a policy of recruiting both male and female staff in homes. More emphasis should be given to making heads of homes and other staff professionally qualified; and this has been a major plank of the Northern Ireland Department of Health's response to the Hughes report. Parity of pay (and by implication status) between residential care staff and field social work should be established. The report also raised the issue of personality and psychological tests in the selection of staff; and we have given much thought to this aspect. The inquiry proposed a variety of changes for giving more emphasis to independent and unannounced visits to homes; and more regular monitoring of homes (including their records) by off-site managers. (A chain of monitoring linking individual homes to the Social Services Inspectorate at Province level has been established as a result.) Complaints procedures were to be strengthened, with the police being brought in at an early stage where there were criminal allegations. Our own inquiry suggests that many of these ideas are not being applied in English children's homes at present.

1.14   The Report of the Williams Inquiry on Ty Mawr Community home in Gwent was published towards the end of our inquiry. The report reviewed a number of incidents of suicide and self-harm and concluded that the home should close as soon as possible. The report said that the Social Services Department must take the blame for the home's failings; and that "there should never in future be an institution....with such an inappropriate mix of residents cared for in large measure by unqualified staff". The report is critical of the Social Services senior management and the role of elected members in appointing staff and recommended that the local authority should "care for its own employees".

1.15   The Wagner Report on Residential Care was concerned with residential provision for all adult groups as well as children. Its recommendations were also less concerned with some of the more detailed staffing and management issues which we have addressed. However, there are several recommendations that are very relevant, particularly those relating to individual rights. These include giving children information about agency complaints procedures; giving children in residential care access to an independent advocate; and not requiring anyone to share a bedroom with another person. (Giving difficult teenagers insufficient personal space and privacy can only make control issues for staff more difficult, and is a matter we return to later in the report.) The Wagner Report wanted every establishment to be required to draw up a staff training plan, and for this to be subject to registration and inspection procedures. The report's central message that entry into residential care should be "a positive choice" is one that we regard as crucial to securing changes of the kind we advocate.

1.16   The 1991 Utting Report on "Children in The Public Care" has been an invaluable source for this inquiry. There are many similarities between that report's recommendations and our own. We share that report's concern that more needs to be done by co-operative working by the agencies concerned to meet the health, educational, employment, leisure and housing needs of children in and leaving residential care. In particular Utting identifies a need for better psychological and psychiatric support for children in residential care that chimes with our own findings. We have elaborated on that report's emphasis on improved management of homes; and share its concern to improve the inspection and regulatory framework within which children's homes should operate. We have picked up the Utting Report's approach to stronger and more integrated guidance from Central Government; greater emphasis on monitoring; and wish for a more coherent approach to planning children's services with the role of residential care more clearly identified within the total framework. We share the Utting Report's concern with securing more professionally qualified staff to run children's homes and to work in them; and to have a training strategy for delivering this that is agreed by all parties involved. Our only reservation relates to the emphasis on social work qualifications; and we explain our arguments on this aspect in Chapter 7.

1.17   The 1991 Review of Children's Homes in Wales, "Accommodating Children" has some interesting ideas. The recommendations on complaints, monitoring and evaluation, good practice and the need for a strategy for residential care are very much in line with our own thinking. The report gives proper emphasis to the design and location of buildings; and not forcing children in residential care to share rooms. The report's major recommendation is that there should be two types of children's homes with "children who are displaying seriously challenging behaviour" being placed in homes separate from children who are in residential care "as a result of circumstances rather than behaviour". We consider this further in Chapter 9.

1.18   The recent Howe Report on Residential Staff, like the Wagner Report, is concerned with staff in adult residential care homes as well as those working in children's homes. We welcome its central emphasis on improving the status, morale, pay, conditions of service and training in residential care. The thrust of its staffing and management recommendations, although broader in scope than ours, are pointing in the same direction (eg., more devolution of responsibility to homes; more emphasis on supervision and training; better support for staff in stressful environments; systematic management training; improved career development opportunities for staff). We welcome the report's support for the new system of National Vocational Qualifications (NVQ) as a means of building towards a better trained and more professionally qualified workforce in residential care. There is also a clear recognition that, as currently constituted, the Diploma in Social Work does not adequately meet the needs of staff in residential care, and this reflects our own concerns. We are very supportive of the broad thrust of the Howe Report, although inevitably we have a more detailed focus on children's homes rather than the generality of residential care.

1.19   We are concerned that there have been so many Inquiries whose findings seem to have gone largely unheeded by the service as a whole.

Our Concerns

1.20   We have not cited these other inquiry reports just to show that we have done our homework. They reflect a growing volume of disquiet with how children's homes are run but also emerging agreement on what needs to be done to put things right. We have been impressed by a sense of resolve in some places - by employers, managers and staff - to try to improve the quality of service in children's homes. We have drawn upon examples of good practice that we have seen in framing our recommendations. However, there is still a long way to go in many parts of the country, and there are still far too many examples of poor or inattentive management. Too many unqualified, and sometimes ineffective, residential staff are left inadequately trained, supervised and managed to deal with some of the most difficult children in our society. It is not surprising that things go wrong and that deeply disturbing events occur. What may be surprising is that disquieting incidents are not revealed more often.

1.21   It is not just a matter of individual employers and managers failing children in particular homes. Society as a whole has shown considerable indifference to the position of children in residential care. There is a tendency to disbelieve that abuse can occur in residential institutions that are assumed to provide higher standards of care than those families from which children have been removed. Until recently there has been less interest in regulating this sector than in inspecting and regulating the adult sector of residential care. National and Local Government has shown a lack of interest in defining the role and purpose of children's homes or in obtaining information about how the sector was changing. Among social work professionals there have been too few champions of children's homes. Too often the profession has seen children's homes as "a necessary evil" - as one current Director of Social Services represented his views to us. It is against this background that children's homes have too often been a backwater neglected by politicians, managers and professionals alike. This has allowed too many well-intentioned staff to flounder and some unscrupulous individuals to abuse the positions of power they have acquired over vulnerable children.

1.22   We believe that the public, professional and managerial mood is changing. It is important to capture the moment with a clear analysis of what is wrong and practical recommendations for improvement that will attract widespread support. It is crucial that managers and staff do not sink into apathy but are given strong encouragement and support to embrace change both by Central Government and their employers, whether local authorities or in the private or voluntary sector.

1.23   The starting point for change has to be a widespread acceptance that society needs a range of well-managed children's homes as an important and permanent part of its system of public care of children. The number, size, purpose and ownership of homes may change over time, but a considerable number will be a permanent part of the child care landscape. Children's homes are there to help those children who would benefit from group care and who cannot stay in their own homes or with foster parents There will always be such children, particularly among the older age groups. The primary purpose of children's homes must be seen as developmental and therapeutic, and not as custodial. Unless there is broad agreement on these basics by politicians at the national and local levels and those responsible for provision, it will be impossible to achieve sustained change and improvement by managers and staff.

1.24   There needs to be general agreement both on the importance of children's homes, and on the major deficiencies in the present arrangements. From the facts and opinions presented to us we believe the concerns to be addressed can be summarised as follows:

- Increasingly difficult children Over the past decade more and more difficult children have been placed in a shrinking number of children's homes. Chapter 2 shows the high proportions of sexually abused and behaviourally disturbed children in homes today, and indicates that there are many substance abusers and victims of violence within their own family in children's homes. Some homes today have many violent, abused, abusing and self-mutilating children, rather than the orphans and truants of a bygone era and popular perception. The management, staffing levels, training and support for staff have to be brought into line with the current realities of the

7

children for whom homes are caring.   The physical conditions of homes and the lack of privacy for children need urgent attention in many places to make it easier to care for children satisfactorily.

- <u>Low esteem</u>   There are two interrelated problems. The low public esteem of children's residential care, and the low self-esteem of the staff working in homes. The Utting and Howe reports both address this issue and we have more to say in Chapter 3. The status of children's homes and their staff has to be raised if the quality of care is to be improved.

- <u>Lack of sustained attention</u>   Children's homes have not received sustained attention from the senior management of many Social Services Departments. Particular scandals may have forced attention on them in some places, but we have been left with an uncomfortable sense that many Social Services Departments are not paying sufficient attention to the possibility of problems. In recent years community care, child protection in the community and the changes in the Children Act have absorbed the attention of Social Services senior management. Children's homes now need their place in the managerial sun. In Chapter 10 we suggest a medium term strategy during which sustained attention by senior management needs to be given to this sector.

- <u>Poor management</u>   There is no escaping the fact that inquiry after inquiry has highlighted poor management as a major contributor to abuse in a home. Poor job definition for staff; inadequate staff appraisal and supervision; lack of accountability; little monitoring or oversight of homes; inadequate complaints procedures; the 'closed' nature of a home with few links with the outside world, are all-too-common features of the homes where things have gone wrong. The senior managers have simply not acted when there were clear warning signals about unsatisfactory behaviour in homes. To many staff working in homes the management superstructure above the home is not seen as relevant to their needs. Overall, too many senior managers have given insufficient attention to ensuring that there are effective management arrangements for homes that provide early warning of problems and means of rectifying situations. We address these management issues in Chapter 6.

- <u>Deficient employment practices</u>   It is clear from the evidence available that not enough attention has been given to the recruitment, selection and appointment of staff. Too often there is a lack of probing into people's previous employment records. Sometimes there is even a failure to check whether staff have a criminal record before they are allowed unsupervised access to children. Insufficient attention has been given to whether people have the personality or aptitude to cope with the difficult circumstances - and sometimes temptations - of life in a children's home. There is poor matching between the requirements of the job and the personality of the person recruited. There is an urgent need for a more systematic and rigorous approach to the recruitment, selection and appointment of staff, as we propose in Chapters 3, 4 and 5.

- <u>Inadequate knowledge and training</u>   A common complaint made by staff is the absence of knowledge about how they should be caring for, controlling and attending to the developmental needs of the children currently in homes. A significant part of the problem is the shortage of specialist support services and training opportunities for many staff. There is also an absence of consensus on the knowledge and skills that staff need to cope in the children's homes of today. We are impressed by the arguments of those who say that the Diploma in Social Work as currently devised will not provide the right skills base for children's residential care in the 1990s, even though sending more staff on Diploma courses will on paper produce a better qualified workforce. We discuss the staff development issues in Chapter 7 and improving specialist support in Chapter 8.

- <u>Problems relating to the policy and planning framework</u> Gaps remain in the policy and planning framework which determines the purpose, standards, range and volume of residential child care to which individual homes and employers have to relate. These gaps can make it difficult to achieve a 'culture of quality'; to plan for the future; or to assess whether standards are rising or falling. We address in Chapter 9 some of the issues involved in achieving a clearer policy and planning framework.

1.25   We have set out our concerns briefly and perhaps starkly in order to focus attention on the key issues. The starting point for change has to be a large measure of agreement on a definition of the current shortcomings. Our concerns are not hypothetical, but are based on the evidence presented to us on visits, and in written submissions, discussions and seminars. We have been particularly impressed by the views of those working in homes and with direct experience of running them. We have paid great attention to the results of the national survey because this reflects the current experience of the people who are running homes. in 1992.

1.26   Implementation of the recommendations in this report will deter a small group of paedophiles who seem to have sought employment in children's homes to gain access to vulnerable children. Society will need to be alert to the danger that determined paedophiles are likely to turn their attention to other vulnerable areas such as education and youth work as it becomes more difficult for them to secure appointments in children's homes.

1.27   The next eight chapters set out in more detail our analysis of the evidence presented and our recommendations for change. In Chapter 10 we summarise our findings and set out our ideas for implementing changes over the next few years. In framing our proposals we have had uppermost two major concerns:

- The quality of care and safety of thousands of children whose only home is a children's home.

- The need to give staff a reasonable chance to succeed rather than set them up to fail.

CHAPTER 2: CHILDREN'S HOMES AND THEIR CHANGING CHARACTER

"I've lived in 'em all - short-stay, long-stay, big, small, lock-ups - the lot. Even one run by a load of nuns. They vary really. Now the last place I lived in was the best home I was ever in. The food was good and the staff were kind and would listen to you. But I had to leave there 'cos I was getting too old." (Girl, 17)

Quoted by David Berridge in 'Children's Homes', 1985.

Introduction

2.1   The starting point for any Inquiry into the staffing of children's homes has to be the purpose of homes and the characteristics of the children resident in them. Those two considerations ought to determine the management and staffing policies for homes. If the purpose of homes and the characteristics of the children change then the knowledge and skills of staff and managers will need to change, which may mean retraining staff for new skills. This is a statement of the obvious, but it has not always been acted upon in the realm of children's homes. In this chapter we set out the picture we have found on the current provision of children's homes; describe some of the changes taking place in provision; and give as up-to-date a picture as we can of the characteristics of children currently in homes.

2.2   Others have commented on the dearth of information about children's homes. In 1985 Berridge pointed out that "many of the decisions on residential care are taken on the basis of inadequate information". In 1991 Utting said "information about the number of institutions accommodating children in care is poor". We have tried to redress the balance a little by commissioning a survey of the children, staffing and personnel/management practices in children's homes. This was conducted for us in April and May 1992 by Price Waterhouse. The result is at Appendix 3 and reference is made to this survey throughout our report. This survey provides a baseline of information for the Department of Health to use for monitoring change. In Chapter 9 we make suggestions on maintaining and updating this information base.

Background

2.3   Children's homes are strongly associated in the public mind with deprived and delinquent children. Dickensian images of 19th century orphanages still linger on. Until the last three or four decades residential provision for children was often seen as having as much to do with protecting society from potentially dangerous children as with child care and development. Less than 50 years ago the Curtis Committee found the following position:

> *"The result in many homes was a lack of personal interest in and affection for the children which we found shocking. The child in these homes was not recognised as an individual with his own rights and possessions, his own life to live and his own contribution to offer. He was merely one of a large crowd, eating playing and sleeping with the rest, without any place or possession of his own or any quiet room to which he could retreat. Still more important, he was without the feeling that there was anyone to whom he could turn who was vitally interested in his welfare or who cared for him as a person."*

Not until the 1969 Children and Young Persons Act were the terms "approved school" and "remand home" replaced by "community home". (Until 1933 they had been "reform schools" - which was certainly an unequivocal statement of intent.)

2.4 However the 1970s and 1980s have seen major changes. Along with many adult institutions such as psychiatric hospitals, children's homes have increasingly been seen as a place of last resort. As a result the number of homes has dropped dramatically. In the early 1960s the Williams Committee estimated there were about 1,850 children's homes in England and Wales with some 30,000 children. By 1970 Beedell found roughly the same number of homes accommodating 25,000 children. In 1990, Utting estimated that the number of homes had dropped to about 1,200. Our survey suggests that there are about 1,300 homes but they are accommodating about 11,250 children. Thus within the working life of some staff in children's homes the sector has reduced by more than 50% in terms of the numbers of children looked after.

2.5 A major reason for the reduction in children's homes has been the growth of alternatives seen as more appropriate, cheaper or both. In the past 20 years there has been a large increase in the number of children in care placed with foster parents, as well as the development of more specialist foster care and independent living schemes for older teenagers. As late as 1980 fostering accounted for only 37% of the children in care in England; but by 1990 57% of these children were fostered.

2.6 In addition the number of children taken into local authority care has reduced significantly. Between 1980 and 1990 the number of children in care in England dropped from just over 95,000 to something over 60,000. This was partly as a result of pressure from research, legislation and professional perceptions of good practice. The growth of fostering, preventative services and community alternatives to custody were all seen as alternatives to residential care. For many children it was seen as less harmful to leave them with inadequate parents and to try to improve parenting skills than to take the children into public care. The development of day care and supervising children at risk in their own home setting has reduced the demand for places in children's homes.

2.7   This is the background against which we view the current provision of residential care for children.

Current Provision of Residential Care

2.8   There is a wide range of residential provision for children in public care:

- Children's homes (including secure units)

- Schools (maintained or independent boarding schools) often meeting special educational needs

- Health establishments (NHS hospitals or psychiatric units; mental nursing homes)

- Youth Treatment Centres

- Prison department establishments.

There are some 1800 children in care accommodated in schools, health establishments, Youth Treatment Centres and penal institutions. Our terms of reference do not cover these other establishments and we do not discuss them further. However much of what we have to say about children's home will in many cases be applicable to these other establishments.

2.9   There are three main types of children's home: community homes provided directly by a local authority or responsibility for which is shared by a local authority and voluntary organisation or trust; voluntary homes which are run by non-profit-making organisations; and private homes (or "registered" homes as they are termed under section 63 of the Children Act 1989). Nearly all the children in voluntary and private homes are placed there and paid for by local authorities. Some community homes have education facilities on the premises; some have secure accommodation; and some provide observation and assessment services.

2.10   Our survey suggests the following pattern of provision in 1992:

TABLE 2.1

	Local Authority Homes	Voluntary Homes*	Private Homes	Total
Number of Homes	950	170	180	1300
Actual number of children accommodated on 31/3/92	7650	2050	1550	11250

* Throughout our report the term Voluntary Homes includes Assisted Community Homes.

2.11   Department of Health statistics suggest that 10% of children in
residential care are in homes which have education on the premises. Children in these
homes will often not go to mainstream schools. About 20% of children are in
community homes concerned with observation and assessment. Thirty two community
homes have secure accommodation.

2.12   The use of secure accommodation is governed by section 25 of the
Children Act 1989 and - apart from children detained under the 1983 Mental Health Act
- no child may be detained in secure accommodation for more than 72 hours without
the approval of a Court. Children under 13 cannot be placed in secure accommodation
without the authorisation of the Secretary of State for Health. Currently there are
about 300 approved secure accommodation places in 32 homes but there are plans to
increase this number by 60 - 65 places over the next few years as a result of changes
in demand arising from the Criminal Justice Act 1991. Most of the homes used for
secure accommodation have observation and assessment facilities.

Regional variations

2.13   A number of researchers have commented on the considerable regional
variations in the availability of children's homes. Our survey showed five local
authorities having no children's homes of their own, including Warwickshire, whose
experience we discuss later in this chapter. At the other extreme Lancashire has 57
local authority children's homes, whereas comparable sized counties have a third or less
of this number. A 1991 strategy produced by the London Boroughs Children's Regional
Planning Committee shows widely varied usage and placement patterns by London
Boroughs; and a little over a third of their children in residential care being placed
outside the London Boroughs. We would agree with a 1991 research finding that
"whether a child is placed with a foster family or in residential care may not so much
depend on the child's needs but on where he or she happens to live".

Recent changes

2.14   We have already commented on the reduction in the number of
children's homes. Our survey suggests that the pace of change in the past three years
has been considerable, although not all sectors are shrinking:

TABLE 2.2

	Local authority homes	Voluntary homes	Private homes	Total
Number of homes 1989	1130	Not known	Not known	Not known
Number of homes 1992	950	170	180	1300
Number of places 1989	12000	Not known	Not known	Not known
Number of places 1992	10350	2750	2000	15100

2.15   Thus local authorities had almost 20% more homes three years ago than they do now, although there are significant variations between types of authority. In 1989 the Counties had approaching 10% more places in children's homes whereas the London Boroughs had over 40% more places. It has not been possible to calculate the exact change in size of the voluntary sector as we were not able to contact those homes which have closed since 1989. However, it is worth noting that those voluntary organisations responding to our survey reported a decrease of around 5% in numbers of homes and 15% in places provided. We would estimate that there has been a reduction of around 15 - 20% in the number of places provided by the voluntary sector.

2.16   However the position in the private sector seems to be quite different. In order to conduct our survey we had to obtain the names of all private homes registered with local authorities. This revealed about 180 homes, although this is likely to be an underestimate because 12 local authorities did not reply. In 1980 there were thought to be about 70 private homes and in 1991 Utting estimated there were about 100. Our survey also shows about 60 homes opening in the past three years, although we do not know how many have closed. We estimate that there are nearly 2000 places available now in private homes, and that there are now more homes in the private sector than the voluntary sector. This is a dramatic expansion of a sector that before October 1991 was never inspected or registered; and about which there is little collective information.

Size of homes

2.17   The Utting Report in 1991 recommended that local authorities should plan their stock of children's homes so that they have a minimum of four or five and a maximum of 14 places. The upper limit was the optimal size of homes for efficient use of resources suggested by research by Knapp at the University of Kent. Our survey reveals that the average number of places per home was as follows:

TABLE 2.3

Local authority homes	....	11
Counties	....	12
Metropolitan Districts	....	10.5
London Boroughs	....	9
Voluntary Homes	....	16
Private homes	....	11

We know that the range in size of individual homes is considerable: from four to 55 places in the private sector; and from 5 to 110 places in the voluntary sector.

Occupancy of homes

2.18   The occupancy level reported in our survey at the end of March 1992 was as follows:

TABLE 2.4

Local authority homes	....	74%
Voluntary homes	....	75%
Private homes	....	78%

The occupancy levels were on average somewhat higher - about five per cent - in Metropolitan District homes than elsewhere in the local authority sector. Overall there has been little significant change in the occupancy levels of local authority and voluntary sector homes in the past three years. However private homes reported an average drop in occupancy levels of about 10% in the past three years, even though the number of homes has increased.

Buildings

2.19   Commenting on the buildings used for children's homes in 1991, Utting said "Little is known about their physical state or the facilities they provide. What data we have is subjective, often impressionistic and not systematic". Drawing upon a survey of 30 Social Services Inspectorate reports on children's homes Utting went on to say that some displayed "good physical standards whilst others show signs of neglect and even decay". He concluded that "purpose-built establishments are, as a class, no better or worse than adapted premises". The buildings themselves are located in very different types of communities. As Berridge put it "some are to be found in densely populated urban areas while others are set in lush countryside and rolling hills, surrounded not by graffiti and petrol fumes but by self-sufficiency and cowpats". What we found on our visits supported the view that the buildings and settings used for children's homes are extremely variable in terms of quality and appropriateness.

2.20   We find it surprising that so little is known about the physical condition and appropriateness of children's homes because this must have an important effect on the behaviour of children and the ability of staff to care for them. We have seen some homes which fall considerably short of desirable standards because of their institutional character and the lack of privacy, through the absence of single rooms. In some places, failure to make repairs and carry out routine maintenance is causing problems. In some homes the decor and furnishings are poor and sometimes there is too little space for privacy and activities. The remoteness of some homes is worrying in terms of the children's isolation from outside influences.

2.21   We welcome the guidance on the structure and layout of children's homes given in Volume 4 of the guidance on the Children Act, with its emphasis on a homely environment, privacy and choice. As well as providing a better environment for children, this can only serve to improve the working conditions for staff. We return to this issue and the need to collect information regularly on the physical state of children's homes in Chapter 6.

Characteristics of Children in Homes

Age

2.22   Our survey revealed that the average age of children in homes across the sectors was about 14, although there are more sixteen year-olds than any other age group. Department of Health figures show the proportion of children in residential care aged 16 or over has increased from 22% in 1980 to 31% in 1990. Research suggests that the children's homes population is getting older; and that the older a child is admitted to care the more likely they are to go into a children's home. Our survey confirms Utting's conclusion that "residential care is now a service mainly for adolescents". Nevertheless there is a considerable minority of young children in residential care.

2.23   A significant minority of individual homes and local authorities report the average age of residents as under 13 and a few as under 10. A number of homes accommodate very young children, including babies, although we recognise that this may well reflect emergency placements. At the other end of the age scale our survey indicates the presence of adults resident in children's homes. Around a quarter of local authorities and individual homes in other sectors report homes caring for people aged 21 or over. This may reflect the practical difficulty of finding suitable alternative accommodation for those young people leaving care who need support well into adulthood.

Gender and race

2.24   There are considerably more boys than girls in children's homes. Department of Health figures show that in 1990 58% of children in residential care were male. However our survey shows only a small proportion - 11% - of children in single sex homes, with about twice as many boys as girls in such homes. The overwhelming majority of children's homes now provide care for both boys and girls. Only about a third of local authorities have any single-sex homes; and the proportions of private and voluntary homes are even lower at 10% and 20% respectively. However about 60% of the secure accommodation places are in single-sex homes, most of them for boys. It is important to ensure sufficient single-sex homes for those who need them, especially girls who have been sexually abused.

2.25   There are no national statistics on the ethnic background of children in residential homes. We are aware that some local authorities and voluntary organisations collect and monitor information to improve the planning and delivery of services. Some have also commissioned small-scale research. We consider that monitoring the ethnic composition of children in residential care is an essential part of the arrangements for providing appropriate care.

Nature of children

2.26   We used our survey to try to identify the primary characteristics of the children in residential care. Respondents were asked to categorise the children in their homes under four primary conditions: physical disabilities; learning disabilities; emotional/behavioural difficulties; other. This approach has limitations, but it did reveal that the overwhelming majority of children - about two thirds - are (in the opinion of those running homes) in a home because they have emotional and/or behavioural difficulties which make other placements inappropriate.

2.27   In summary our survey revealed the following picture:

TABLE 2.5

Primary Characteristic Reported	Local authority Homes	Voluntary homes	Private homes
Physical disabilities	4%	19%	c.1%
Learning disabilities	14%	11%	c.2%
Emotional/behavioural difficulties	64%	57%	71%
Other conditions	18%	13%	26%

Children with physical disabilities are looked after equally by the local authority and voluntary sector but the former provide nearly all the care for children with learning disabilities. About 75% of the work of the private homes is concerned with children with emotional and behavioural difficulties. It looks as though the growth of this sector has been in response to a demand for services for this group of children.

Sexual abuse

2.28   It is not surprising to find such a high proportion of children in homes have emotional/behavioural difficulties given how many of them have been sexually abused. Most respondents to our survey felt able to provide estimates of the number of children in their homes who had been sexually abused, although many indicated that their estimates were probably on the low side. The picture is a disturbing one:-

TABLE 2.6

Estimates of numbers of children sexually abused

Local authority homes	Almost one third
Voluntary homes	Around one third
Private homes	About one quarter.

2.29   Our survey's findings were supported by other evidence presented to us. We believe that currently there are likely to be approximately 4,000 sexually abused children in children's homes in England. This has major implications for the staffing and management of homes. The implications are particularly serious given what research has revealed about the propensity of abused children to become abusers in turn, including abusing other children; or to unconsciously re-enact their pre-care experiences or transference of anger. These children may also be more likely than others to make unjustified accusations against staff. We discuss these implications in Chapter 8.

Abuse in institutions

2.30   The significant number of sexually abused children in children's homes poses problems not only for staff but for other children where the abused child seeks to become an abuser. Moreover the growing knowledge about institutional abuse of children by adults shows that society cannot assume that once placed in a home children are safe. This Inquiry was established following the systematic sexual abuse of children in residential care in Leicestershire by Frank Beck, the head of a children's home. The Kincora report was concerned with sexual abuse in Northern Ireland boy's hostels. During the course of this Inquiry there have been several prosecutions of staff in children's homes for sexual abuse of children in their care.

2.31   We have tried therefore to form some picture of the vulnerability to sexual abuse of children in residential care. American research studies consistently document the existence of sexual abuse of children in institutional settings. There is no full-scale study of abuse in institutions in the United Kingdom but there is some work by The National Association of Young People in Care (NAYPIC) and The National Society for the Prevention of Cruelty to Children (NSPCC) to draw upon. In 1990 NAYPIC produced a small sample of 50 young people in care - mostly in institutions - who had complained to them of abuse, and two-thirds of the complaints related to sexual abuse. In July 1992 the NSPCC published a survey of 28 of its teams/projects which revealed 84 children abused in 43 different institutional establishments. Over half the children were abused in children's homes and most of the rest were abused in schools. Over 80% of these children were sexually abused and one third of them had a learning disability. About half the perpetrators of abuse were staff, overwhelmingly male; and the other half were other children.

2.32   We have received anecdotal evidence of abuse in private homes and independent boarding schools. Given that these establishments have never been inspected or registered until recently it is less than surprising that abuse is starting to come to light. As children become more confident about using complaints systems and society becomes better at listening to children it would seem likely that more abuse within institutions will come to light. Sadly we are led to the conclusion that it is probable that much sexual abuse of children in homes has gone undetected but that as public and professional awareness increases more is likely to be investigated. As the number of sexually abused children in homes increases then so does the vulnerability to abuse of other children, unless special care is taken by managers and staff.

Looking to the Future

2.33   We have tried to present in this chapter a picture of the changing world of children's homes. In the future that world will not remain static. The new Criminal Justice Act will produce changes; and there will be a growth in secure accommodation over the next few years. It is unlikely that the existing proportion of deprived, difficult, disturbed and abused children will reduce. They are more likely to form an even larger proportion of those in children's homes. Given the uneven geographical spread of children's homes, it is difficult to imagine that those areas with more homes will not review their provision - if only from financial pressures - to see if they can make do with less. This will be facilitated by the ability to use fostering more extensively in some places and a possible drop in the numbers coming into care as a result of the Children Act.

2.34   This is inevitably speculative, but we consider that it is important for employers to think about their likely future needs as they look at their services in the light of our recommendations. They need to ensure that the management and staffing is likely to be able to cope with possible changes. In looking to the future it is useful to draw on the recently published work evaluating Warwickshire County Council's decision in 1986 to close the last of its children's homes - "Closing children's homes: An end to residential child care?" by David Cliffe and David Berridge.

2.35   The conclusions of this book provide important pointers for others reviewing the future of children's homes. Cliffe and Berridge say that Warwickshire did not take the position that there was no role for residential child care, but continued to make a small but not insignificant use of children's homes. They reveal that Warwickshire ploughed back the savings from closures into other forms of child care, so closures are not necessarily a simple option for making savings. Perhaps more significantly, Cliffe and Berridge show that closure of homes can produce difficulties for the fostering services. Although Warwickshire placed the vast majority of young people in foster homes (including some difficult teenagers), children from minority ethnic groups were often placed with white foster parents; in over half the cases there was only one foster placement available so there was limited scope for matching children carefully with foster families; and the turnover of foster placements was higher than the national average. The closure of children's homes was also accompanied by an unusually large surge in the placement in residential schools of children with emotional and behavioural difficulties, although the research is inconclusive about whether there is a causal link between the two events. Thus closing children's homes is likely to have a significant impact on other services.

2.36   In the past too little attention has been paid to the views of the young people in residential care. Children from homes consistently draw attention to their sense of stigma and feeling different from other children. A strong sense of instability emerges as staff and children in homes come and go; and there is no one adult providing any continuity of care akin to a parent substitute. Many children feel ill-equipped to leave residential care and cope with life as a young adult. The continuing dilemma for residential child care was well put to us by one person in evidence:

> *"To expect young people from a variety of backgrounds*
> *experiencing very different problems and needs to live with any*
> *degree of harmony cheek by jowl with each other competing for*
> *staff attention and finding their own identities in the process was*
> *an impossible expectation."*

In future more attention needs to be paid to the views of young people about the care provided in homes and the way they are run.

2.37   Children's homes are seen by many as a place of last resort and find it difficult to refuse placements. Yet they may not be equipped to meet the needs of all the young people placed under their roofs. Too often the provision of residential places may mean providing a good service for social workers but a less good one for children. The result can be, as Rutter has pointed out, that adults who have experienced long periods of institutional care as a child go on to encounter considerable social problems and often make poor parents.

Summing Up

2.38   We recognise that we are not presenting here a simple or particularly encouraging view of children's homes either now or in the near future. However we consider that we do children and staff no favours by presenting a misleadingly simplistic or optimistic view. We have seen on our visits and encountered in our evidence many examples of homes and staff providing good quality care for the children in their charge. There are many well-run homes in all sectors with competent, caring staff providing children with a positive developmental experience while they are in public care. Most of the staff respect children as individuals and do not abuse them. However sometimes positive outcomes are more by luck than judgement. As we shall show later in the report, there is a long way to go before people can be confident that everything that can reasonably be done to improve management and employment practices has been done.

2.39   When considering the future staffing, management and training aspects of children's homes we believe that the features to be kept uppermost in people's minds are:

- The recent rapid reduction in the number of homes and the uncertainty that this is likely to produce in the minds of managers and staff, particularly if homes continue to close.

- The small size of many homes and the difficulty that this may produce in staffing and managing them well and cost-effectively.

- The wide regional variation in the number and nature of homes and the difficulty of reconciling this with any notion of a planned assessment of need.

- The apparent rapid increase in the private sector, about which there is little information and which until this year has never been inspected or registered.

- The mixed-sex nature of most homes and the implications this has for mixed-gender staffing of homes.

- The mix of ethnic origins of children in many homes, which requires an appropriate ethnic balance in the staffing of homes.

- The overwhelmingly adolescent clientele in children's homes and the implications this has for the knowledge, basic skills and training of staff.

- The low priority and regard given to children's homes within the range of Social Services, and the resulting difficulty of attracting or retaining appropriately qualified and temperamentally suited staff.

- Doubts about the layout and conditions of some buildings (particularly in relation to privacy) and the difficulties that unsatisfactory buildings can cause for the successful care of children.

- The high proportion of emotionally and behaviourally-disturbed children in homes and the implications that this has both for the training of staff and the specialist support provided to homes.

- The large number of sexually abused children in homes and the implications this has for staff competencies and training and for the protection of staff and other children.

- The lack of perceived beneficial outcomes for many children who experience residential care in terms of stigmatization, lack of emotional support, poor preparedness for the adult world and possible experience of abuse of children within the institution.

- The wide variety of children likely to end up in a facility of last resort and the difficulty of making homes more effective without greater specialisation and greater clarity in identifying areas of specialisation.

- The likelihood that much abuse in institutions has been undetected and that with greater awareness more will come to light with adverse implications for the staffing, morale and esteem of children's homes.

- The need to listen more closely to the views of young people about the running of children's homes.

2.40   We consider that if Government, employers, managers, staff and training bodies face up realistically to the situation as it is then much can be done to improve the whole residential care sector for children. This will mean recognising the needs of the sector; actively promoting the meeting of those needs in the interests of children and society; and recognising the value and worth of children's residential care. The evidence available to us is that people at all levels want to tackle the problems and achieve improvements. They are looking for guidance and leadership on achieving change. In the following chapters we set out our own analysis and recommendations on what can be done, provided that there is the will to do it.

_____

CHAPTER 3:   RECRUITMENT OF STAFF

*"Half the money I spend on advertising is wasted
and the trouble is I don't know which half."*

Quoted by David Ogilvie in 'Confessions of an
Advertising Man', 1963

Introduction

3.1   A lot of money and effort is spent on the recruitment of staff but for many employers the money and effort is unproductive or poorly directed. In this chapter we examine the various stages of the recruitment process up to the point of issuing application forms to prospective candidates. The later stages are dealt with in Chapter 4 on Selecting Staff and Chapter 5 on the Appointment of Staff. What we say throughout the report relates to heads of homes, their deputies and care staff, although some of our findings are applicable to other staff in children's homes. We have tried to make clear and constructive recommendations for change, and where possible these recommendations are in the form of good practice that we believe employers - public, private and voluntary - can and should attain. First however we discuss the background against which the recruitment of staff is taking place and some of the difficulties to which employers have drawn attention.

Employer's Perspective and Difficulties

3.2   Respondents to our survey from all sectors report recruitment difficulties arising from the unattractive image of residential child care. This survey was undertaken at a time of recession and high unemployment, so the position is likely to be worse at a time of economic buoyancy. The main factors seen by employers as contributing to this unattractive image are poor pay, limited training and career development opportunities, insufficient recognition of and compensation for anti-social hours, inadequate supervision and unsatisfactory support arrangements. The point was starkly put by one employer that recruitment problems arose from "the association of residential child care with poorly paid women's work". Many employers then see recruitment difficulties as accentuated and perpetuated by retention difficulties, as staff who obtain social work qualifications move into fieldwork positions. The point was made to us repeatedly that the policy of seconding residential staff to Diploma of Social Work training guaranteed them an exit visa from residential work.

3.3   Labour market conditions vary in different parts of the country and some employers find it easier to recruit than others. In many areas employers make use of agency staff, even though this can mean the payment of a substantial premium. (We were told of cases in London where the premium is 30% above the local government rate for the job.) Our survey shows considerable variation in employer attitudes to agencies with some not using them at all and others having a heavy reliance on agencies. The picture to emerge is:

- In local authorities over 10% of heads of homes and a similar proportion of care staff are from agencies. Use of agency staff is particularly pronounced in the London Boroughs, where 13% of heads of home and 21% of care staff are from agencies.

- In the voluntary sector around 5% of heads of home and 8% of care staff are from agencies.

- For private sector homes agency staff account for around 3% of all types of staff.

We discuss the issues of using agencies later in this chapter (see paragraphs 3.39 - 3.42).

3.4   To alleviate recruitment difficulties some employers report local initiatives such as career grade progression, integration of field and residential grades and the promise of training. Throughout this report we have tried to support such initiatives in the recommendations we have made. Although such measures appear to have helped to some extent, the reality remains that, as one respondent said, "One is forced to employ the best on the day rather than be too selective." Employers want to see the unattractive image of children's homes tackled by positive action at both the national and local level. Before making suggestions about this we want first to provide a picture of the current staffing in children's homes.

Characteristics of Staffing in Children's Homes

3.5   The Utting Report estimated that in September 1989 there were 10,800 (whole time equivalents) care staff (including heads of home) employed in local authority children's homes. We estimate that their number is nearer 11,300. We also estimate that there are some 2,100 care staff in voluntary homes and about 1,600 in private homes. Thus the sector as a whole has about 15,000 care staff and heads of homes looking after children.

3.6   In our survey we tried to obtain some picture of the age, experience, qualifications and working patterns of staff in children's homes. The position on age and experience was as follows:-

TABLE 3.1

	Local authority homes	Voluntary homes	Private homes
Average age (years):			
Heads of home	39	40	39
Other care staff	35	33	30
Length of time in post (years):			
Heads of home	4	6	4
Other care staff	4	4	2

This shows that, contrary to the belief of some, many of the staff in children's homes are people of some maturity, although in the fast-developing private sector there would seem to be a higher proportion of less experienced and younger staff. There is no significant variation in the age and experience of the heads of home in all three sectors, although those in the voluntary sector have been longer in post.

3.7   However there are some significant differences between the sectors when one examines the survey's results on qualification:

TABLE 3.2

	Local authority homes	Voluntary homes	Private homes
% with Social Work Qualifications:			
Heads of homes	41	38	30
Other care staff	6	9	7
% with other relevant Qualifications:			
Heads of homes	7	40	50-60
Other care staff	14	23	30-40
% with no relevant Qualifications:			
Heads of homes	41	22	10-20
Other care staff	80	68	45-50

(Some inconsistencies in the returns from private sector employers about staff having no relevant qualifications have meant that range figures are shown for their staff.)

3.8   It is clear that both the private and voluntary sectors attach much less importance to social work qualifications for residential child care work than does the local authority sector. Employers in the independent sector have a much higher proportion of their staff with a qualification that <u>they</u> consider relevant to the work than does the local authority sector. These findings have some important implications for public policy in the light of the Utting and Howe Reports' recommendations on social work qualification as the desired professional qualification for both heads of home and care staff. We explore these implications further in Chapter 7.

3.9   There are also significant differences in the working pattern in the three sectors:

TABLE 3.3

	Local authority homes	Voluntary homes	Private homes
Average hours worked weekly:			
Heads of homes	41.8	44.8	42.4
Other care staff	45.6	41.7	35.7
% of working days lost through sickness:			
Heads of homes	3.4	3.1	1.8
Other care staff	6.4	2.9	2.1
% of working days post left unfilled:			
Heads of homes	7.0	4.6	2.6
Other care staff	5.0	2.5	2.1

3.10   The survey suggests that on average local authority care staff have much longer working weeks than their equivalents in the other sectors. They also work longer each week than the heads of home, which is the reverse of the situation in the private and voluntary sectors. Local authority homes lose many more days through staff sickness than other types of home; and also have posts unfilled for longer. This means that in local authority homes an average of one month's work is lost annually for each care staff post through sickness or other reasons.

Improving the Recruitment Climate

3.11   To provide good quality care and a safe environment for children requires a sufficiency of competent and well-motivated staff and managers. The position we have described shows a quite different situation in some parts of the country. The recruitment position generally will improve if there are improvements in conditions of service, working environment, training opportunities and staff support and supervision. Perhaps most significantly of all, as staff competency increases then pay must reflect the complexities of the job in children's homes.

3.12   We welcome the changes in pay and conditions of service recommended in the Howe Report and the new national agreement affecting local authority homes. In particular the move towards local determination of pay and grading in the light of local job responsibilities is a move we endorse and want to build upon. We explain how this approach could with advantage be taken further later in this chapter. In other chapters we set out proposals for improving supervision, training and support which we believe over time will improve recruitment prospects for children's homes. It will require advances in all these areas to achieve a more favourable recruitment climate for staffing children's homes.

3.13   It has been put to us that the Government should do more to aid the recruitment of staff for children's homes even though they are not the direct employers of staff. In support of this argument people have cited the nurse recruitment campaigns funded by the Department of Health even though nurses are employed directly by health authorities and family doctors. (In 1989-90 and 1990-91 over £7.5 million was spent by the Department on nurse recruitment campaigns.) We have some sympathy with the argument that the Government should mount a similar campaign for children's residential care staff. Such a campaign would be considerably strengthened if progress has been made in implementing the many recommendations for improvements in this report.

3.14   Once steps have been taken to improve training opportunities for staff in children's homes, there will be a role for central government in promoting the positive aspects of the job. Ideally this will take place after the introduction of the new training approaches outlined in Chapter 7. The Committee recognises that the Government's role should be one of raising public awareness of the beneficial aspects of the service rather than a specific recruitment campaign because recruiting staff for particular homes will remain the employer's responsibility.

3.15   Although the Government can aid the recruitment of staff for children's homes, employers can do much more to help themselves by scrutinising their own recruitment processes and making these as professional as possible. The recruitment process covers all those steps from the identification of a vacancy in a particular home to the issuing of application forms to prospective applicants. Recruitment procedures should be as open as possible, with the aim of ensuring the best field of candidates appropriate to the needs of the individual home. This is not to say that procedures should simply aim to attract as many applicants as possible. Instead there should be careful analysis of the requirements of the home and of the type of candidate needed in terms of their skills and experience. Employers need to adopt an approach of recruitment to specific vacancies in children's homes. By opening up the field to candidates external to the employing authority a wider range of <u>appropriate</u> candidates is likely to be obtained. Open recruitment procedures are vital also to ensuring that an individual home does not become a 'closed' institution. In the remainder of this chapter we set out our proposals on good practice which we consider will assist employers to recruit more good quality staff.

Recommendation 1

The Department of Health should, within two years, fund a centrally run campaign to raise the public's awareness of children's residential care, and to promote the positive aspects of working in children's homes as a career.

Defining the Job and Postholder

Statement of purpose and objectives

3.16   We consider that a major problem in recruiting staff has been the lack of clear objectives for homes either collectively or individually. Other Inquiry Reports have recommended the production of statements of aims and objectives for homes. Regulation 4 of the Children's Homes Regulations 1991 now requires the preparation of a statement of purpose and function for each home. At present many staff enter employment in children's homes with no very clear idea about the purpose of their job and what they are supposed to achieve. This is not a good basis for recruitment. We consider that employers must change their approach by using clear statements of purpose and objectives as the starting point of the recruitment process.

3.17   For each home we consider that there should be a clear statement of purpose and objectives drawn up in accordance with Volume 4 of the Guidance on the Children Act 1989. This needs to be approved by the employer and kept up-to-date. We discuss this issue in much more detail in Chapter 6, where we set out what should be incorporated in these statements. In the meantime we recommend that each employer should agree and keep up-to-date a statement of purpose and objectives and use this as the basis for preparing job descriptions for staff working in children's homes.

Job description

3.18   The up-to-date statement of purpose and objectives should form the basis of job descriptions for heads of homes and care staff. These job descriptions should set out the main duties, responsibilities and accountabilities of each job. They will form the basis of the person specifications we discuss below, but are quite separate documents. At Annex 3A to this chapter we provide an illustrative model job description for the head of a particular type of children's home. We hope that this will be useful to employers although it should not be followed slavishly in all homes.

3.19   As homes change, as a result of revised policy objectives within the organisation, or because the client group is changing, the statement of purpose and objectives for the home will change. Each time a new member of staff is recruited the job description should be reviewed in the light of any changes in the statement of purpose and objectives, and revised as necessary. Staff appointed should be aware that the job description may change in the future, and that further training may be needed for them to fulfil the requirements of any new job description.

Job descriptions and grading

3.20   It is important that job descriptions are related to the characteristics, objectives and needs of individual homes and are not constrained by national pay and grading schemes. In future the characteristics and objectives of homes should play a greater part in the grading of heads of homes than traditional measures such as number of places, number of staff or size of budgets. The "professional" as well as the "management" component needs to be adequately recognised in the job description, person specification and grading of heads of homes. There seems to be no difficulty in recognising this "professional" element in medically-based establishments managed by doctors so we can see no objections to doing so in respect of children's homes.

3.21   This means in our view that employers have to take more trouble to relate the pay and grading of posts - particularly those of heads of home - to their local circumstances as defined in their statements of purpose and objectives, job descriptions and person specifications. We have already drawn attention in Chapter 2 to the considerable variation in the circumstances and approaches of children's homes but we are not convinced that this is properly reflected in the pay and grading of staff. This may well explain why some employers have more recruitment difficulties than others.

3.22   We welcomed in Chapter 1 the recommendation in the Howe Report for making the pay of residential care staff more responsive to local definitions of duties and responsibilities. However the concept of a "benchmark" job in the new national agreement could be used as a means of constraining the responsibility of employers to ensure that the pay and grading of staff in children's homes reflects not just a broad description of tasks involved in a particular job, but also the level of competency and skill required to cope with the difficulty of the job as defined by the characteristics of the children, the objectives of the home and the skills and competencies required of job applicants. Given the circumstances of children's homes and the history of recruitment difficulty, we see no alternative to moving further and faster along a road of more local autonomy for employers to determine the pay and grading of children's homes staff in the light of their local circumstances.

Person specification

3.23   The person specification should be drawn up with a view to it being used during the selection process, providing a set of criteria against which to measure the suitability of candidates. It should distinguish between essential and desirable attributes. These two categories are frequently confused, resulting in wrong judgements about suitability. The person specifications for heads of homes will be significantly different from those for care workers because of the managerial content of the job.

3.24   A person specification should be produced each time a vacancy arises to take into account any changes in the home's statement of purpose and objectives. It should be prepared in parallel with the job description and should consider the competencies (ie, skills and personal attributes) and experience needed for the particular post, covering both professional and management responsibilities where appropriate. Person specifications should define the range of qualifications acceptable for a post where a qualification is to be a requirement. We discuss in more detail in Chapter 7 the issue of looking wider than social work qualifications for residential child care. An illustrative model person specification is provided at Annex 3B to this Chapter, to be read in conjunction with our model job description. We believe this will assist employers, not least because some respondents to our survey have advocated greater use of person specifications.

3.25   From the evidence presented to us we are convinced that it is impossible to make simplistic statements about the type of person who would make the ideal care worker in a children's home. Much of the written evidence we have received suggests that people from a variety of backgrounds can be appropriate for working in children's homes. The British Psychological Society suggested that a number of characteristics can be identified, including the ability to provide a role model for young people, and to demonstrate a wide range of life experiences; and that staff in a home should reflect a wide variety of experiences, interests and activities. This view was supported by the Association of Metropolitan Authorities (AMA). Childline suggested that "Staff should be recruited from a variety of professional backgrounds so that they have vehicles other than 'casework' through which to interest and engage children". We support these views.

3.26   In our view the precise nature of the staff required in a particular home at a particular time will depend upon the type of children in the home, the purpose and objectives of the home, and the composition of the rest of the staff team. There are some staff who should not be working with children and in Chapter 4 we suggest more rigorous selection procedures to enable employers to weed out applicants who exhibit unacceptable traits. Experience of using more effective selection procedures will enable employers to determine what traits are desirable in staff, and whether staff from particular backgrounds are more appropriate to particular tasks. This approach means that employers have to consider carefully what type of person they want each time a vacancy occurs, so that newcomers balance and complement existing staff in the home.

3.27   It is especially important to balance the gender and ethnic needs of the home in filling vacancies. A point made to us both in evidence and on our visits to homes was that too often equal opportunities policies were being applied so rigidly that homes were unable to appoint person of a particular gender when a staff team needed a man rather than a woman or vice versa. We recognise the importance of equal opportunities policies but such a narrow approach is quite contrary to the spirit and letter of the Children Act and Department of Health Guidance. We return to this issue in Chapter 4 (see paragraphs 4.64 - 4.67).

Recommendation 2

Employers should only recruit staff after preparing a job description clearly related to the home's current statement of purpose and objectives; and a person specification for each post to be filled setting out clearly the competencies (ie, skills and personal attributes) and experience required to discharge satisfactorily the responsibilities in the job description.

Recommendation 3

Employers should use as a basis for job descriptions and person specifications an agreed up-to-date and publicly available statement of purpose and objectives for each home that makes clear the type and characteristics of the children in the home and the objectives of the care and treatment programmes it is providing.

Advertising

3.28   When job descriptions and person specifications have been prepared then vacant posts can be advertised. Advertising vacancies widely not only helps to secure the most appropriate candidates but is a means of ensuring openness in recruitment procedures and avoiding a home's staff becoming excessively inward-looking. A feature of children's homes where disturbing episodes have occurred has often been a reluctance to fill vacancies from a wide field of competition. Filling vacancies on a basis of personal referral or narrow advertising will only foster the development of a 'closed' institution, as the Pindown Report emphasised; and it may not result in the appointment of the best available person for the job, to the detriment of the care and development of the children in the home.

3.29   In evidence to us and on visits some people advocated personal referral as a basis for recruitment and told us that they invariably filled vacancies from within the employing authority. Both approaches have dangers which employers need to recognise. We are strongly against unfettered personal referral as a basis for appointment as this only facilitates abuse of power by an unscrupulous head of home. It is also inconsistent with equal opportunities policies. In our view if people are personally referred they must compete on equal terms with applicants responding to advertisements, despite the delays this may cause in some instances.

3.30   Openness is not guaranteed by internal advertisements, although this might be acceptable when employing authorities are seeking to avoid redundancies. Our preferred option for all heads of homes and care staff posts is external advertising of vacancies, although internal staff still also have a right to apply and be considered. We accept that if there are large numbers of staff from within a local authority who are facing redundancy it is difficult not to consider them in the first instance for any vacancies which arise.

However, this may lead to appointments being made which are contrary to the best interests of the home and of the children being looked after. Employing authorities might reasonably attempt to make appropriate appointments from within the pool of staff to be redeployed but should not, in our view, make any appointments from that pool unless the person appointed satisfies the requirements of the person specification for the post or, with appropriate training, will be able to satisfy them.

3.31   There are those who argue that external advertising of posts is unfair to good internal candidates who deserve promotion. We can see that there will be circumstances where somebody has performed well, is ready for promotion and that there is a strong temptation to reward them with a promotion in the home. Supporters of this view will argue that it is unfair to force such staff into a situation where they find themselves in competition with other more experienced external candidates. However we consider it would also be contrary to the best interests of the children in a home if vacancies were to be filled solely by internal promotees. Instead, systems of training and staff development should be seen as preparation for open competition for posts. If a member of staff has received appropriate training, and has had access to proper development, then he or she will be able to compete on level terms with external candidates who have previously worked at that grade. 'Grooming' of internal staff for promotion within a home - in the sense of preparing them to take up a particular post without opening recruitment to wider competition - works against openness and in favour of a 'closed' institution. It also discourages the movement of staff between homes which rightly other inquiries have emphasised as one of the checks on abuse of power by like-minded cliques in a home. As one person giving evidence put it, switching staff between homes "diminishes the likelihood of bad practice being cultivated and institutionalised".

3.32   In our view when it comes to filling vacancies in children's homes then the best interests of children are served by openness and competition. This means advertising posts externally to the home in all cases and, except where an employer faces redundancies, advertising externally to the employing authority. In the case of heads of home special considerations apply. We consider that wherever there is a vacancy for a head of home it should be advertised nationally and we were pleased to see from our survey that this is already the approach of the majority of employers - although significant numbers of private homes do not do so.

3.33   We accept that deciding the appropriate media for advertisements is a matter for employers in the light of local circumstances. Our survey shows that 50% of local authorities and voluntary homes always use the professional/social work press for recruitment of heads of homes. This is nearly double the equivalent private sector figure. Use of the professional/social work press is significantly greater in the London Boroughs than elsewhere. Local newspapers are more commonly used in all sectors than either the professional press or national newspapers to recruit care staff, although many London Boroughs find the local press less effective than the professional/social work press.

3.34   Our position is that we recommend that all care staff posts should be advertised at least in the local press and any local publications serving ethnic minorities, except where an employer facing redundancies chooses to limit advertising of vacancies to internal staff from outside the particular home. Where vacancies are advertised internally an external element in the selection process would be an important safeguard and we discuss this in Chapter 4. We hope that employers will explore local radio (and possibly television) as a means of advertising vacancies.

Recommendation 4

Employers should ensure that all vacancies are advertised - usually externally - and are open to competition; and that all heads of home posts should be advertised externally and nationally.

Advance Recruitment

3.35   There are striking contrasts between the recruitment of residential care staff for children's homes and foster parents. The latter are selected and trained and placed on an approved panel before being employed, but this is not usually the case with residential care staff. In their written evidence, the Association of Directors of Social Services (ADSS) commented that "The standards required for the selection of staff in residential care should be no less rigorous and detailed than those for the recruitment of foster parents given that the children and young people to be cared for are, in both cases, being provided with substitute family care". It is inconsistent that a local authority may be taking great trouble to ensure that foster parents are carefully selected and trained before having unsupervised access to children and yet may be prepared to give that same access to casually-recruited and ill-prepared staff in a children's home. There should be greater consistency between the way foster parents are recruited and prepared before undertaking fostering and the arrangements for new residential care staff to ensure that children in residential care are not exposed to inadequately prepared or inexperienced staff.

3.36   An important lesson to be learned from fostering is the notion of advance recruitment and preparation before having unsupervised access to children. Advance recruitment and training against vacancy predictions (ie, creating a pool of care staff) would be a way of ensuring that residential care staff were more appropriately prepared before they take up a post. This would also reduce the need to use agencies and save agency fees for temporary staff.

3.37   We recognise that some employers may not be able to create and sustain a pool of staff awaiting appointment to a post in a children's home. However there may well be scope for organisations from all sectors to create a regional resource. This could be arranged in several ways. Employers from the statutory, private and voluntary sectors could form consortia to use financial resources jointly for the operation of a pool of staff, which could lead on to the setting up of a regional agency, operating in a similar way to commercial agencies. Evidence submitted from a member organisation of the National Council of Voluntary Child Care Organisations (NCVCCO) supports this proposal; and urged that if such pools of staff were to be created, the independent sector should have access to them.

3.38   The use of part-time staff, or staff who are willing to work on a locum basis, should be explored by employers or consortia of employers. Part-time staff would be subject to the same recruitment, selection and appointment procedures as full-time staff. We have seen a system in operation, where part-time staff form a group of available relief staff who can be drawn upon to fill vacancies, whether unexpected or planned. We consider that employing authorities acting in consortia could benefit from similar arrangements.

Recommendation 5

The Local Authority Associations should establish a number of carefully monitored pilot projects for the advance recruitment of children's residential care staff against predicted vacancies and encourage the formation of consortia of employers in all sectors for this purpose.

Use of Commercial Agencies

3.39   We have considerable reservations about the current use of commercial agencies for recruiting staff for children's homes. The National Children's Bureau noted in their evidence to us that employment agencies are a natural point of entry to the service for someone who may have a questionable background. Others pointed out the difficulty of checking on the recruitment processes used by agencies. As paragraph 3.3 indicates our survey revealed considerable use of agency staff by employers, particularly London Boroughs. There is to our mind something rather perverse about paying 25% or 30% more to an agency to hire staff rather than an employer simply using the money to increase their own rates of pay or improve their recruitment procedures. Apart from the costly nature of agencies, excessive reliance on agency staff can mean high turnover of staff in homes and a corresponding discontinuity in the care relationships with children. Stability of staffing is an important factor in the proper care of many of the disturbed children we have shown to be in children's homes today.

3.40   Perhaps even more worrying is our survey's findings on the vetting of agency staff. About 15% of local authorities made no background checks for agency staff. The figure was slightly lower for private homes but even higher - at around 25% - for voluntary homes. Although several respondents noted that they required agencies to undertake prior checks this is not particularly reassuring because many employers do not know how much checking has been done by agencies. The police will not accept requests from agencies for checking criminal records; and there have been some instances where agency staff who have committed offences or misdemeanours have been found not to have been vetted. In our judgment the use of agency staff under current arrangements could be seen as a threat to the safety and proper care and development of children in homes. We are also concerned that most commercial agencies do not accept full responsibility as employers for the staff they provide.

3.41   We can see no grounds for paying premiums to agencies and then allowing staff from them to have unsupervised access to children without having gone through the same processes as an employer's directly recruited staff. If agencies are to be used to recruit staff for children's homes then they should demonstrate to employers that they are adopting selection and appointment procedures and practices as rigorous as those proposed in this report. A requirement to meet these standards should be included in contracts with agencies.

3.42   Whatever general attitudes there may be to agencies we do not consider that they should be used to fill vacancies for heads of homes. To do so would reduce the employer's commitment to and the standing of these key posts. Heads of home are essential to ensuring the continuity of care within the home as a whole and for specific children. To fill such posts by using agency staff cannot be in the best interests of the children. If the reason for taking on agency staff to fill a head of home post is the inability to recruit suitable applicants, then the problem will clearly need to be addressed in a more fundamental way by an employer. They will have to look at the role of the home, the characteristics of the children, the rates of pay offered, the way the post has been advertised, the job description, even whether the home is needed. Using agencies as an expedient for filling head of home posts, in our view, means that employers are not discharging their responsibilities to the children and staff in their homes.

Recommendation 6

Employers should appoint all heads of homes on direct employment contracts, and should not use agency staff as heads of homes.

Recommendation 7

Employers who wish to use agencies should satisfy themselves that they represent good value for money and do not have an adverse effect on the resources available for the care of children; and should require any agencies used to adopt selection and appointment procedures as rigorous as those for directly employed staff set out in this Report.

ANNEX 3A - SPECIMEN JOB DESCRIPTION
(To be read in conjunction with specimen Person Specification)

JOB TITLE:	Head of Home
RESPONSIBLE TO:	Locally-determined Senior Manager
RESPONSIBLE FOR:	Residential Staff Cook Care Staff
LOCATION:	(Name of Home)

PURPOSE OF JOB:

To manage the resources of the Home and to provide a positive living experience for resident young people.

ORGANISATION CHART:

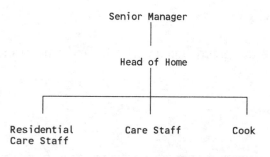

KEY RESPONSIBILITIES/DUTIES:

1. To advise on policies and procedures to reflect the aims and objectives of the Home and to develop systems for monitoring progress towards the achievement of such aims and objectives.

2. To assess the developmental needs of residents and to monitor and improve the Home's care plan and practices for each young person.

3. To generate an open and supportive atmosphere within the home, between staff members, between staff and residents, in order to enable the growth and development of both staff and residents.

4. To ensure children and young people and staff are aware of all procedures relating to complaints and concerns and know how to activate them.

5. To recruit, train and develop staff to meet the objectives of the home in accordance with agreed principles.

6. To manage and operate budgets within the agreed guidelines for the home.

7. To create and develop links between the community and the home and enable children and young people to participate fully in the life of the local community.

8. To ensure the physical standards of the home provide a safe and good quality environment for children and young people.

DECISION MAKING AUTHORITY:

To make appropriate decisions within agreed financial limits and care policies, e.g...............

FINANCIAL LIMITS OF AUTHORITY:

To authorise expenditure within the approved overall budget for the home and the employer's financial policies and procedures not exceeding £........

ANNEX 3B - SPECIMEN PERSON SPECIFICATION
(To be read in conjunction with Specimen Job Description)

JOB TITLE:

Head of Home

AIMS AND OBJECTIVES OF THE HOME:

To provide task-centred care to children and young people between the ages of 12-16 in order to assist them in preparing for adult life.

DESCRIPTION OF THE ROLE:

The Head of Home has two main accountabilities:

1. To provide the appropriate environment for the development of children and young people
2. To manage the resources within the Home cost-effectively and efficiently to achieve the Home's aims and objectives

MANAGEMENT SUPERVISION AND SUPPORT:

To formulate, implement and review personal development contracts and performance appraisal targets with all staff in the Home

DESCRIPTION OF CURRENT RESIDENTS:

10 children between the ages of 12-16, most with disturbed behaviour patterns.

TYPICAL ISSUES FACED BY JOB HOLDER:

The need to maintain an open and supportive atmosphere while, at the same time ensuring the care and safety of staff and young people.

TRAINING PROVIDED:

Induction: A 3-month training programme including introduction to financial systems and procedures, familiarisation of childrens' care plans, introduction to social workers, appreciation of the employer's overall aims and objectives.

Further development needs to be considered as part of the jobholder's personal development contract.

	ESSENTIAL	DESIRABLE
Education & Qualifications: **Explanation:** List the minimum education and qualifications required for standard performance.		
Knowledge: **Explanation:** Knowledge of a particular function, field, legislation, regulations, procedures.		
Experience: **Explanation:** The range and level of experience, e.g. work in residential child care, supervising a small team, managing expenditure budgets of £.......... and applying employment procedures.		
Key Skills: **Explanation:** Critical reasoning, written and oral communication, numeracy.		
Personal Attributes: **Explanation:** Key personal characteristics, e.g. stress tolerance, integrity, resilience, flexibility, ability to relate to children and young people, including children and young people from different ethnic and cultural backgrounds.		

CHAPTER 4:   SELECTING STAFF

"The degree to which an organisation selects its participants affects its control needs in terms of the amount of resources and effort it must invest to maintain the level of control considered adequate ...."

A Etzioni 'Modern Organisations', 1964

Introduction

4.1   Arbitrariness, lack of information and inconsistency are the enemies of good staff selection, whether for children's home or elsewhere. The picture to emerge from our survey is one in which the number of candidates from which a selection can be made is limited; too often insufficient information is obtained on candidates; there is excessive reliance by most employers on the chance performance of a candidate at a formal interview; and there is considerable inconsistency of selection practice between employers. On the evidence available to us most employers need to revise their selection procedures for appointing staff in children's homes, particularly for heads of homes. They need to draw upon a wider range of selection techniques in order to obtain a fuller picture of candidates. This chapter reviews the various selection techniques and processes available to employers up to and including final interview and makes recommendations on good practices that employers should adopt.

4.2   The approach to staff selection in children's homes was well-described in evidence from the Social Care Association. They suggested that assessment of candidates should be capable of considering the ability to contribute to the social, emotional, physical and spiritual needs of children, and that the methods used should focus on the values of staff, their commitment to working within and contributing to a team, their ability to work with others, including parents, and their self-confidence as people. Of course this is not an exhaustive list of the areas to be probed but it illustrates the territory to be explored in selecting staff to work in homes. The process of assessment should be aimed at gaining a full picture of a candidate's personal attributes, skills and experience, to enable those making the appointment to consider the information and decide which candidate best meets the requirements of the person specification. There may indeed be occasions when a decision has to be taken to appoint none of the candidates, if nobody adequately meets the criteria in the person specification. In such cases the recruitment procedure should be reconsidered, in particular looking at the need to attract a wider range of candidates, taking account of the race, language and culture of children in care.

4.3   Our survey shows that the selection processes used by most employers do not enable them to adopt the approach described by the Social Care Association. Most appointments are made on the basis of an application form and a formal interview. In many cases the interviews are conducted in panels of four or more people, which is hardly a forum for exploring aspects of personality. Control and punishment issues and equal opportunities are the main subjects discussed at the formal interview; and exploration of personal issues or spontaneous follow-up questioning are seen as difficult by some employers, particularly local authorities.

4.4   We asked employers to what extent they used particular selection techniques other than formal interviews in selecting both heads of homes or care staff. Their replies - to the question of whether they <u>sometimes</u> or <u>always</u> use specific techniques - suggest considerable reluctance to use methods other than the interview).

TABLE 4.1

<u>Employers' Use of Specific Selection Techniques</u>

	Group Discussions/ Interviews	Candidate Presentation	Skills Assessment (eg In-Tray Exercises)	Personality Assessment
Local authorities				
Heads of homes	71%	71%	35%	17%
Care officers	51%	31%	28%	5%
Voluntary homes				
Heads of homes	43%	44%	36%	21%
Care officers	48%	42%	36%	11%
Private homes				
Heads of homes	83%	74%	74%	61%
Care officers	82%	69%	67%	57%

In the London Boroughs these techniques were rarely used for any appointments in children's homes - head of homes or otherwise. Ninety-five percent of Boroughs never used any personality assessment. There is much less reluctance to use candidate presentation and group interviews/discussions among County Councils, who also make some use of personality profiling for heads of homes. The private sector makes much more use of these other selection techniques than does the voluntary sector or local authorities. One employer said, "Our procedures rely upon good sense, gut reactions and sharing the decision-making." We consider that it is possible to make selection of staff more systematic and objective than this.

A New Approach to Selection

4.5   We do not believe that it is in the best interests of children or staff to allow the present situation to continue. The process of staff selection must be adapted to achieve more effective gathering of information about candidates. Procedures should aim at all stages to collect as much relevant information as possible about a candidate and enable those responsible for taking the decision on the most appropriate candidate to make that decision on an informed basis. We do not believe that we are suggesting anything revolutionary, because all the techniques we discuss below are being used already by some employers for selecting staff.

4.6   The aim should be to achieve a full and rounded picture of the candidate, providing more detailed and complete information than is possible with the traditional application form - interview system. The Institute of Personnel Management (IPM) noted in their written evidence that on its own "the interview is not a good predictor of future job performance". Research findings quoted in the evidence suggested that the interview has a validity coefficient of 0.14 (ie only 14 in 100 appointments based on interviews will meet employers' expectations on job performance). The IPM commented that this is somewhat worse than making decisions on the toss of a coin. They and others also referred to the 'halo effect', where interviewers react to one positive or negative aspect of the candidate's performance, and allow this to overshadow other aspects perceived as less significant. For example, our survey has shown that attitudes to control and punishment emerges as the most frequent interview question, and can determine the outcome. Although this is an important area for exploring with candidates, we seriously doubt whether this can be explored effectively in a formal interview setting. The tools and techniques discussed below are all designed to increase the information gathered about candidates and to evaluate it more effectively. At the end of the chapter (paragraph 4.70) we discuss the possibility of using selection assessment centres to enable the process of information gathering to be carried out in a rational and systematic way.

4.7   We set out in the remainder of this chapter the selection techniques we recommend for wider use by employers. Some are adaptations of present arrangements. All are being used by an employer somewhere in the country. We hope that employers who are not using them currently will see them as helpful tools for ensuring that all the relevant information on candidates is collected before the final decision to appoint is made. It will not always be necessary to use all the techniques, although heads of homes posts will invariably require that more be used, given the important additional responsibilities which these posts carry. Extra investment of time and effort in selection will, in our view, prevent inappropriate appointments and avoid wastage.

Application Forms

4.8   Application forms are an important part of the selection process and provide an opportunity to collect much relevant information about candidates for jobs. Although all local authorities use application forms for children homes posts, our survey shows that about 10% of independent sector homes do not use them. Moreover local authorities generally use a single application form for all types of jobs in the authority except manual jobs, top management posts and teachers. Thus most employers are not using an application form designed specifically for children's home work and related to the job descriptions and person specifications for posts in that sector.

4.9   In the private industrial and service sectors the position on application forms has been changing in recent years towards the use of specific forms for specific job categories. The application form is based on a thorough analysis of the job, and can be used to collect data to compare candidates <u>and</u> as the first stage in the selection process. We believe that this practice should be adopted in the residential child care sector. We have recommended in Chapter 3 that job descriptions and person specifications should be thoroughly reviewed to accord with the statement of purpose and objectives for the home; and this process should feed into the design of the application form. As it is already common practice for local authorities to use separate application forms for one category of employees who work with children (ie, teachers, because special information is required - as is also the case with candidates for posts in children's homes), there should be no difficulty with extending this practice to residential child care staff.

4.10   The core information that should be provided in an application form for posts in children's homes is shown at the end of this chapter (Annex 4A).

Information issued with application forms

4.11   Our survey showed that the vast majority of employers always send job descriptions out with information to potential applicants, although local authorities do better than the independent sector in this respect. However person specifications are distributed far less frequently - in only about 50% of cases in the public, private and voluntary sectors. We consider that applicants should be aware from the earliest possible stage of the requirements of a post. This will mean sending a copy of the job description and person specification for the post with the application form. As much information as possible should be provided on such subjects as working hours and arrangements for shift working, location of the job, the task of the home (including a copy of the statement of purpose and objectives), the staffing of the home and the type of children looked after. The aim of this will be to enable the prospective candidate to make an informed decision on whether he or she will be suitable for a post, can fulfil all the requirements and would enjoy working in the home. This will mean that there will be an element of self-selection from the point that an application form is issued. Comments from some respondents to the survey suggest that some employers withhold information about poor or unattractive working conditions in the belief that if candidates find out about them at a later stage they are less likely to withdraw their applications. We believe this to be a misguided approach and not one designed to secure appropriate staff to work in children's homes.

Recommendation 8

Employers should require applicants for posts in all children's homes to complete application forms specifically designed for these posts and that collect core information relevant to the posts, as defined in the job descriptions and person specifications.

Recommendation 9

Employers should send applicants job descriptions, person specifications and full information about the home where they have applied for a post.

Written Exercises

4.12   Muddled managers produce confused staff. Staff who cannot express themselves clearly are likely to make young people in their care confused and possibly angry. Irrational responses to children and young people are likely to worsen problems of control in homes. Most managers and many staff have to write reports and many of these affect children's future. All this suggests that the selection process should test candidates' ability to think clearly and to express themselves well, both orally and in writing.

Format

4.13   Written exercises can be designed to test clarity of thought and expression; and some respondents to our survey want to see more use of written exercises. The qualities mentioned are particularly important for posts where there is a significant management element. Exercises should take the form of asking applicants to write a short piece on a subject relevant to residential child care practice or management. Candidates should be asked to complete the written exercise and return it with the application form. The subject of the written exercise should be sent out with the application form, and should state a maximum length of reply. Usually 1,000 words should be sufficient length.

Results

4.14   The results of written exercises should be used in the shortlisting process. They will provide evidence not only of candidates' ability to think clearly and to express themselves cogently, but will often reveal underlying attitudes. The issue to be addressed by candidates should be relevant and designed to test attitudes - for example to control of children; philosophy of residential child care; or knowledge of child development. Responses should be drawn upon later in the selection process, most appropriately in interview or discussion with the candidate. It is particularly important to ensure that responses to a written exercise are the work of a candidate and not a 'helper'. Candidates should be told at the outset that their written exercises will be discussed in the interview.

Recommendation 10

Employers should use written exercises in the selection process (including shortlisting) to test the ability of candidates to think clearly and to express themselves.

Visits to Homes

4.15   An important initial stage of the selection process should always be a visit to the home. This is already common practice with many employers, although we note from the evidence and visits that a number of employers mistakenly consider this contrary to equal opportunities policies. We believe that, if properly planned, these visits are a valuable source of information both about and for the candidate. Candidates will be able to reconsider their own application in the light of their experience on these visits, and the employing authority will be able to observe the interaction between candidates and staff and children. A number of people providing evidence wanted to see more testing of the ability of candidates to work with young people and more involvement of young people in the selection process. We support such developments.

Requirement to attend

4.16   A number of safeguards must however be built into the visits. The first of these is that all shortlisted candidates should be required to attend. This can only be achieved if the employing authority pays the necessary expenses of candidates, including costs of travel and, where necessary, of overnight accommodation. This will of course involve extra costs for the employer, but avoiding inappropriate appointments will save money in the long term.

Structure of visit

4.17   Some people think that children should not be involved at any point in the selection process; and there are concerns that informal discussions between staff and candidates could lead to appointments being made on the basis that a candidate's 'face fits'. Current practice varies considerably, with some employers insisting that informal visits take place, while others forbid them. Greater uniformity of practice would improve equal opportunities. Moreover, to ensure adherence to equal opportunities principles, there need to be safeguards on the use that is made of information gained from a candidate's visit to the home. We believe nevertheless that these visits should take place.

4.18   A properly structured visit should involve candidates being shown round the establishment (either by a group of young people and/or staff), and candidates meeting groups of children and staff (rather than individuals). These meetings should be attended by a person involved in the appointment process, ie. in the case of a care officer by the head of home; and in the case of a head of home post by the line manager for the home. This person should then make available to others involved in the appointment process information about the interaction between all the candidates and staff and children.

Recommendation 11

Employers should require all shortlisted candidates to visit the home and meet staff and children in advance of the interview. Information about the interaction on visits between candidates and staff and children should be made available to those involved in deciding the appointment of candidates by a person involved in the appointment process.

Group Exercises

General

4.19   We consider that selection processes which most closely simulate the actual experience of working in a post are the most effective. We recognise that effective simulation of work in a children's home will be extremely difficult to achieve. However, it should be possible to simulate the <u>environment</u> in the home, and to consider how candidates respond to it. The most appropriate means of doing so is through group exercises and discussions.

Format

4.20   Three forms of group exercises can be identified: with other candidates; with staff; and with children. The latter two to a certain extent overlap with visits to children's homes; and there is scope for combining these two exercises. This may take the form of, for example, asking candidates for a head of home post to chair a staff meeting, or allowing candidates to be questioned by the young people in the home. We note that a number of employing authorities are already doing this.

4.21   Group exercises need to be carefully planned: questions or topics should be set that will test for what is required in the person specification; that are based on realistic or practical situations; and that can be readily and fairly scored. There is a maximum number of candidates who can be involved in any discussion, and It would be difficult for any assessor to observe more than two candidates at a time.

Assessment

4.22   Assessors need to be properly and thoroughly trained in running group exercises. This may create difficulties, in particular for small voluntary or private organisations whose recruitment needs are low. We are recommending therefore that further development work be undertaken to make this technique more widely available. Those employing agencies which are currently using group exercises and discussions are encouraged to continue to develop these; and a pilot project should be set up to evaluate their experience and promulgate good practice.

Recommendation 12

The Department of Health and the Local Authority Associations should establish a project to evaluate existing experience on group exercises and discussions and to develop ways of ensuring that these techniques are available to all employers with children's homes, particularly for the appointment of heads of homes.

Tests

General

4.23   Before making recommendations on aptitude tests and personality profiling questionnaires (known collectively as psychometric tests) we need to clarify where we stand in the debate on these tests that has taken place in occupational psychology circles. We have received conflicting views on these tests in the evidence presented to us; and there is clearly some reluctance on the part of many employers to use them. We have tried to weigh all the arguments and make a judgement about their validity and use in selecting staff for children's homes.

4.24   The conclusion we have come to on such tests is that providing the appropriate level of tests are used for particular jobs and are administered and interpreted by qualified people, they are valuable in assisting the selection of staff for children's homes. In particular they have three main roles:

- To provide information about the possession of certain skills and competencies important in the person specification.

- To assess personality against the profile sought in the person specification.

- To provide information about personality characteristics or abilities that need to be probed further at interview.

The tests should never be used on a straight "pass/fail" basis. We discuss in the following two sections our recommendations for their use. These tests are never going to provide an accurate prediction of whether a person will abuse a child, for reasons we discuss in paragraphs 4.32 to 4.34.

4.25   Concerns were expressed in evidence from the local authority sector. The Association of Directors of Social Services (ADSS) pointed out in their evidence that some tests may contain a bias against people for whom English is not their first language; and some tests measure performance against populations which do not necessarily reflect the need for the staffing of children's homes to reflect multi-racial communities. In their evidence the Association of Metropolitan Authorities (AMA) expressed their concern that the selection process "should not become too dependent on psychological/aptitude decisions". We understand these anxieties and accept that testing can never be an exclusive determinant of selection. We also note that in their publication 'Psychometric Tests and Racial Equality', the Commission for Racial Equality warn that "Tests that are badly designed, inappropriate, poorly administered, or improperly scored may not only result in unsatisfactory selection decisions, but may also be a cause of indirect racial discrimination". Nevertheless the Commission make it clear that "Used properly, tests can be a valuable and cost-effective method of getting information...". Our views on psychometric tests are similar to the Commission's and as we explain below, we believe that they have an important part to play in gathering information about candidates and informing the selection process.

Aptitude Tests

4.26   Aptitude tests provide a measure of more or less specific skills such as numeracy, comprehension and reasoning capability. They can be selected for different levels of educational attainment and can be used in selecting staff for, on the one hand managerial/professional posts and on the other for semi-skilled or unskilled jobs.

4.27   Within the sphere of children's homes, we received evidence that some tests of aptitude have been identified as the best method of obtaining information about specific skills considered to be of major importance in the job of care staff there. These were: high levels of literacy; good and accurate written English; and the general ability to reason using verbal skills. We do not wish to cite the particular tests used, in order not to promote particular commercial products. However we found the evidence on these tests convincing, despite some scepticism expressed by others. The conclusion we have come to is that if person specifications for jobs identify key qualities and skills that can be measured by aptitude or ability tests it would seem sensible for employers to use them provided the costs are not exorbitant. We would like to see a larger and properly validated project drawing on current experience of these tests.

4.28   As we have indicated, aptitude tests can be a useful tool for assessing competency in various fields. The recognition that there is an increasingly large management component in heads of homes posts has led us to the conclusion that for all these posts there should be some form of assessment of competencies; and that aptitude tests are the most efficient, effective and fair means of doing so. Specifically, there should be tests of verbal and numerical reasoning. As the management component grows heads of homes will assume responsibility for controlling budgets, for example; and report writing has always been a component of the job. The British Psychological Society noted in their written evidence that prospective staff should also "demonstrate an ability to concentrate on and learn the academic tasks necessary to benefit from post-appointment training". It will be important for anyone appointed to have proven ability to cope with the demands these will impose. However, the Institute of Personnel Management have pointed out that "...occupational testing is only successful if based on a thorough job analysis and identification of the skills needed for satisfactory job performance". We suggest that any aptitude tests used must relate specifically to the requirements of the job description and person specification. We are recommending that these tests should always be used for heads of homes appointments, and those responsible for the selection processes for other posts should be encouraged to use verbal reasoning and numeracy tests.

Recommendation 13

Employers should use appropriate aptitude tests as part of the normal selection process for shortlisted candidates for heads of homes and other senior management posts in residential homes.

Recommendation 14

The Department of Health and the Local Authority Associations should commission work to evaluate currently available aptitude tests; and to devise more appropriate tests where necessary for use in the selection of staff for children's homes.

Personality Profiling

4.29   In an article in 1991 Blinkhorn and Johnson argued that it rarely happens that better selection or promotion decisions are made when personality tests are used. Six experts replied to their article. Professor Clive Fletcher of the University of London asserted that "It is extremely difficult to see any justification for the Blinkhorn and Johnson view on statistical, empirical, conceptual or practical grounds". He went on to say that personality tests can never be seen as a stand-alone method of selection, but are useful when taken in conjunction with other approaches and, perhaps most important of all, when the users have been properly trained. This is very much the position taken by the British Psychological Society in their evidence to us, although they have emphasised also that tests need to be adapted for the setting in which they are to be used.

4.30   The professional advice given to us is that reputable personality tests do give a reasonably accurate picture of the so-called "big five" elements of personality - extroversion, emotional stability, agreeableness, conscientiousness and culture. Some will argue that these "big five" are too crude to be used for personnel selection. It is true that they are not the only factors in choosing people for a job. However, they are important considerations in choosing people to work in children's homes - particularly emotional stability, agreeableness and conscientiousness. If reliable tests are available for assessing these factors then it would seem perverse not to use them. They enable interviewers to ask more probing questions on the responses received.

4.31   The other main argument used against personality tests is that they have not been validated against staffs' subsequent performance. Although there are few studies in this, we are aware of a four-year study of 750 managers in two different types of organisation (a bank and an electrical engineering company) completed in 1991. This reported a high correlation between the results of personality profiles and subsequent performance.

4.32   It is important to recognise what personality tests will <u>not</u> do. They will not identify potential sexual abusers of children. The Kincora Report asked for this issue to be examined; and the Northern Ireland Department of Health and Social Services commissioned a review by Queen's University Belfast and the University of Ulster's Psychology Department into the scope for assessing the propensity for child sexual abuse of applicants for posts in children's homes. As a result of this review the Department of Health and Social Services concluded in 1988 that "there is no acceptable test currently available or likely to become available in the near future which could be used with any degree of accuracy to screen applicants for their potential to abuse children sexually". We have looked again at this issue.

4.33   Research has identified four processes that influence paedophile tendencies and the propensity to initiate sexual interactions with children. The first is 'emotional congruence', where children have a powerful emotional meaning for people, so there is a congruence between the emotional needs of the abusers and the characteristics of children. The second is 'sexual arousal' by children. The third, 'blockage', refers to the thwarting of sexual relationships with adults; and the fourth is 'disinhibition' (ie, overcoming society's sanctions). The major psychological processes which define these characteristics are :

- relatively high levels of introversion, anxiety and psychoticism;

- low self-esteem and poor social competence, particularly in heterosexual relationships;

- distorted perceptions of the female role and associated dysfunctions of sexuality.

However, our professional advice is that there are no valid instruments for measuring these sets of attributes in relation to paedophilia. The conclusion of the University of Ulster researchers was that "At best the available instruments are able to assess some of the psychological characteristics which make people vulnerable to paedophilia but these cannot be said to be determining factors".

4.34   It may be that in time further research will produce reliable tests for predicting propensity to initiate sexual activities with children. Certainly we would encourage Government to assist research in this area. However, no test is likely to be available in the near future. The best that can be achieved at present is the exploration by a skilled interviewer of some of the aspects described in paragraph 4.33. We discuss this further in paragraphs 4.37 - 4.40.

4.35   We recognise that there has been a level of resistance to the introduction of personality tests. We note also that in many local authorities personality profiling is used in the selection of senior staff, although it is much less common in more junior grades. Some 17% of local authorities make some use of them for heads of homes posts, but only 5% of authorities reported using them 'sometimes' for care staff. However, their use is much more common in the voluntary sector; and within the private sector less than half the homes say they never use these tests for either heads of homes and care staff.

4.36   In our view personality tests should be used to help determine the extent to which a candidate fits a person specification. This will invariably have been prepared to require that candidates have certain characteristics and an affinity to work in the particular environment of a children's home. Initially therefore we are recommending that personality profiling is used for heads of home and other management posts in homes, as a means of gaining a fuller picture of the candidates. However we recognise that the field of personality testing is continually developing; and we consider that it is important that the potential for tests to be used in selecting staff in children's homes should be further explored. The British Psychological Society have stated in their evidence that they are not able to endorse any psychometric tests which are not specifically adapted to the recruitment and selection of staff in children's homes. This points to the need for more development work being encouraged by the Department of Health and employers.

Recommendation 15

The Department of Health and Local Authority Associations should evaluate current personality tests; and consider commissioning the design of the most appropriate tests for posts in children's homes.

Preliminary Interviews

4.37   We recognise from our survey and visits that any interviews other than final interviews are frowned upon by some employers, often on the grounds that they infringe equal opportunities policies by, for example, asking different questions of different candidates. We consider these reservations to be misplaced. Indeed we would say that an employer could be regarded as negligent in not using a preliminary interview to explore many of the sensitive personal issues we discuss below in order to ensure candidates' suitability for work in children's homes. We consider that it is totally unrealistic to expect large interview panels to be able to probe these issues effectively in a formal and final interview. As long as the staff conducting the interviews are properly trained and are aware of the equal opportunities implications of the preliminary interview, and a proper record is made of the discussions, then there should be little difficulty in ensuring that the process is fair to all candidates.

4.38   In our view, the preliminary interview can be thought of as a less structured and more informal process than the final interview (see paragraphs 4.55 to 4.63 below). The purpose of this preliminary interview is to explore questions raised by any of the earlier selection processes and, more particularly, to consider questions which are inevitably less easy to discuss in a formal situation. For example, as we have indicated, it will be important to look at whether a candidate has a propensity to form sexual relationships with children and young people. This would be a very difficult issue to discuss in any situation other than that of an informal setting. It will be a difficult subject to probe properly at interview, and will need highly skilled interviewing techniques. There may be lessons which can be learned from the recruitment of foster carers, which is a very detailed process, involving group and individual interviews by specially trained staff, who explore with would-be foster parents issues - amongst others - around sexual relationships.

4.39   Thus preliminary interviews should be used - as with foster parents - to ensure shortlisted candidates have a full understanding of the requirements of the job and its difficulties. They can explore candidates' attitudes to control and punishment issues involving children; probe the extent to which they have characters strong enough to resist sexual temptation from children in their care; and whether their sexual interests were likely to cause them to pursue children for purposes of sexual gratification. This is likely to take interviewers into the territory of the stability of candidates' emotional and sexual relationships. They can look also at other issues such as motivation and attitudes to power and authority.

4.40   It will be for individual employing authorities to determine who are the most appropriate people to conduct such interviews. Again, the link with procedures for recruiting foster carers is evident. It may be that preliminary interviews would be carried out by staff with similar skills to those who interview potential foster carers. In order to retain an informal atmosphere, these interviews should be carried out by no more than two people. A written record should always be made of the interview, and should be made available to those making final decisions on appointments. Independent sector employers may need to 'buy in' these skills if they do not have them in-house.

Recommendation 16

Employers should use preliminary interviews as a standard part of establishing a fuller picture of the character and attitudes of shortlisted candidates for <u>all</u> posts in children's homes.

References

General

4.41   The current position on the pursuit and use of references is unsatisfactory, even though potentially information from previous employers can be very revealing about candidates. Although employers in all sectors seek references from two or three previous employers, many do not seek or obtain references until after the final interview. The norm in all sectors is to seek references between shortlisting and interview (except in London Boroughs, where it is the norm to seek references after interview). In about a quarter of local authorities and voluntary organisations references are sought after the final interview. In the private sector this is the practice in nearly 40% of head of home appointments and over 50% of care officer appointments. Thus a high proportion of appointments are offered - subject to references admittedly - without any information from a previous employer. Although some appointments are terminated when unsatisfactory references are received the opportunity to probe ambiguities at interview has been lost. We suspect also that this approach encourages employers to give questionable candidates the benefit of the doubt because following up references after appointment is more difficult.

4.42   The evidence presented to us suggests that the current system of references is of little value to many employers. In particular, employers may continue to give good references to help difficult or poor quality staff to find employment. This was noted by both the AMA and the National Association of Local Government Officers (NALGO) in their written evidence. A common method of obtaining references is to simply request the names of one or two (sometimes more) referees from the applicant and at a relatively late stage in the selection process write to the named referees asking for a general statement about the character of the applicant. There is very little follow-up of references by telephone calls. In most local authorities this practice is forbidden on the grounds that it is inconsistent with equal opportunities policies because some candidates may be treated differently. Phone calls are used in only 15% of local authorities, although the figures for the voluntary and private sectors are 20% and 35% respectively.

4.43   We do not consider that the present inconsistencies between employers should continue. In our view appointments should never be made 'subject to references'.

Prospective new employers should take the initiative in obtaining information about candidates from previous employers or line managers before final interview. Previous employers have the information that enables a new employer to form a rounded picture of a candidate's strengths and weaknesses, and this information should be sought by letter and telephone. Information obtained by telephone is often more accurate and revealing, and to forbid the obtaining of it by this means through some misguided view of equal opportunities policies is simply to neglect the interests and safety of children. We consider that local authorities should abandon any embargoes on obtaining information about candidates by telephone.

4.44   The basis for our approach is that candidates should be asked to name all previous employers (with dates and other details, such as the address and the nature of the work) on their application form. This will reveal any gaps in employment that need further inquiry. They should be told when applying that the new employer reserves the right to approach any previous employer and will specifically ask about disciplinary offences. This should encourage applicants to be more forthcoming in their applications and prevent them from 'selecting out' referees who are less likely to provide a satisfactory reference. It should also deter candidates who have something to hide from applying. What we are proposing is a more 'positive vetting' approach by employers for staff working in children's homes, because of the vulnerability of the children, even though this may not be necessary for other staff employed by a local authority.

4.45   Even though in future the emphasis should be on finding out about a candidate's previous employment record, applicants should still be able to provide the name of a referee other than a previous employer. This may be for example, someone who has worked with the candidate in a voluntary capacity, or an academic referee. Generally this reference should be taken up by the employing authority.

Information requested

4.46   Employers must be specific about the categories of information required from referees. This will be best achieved by sending a copy of the job description and person specification for the job with the request for information; and asking for comments to be related to the needs of the post. Referees should also be asked specifically about the candidate's weaknesses as well as their strengths. Requests for references should also ask for information about previous disciplinary offences. This may cause some difficulties for employers where records are 'time-expired', ie destroyed after a fixed period of time. However, a parallel may be drawn with police checks where, in order to protect the welfare of children, criminal offences committed by people working with children are exempt from the provisions of the Rehabilitation of Offenders Act, and details of expired offences are passed on. We consider local authorities should retain records of disciplinary offences where they would be relevant to employment with children, and pass on information to a future employer where it is requested in connection with a post involving work with children.

4.47   It is important that references are provided by people with direct experience of the candidate. Many candidates will come from a local authority background and it should be possible to use personnel networks to ensure that references are provided by people with direct knowledge of the candidate. It is important that internal candidates have proper references sought as well, particularly if they are moving to work in a children's home for the first time. We do not believe that senior managers should be discouraged from using their informal networks to find out more about candidates and making this information available to those responsible for making appointments.

Timescales

4.48   Sufficient time should be allowed for references to be available to those making final decisions on appointments. Employers should be free to contact a referee where they feel that more information is needed after the reference has been received. Where such informal contact does take place, a written record of the conversation should always be made and retained with other papers relating to the candidate's application.

4.49   We recognise that the more rigorous and pro-active approach to references that we are proposing will cause difficulties and probably irritation in some quarters. Many local authorities will need to change their attitudes. Record-keeping in the independent sector will need to improve. There will be anxieties in the many local authorities where there is an 'open file' policy, whereby applicants are able to gain access to references - both those which were provided in the course of their application for their current post, and those which their current employer has provided in respect of an application elsewhere. This makes it important that references should not say anything which the candidate has not already been told by line management; and this should improve the quality of management. More time will need to be spent on checking previous employment records. Telephone inquiries and informal networks will have to become respectable with those employers who are opposed to their use. We do not make these proposals for change lightly but consider the safety and welfare of children justify them.

Legal considerations

4.50   No doubt there will be some who will argue against what we are proposing on legal grounds. There will be anxieties about the practice by local authorities of putting disclaimers on references with respect to their liability if the appointment made turns out to have been unsuccessful. The legal liabilities of referees is a matter to which we have given some consideration.

4.51   There is a clear legal liability for references. The person giving the reference should ensure that it contains no material misstatement or omission relevant to the suitability of the applicant for the post. A person providing the reference can be held liable if the reference is defamatory. A statement is defamatory if it is false and lowers the person in the eyes of right thinking members of society. This should not discourage referees from revealing relevant information. Providing the reference has been given with due care and without malice the referee will have a defence - known as 'qualified privilege'- against an action for damages by a claimant who thinks that he or she has suffered as a result of the reference. If a reference omits relevant information about an applicant, a new employer who suffers resulting damage may have a cause of action against the referee. Referees should draw to the attention of prospective employers any concerns they have about applicants, whether or not they have been the subject of disciplinary proceedings. The applicant should then have an opportunity of dealing with the concerns. Employees do not generally have a right to see a reference, but disclosure cannot be resisted on the grounds that it was given in confidence.

4.52   We do not consider that this legal context should prevent an employer from providing honest, frank or timely references for a person seeking employment in a children's home. It is in the best interests of children that they do so and this should override any concerns about making critical remarks about a current or previous employee.

Recommendation 17

Employers should require candidates when applying to provide a full employment history, including periods of unemployment, with dates (to the nearest month) and the names and addresses of past employers. Candidates should be free to provide the name of a referee in addition to an employer if they wish.

Recommendation 18

Employers should always approach an applicant's present employer; should tell applicants that they reserve the right to approach any previous employer (or line manager) about a shortlisted candidate's character and performance before interview; should seek written references on the basis that referees have the job description and person specification and are encouraged to comment frankly on shortlisted candidates' strengths and weaknesses in relation to those two documents; and where necessary should explore any aspects of references by telephone with a current or past employer.

Recommendation 19

Employers should keep a record of conversations with referees and pass the result to those responsible for making appointments; and they should retain records of disciplinary offences or concerns that enable them to be passed on to a potential employer when requested in connection with a job which involves working with children.

Shortlisting

4.53   Shortlisting from application forms should be an objective process based on comparing the information on the application form with the requirements of the job description and person specification. We do not consider it appropriate to make an authoritative statement of the correct ratio of shortlisted candidates to posts, as this has to depend upon the number and quality of candidates, which will vary according to the local labour market. However, good practice would suggest that if possible there should be at least three candidates shortlisted for each post, to enable a reasonable choice to be made.

Shortlisting panel

4.54   Shortlisting is an important part of the selection process and should be seen to be undertaken in a fair and objective way. Theoretically there is little difficulty in one person undertaking the shortlisting process if the person specification and application form have been properly designed. However, we recognise that many employers will consider that the process can only be undertaken fairly and equitably by a shortlisting panel, as is current practice. We recommend therefore that the shortlisting panel should comprise three people, ideally those who will be responsible for taking the final decision on appointment. There should always be an element independent of the line management of the post on the panel, but line managers should always take part in shortlisting candidates. As far as practicable the panel should be balanced by gender and the racial balance should reflect the local population. This is particularly important as many of the respondents to our survey reported failing to achieve gender and ethnic balance on interview panels.

Recommendation 20

Employers should ensure that, wherever possible, shortlists have at least three candidates; that shortlisting panels should include line managers and a person independent of the line management of a home; and a that the panel should have no more than three members balanced by in gender and, where appropriate, race.

Final Interviews

4.55   Final interviews form the basis of the majority of current selection procedures. All employing authorities use them, and they are usually the only method of selection apart from application forms and references. We have already expressed our reservations about this. We have already made a wide range of recommendations to enable employers to achieve a fuller picture of candidates before they come to a final interview. It is essential that those conducting the final interview have all the information on candidates so that they can use the occasion to clarify and expand upon any points or issues emerging from earlier stages in the selection process. We believe it essential that a number of ground rules are established to ensure a minimum standard of interviewing and fairness and equity for candidates. The recommendations below are designed to achieve this.

Composition and size of panel

4.56   We consider that panels should always contain the line manager for the post, his or her line manager and at least one other person independent from line management. One of these people should be the designated appointing officer for the post (see Chapter 5). Our survey shows that the most frequently occurring member of interview panels is the line manager, followed by the person senior to that manager, so this approach should cause no problems. People from outside the line management structure could come from the personnel department (if a local authority or large voluntary organisation); from elsewhere in the social services department; or from outside the organisation. The decision on who should be involved must be a matter for the discretion of the employing authority. The use of external assessors (see paragraphs 4.60 and 4.61 below), particularly in the small employing authorities, might well improve the quality of judgements being made after interview, and will enhance the objectivity of the decision-making process.

4.57   Our survey shows that in local authorities elected members interview candidates in one-third of the appointments for heads of home. The evidence available to us leads us to the conclusion that elected members of local authorities should not participate at all in the selection of any staff working in residential care. This is seen by many as essentially a management task in which it is inappropriate for elected members to be involved. We do not believe elected members should be involved in the appointment of staff in children's homes. We discuss the appropriate role of elected members in Chapter 6.

4.58   Large interviewing panels are unwieldy and tend to achieve little in terms of gaining further information about a candidate. Evidence suggests that there is little need for more than two people on an interviewing panel. In practice we recognise that in a large organisation such as a local authority this is likely to be unrealistic. We consider that interviewing panels should include a <u>maximum</u> of three people. Only around 10% of local authorities report interviewing panels of more than four people now, although panels are larger in the independent sector. All those who will be involved in making the final appointment decision should be involved in the formal interview.

4.59   Forty percent of respondents to our survey report failing to achieve an appropriate gender mix in interview panels, with the local authorities much worse in the Counties and Metropolitan Districts than in the London Boroughs. Local authorities also report less achievement of ethnic mix on panels than do the independent sector - one third compared to a half. Again the London Boroughs are doing far better than other authorities - three times as well. We consider that, where the local population includes significant ethic minorities, employers ought to be able to do better and at least achieve what has been achieved by the London Boroughs. In terms of gender <u>all</u> employers should aim to emulate the achievements of the London Boroughs. Although the composition of interview panels has to be left to employer's local decisions, we urge employers to strive to achieve interview panels which are more balanced in terms of race and gender.

External assessors

4.60   External assessors can play an important part in selection procedures where an organisation is so small as to make the presence of an independent element from within that organisation difficult if not impossible. Thus most private children's homes and many of the smaller voluntary organisations would need to make use of external assessors. External assessors could be drawn from any body not directly involved in the line management of the post in questions, and it is difficult to be prescriptive about who might be appropriate. Clearly some knowledge or experience of residential child care issues would be important, as would a degree of knowledge of selection and recruitment procedures. External assessors would also need to have received the appropriate training (see paragraph 4.62 below).

4.61   We recognise that there may be a number of difficulties in obtaining appropriately qualified external assessors. It would be difficult for local authorities to be involved with providing this service. Their roles of inspecting and registering body (in respect of the private sector) and of placing agent for children (In respect of both sectors) could well lead to a conflict of interest. We suggest therefore that there may be a role for the regional Social Services Inspectorate in providing or approving external assessors for homes in the private sector; and a similar role for the National Council for Voluntary Child Care Organisations in respect of the voluntary sector.

Training of interviewing panels

4.62   Interviewing is not necessarily a skill which everyone possesses. Our survey shows that most local authorities have recognised this. Interview training is generally provided for elected members; and 80% of local authorities report it as "always" or "usually" provided for officers who interview. In the independent sector only about one-third of those interviewing have been trained to do so. We consider that it is essential that those conducting interviews are properly trained to undertake them. No person should be allowed to take part in interviews without having received thorough training in interviewing techniques and the proper application of equal opportunities policies.

The nature of interviews

4.63   Possibly because of their preoccupation with equal opportunities issues, local authorities explore few other specified areas such as significant childhood events or the stability of candidates' personal relationships. Given their reluctance to use preliminary informal interviews, the evidence suggests that local authorities simply do not probe some of the crucial areas for people to be appointed to children's homes. The independent sector does not have the same inhibition about probing these more sensitive areas. We are not recommending that final interviews should be used to begin in-depth probing of attitudes to areas such as control and punishment, significant childhood events, stability of personal relationships or sexual attraction to children. These are for earlier stages in the selection process as we have indicated. The information collected in the earlier stages of the selection process should be made available to the final interviewing panel, and unresolved concerns should be taken up at final interview. Indeed the final interview should be used to explore all areas of doubt and concern arising from earlier stages of the process, and in order for this to be possible the interviewing panel must have access to all available information about a candidate. It is important therefore that all information contributing towards a fuller picture of candidates be provided in advance of interviews to the interviewing panel. The person specification should be used to guide the area of questioning and to structure the panel's assessment of a candidate's performance against the requirements of the job.

Recommendation 21

Employers should ensure that final interview panels consist of no more than three people balanced by gender and race as far as possible and appropriate; and should include an independent person as well as the line manager and person senior to the line manager - one of whom should be authorised to make the appointment.

Recommendation 22

Employers should ensure that final interview panels should have available to them and use all the information about candidates from earlier parts of the selection process; and that panels are free to explore areas of doubt and concern in order to discharge their overriding responsibility to make safe and competent appointments in children's homes.

Recommendation 23

Employers should only assign people to interview panels if they have had appropriate training, and should consider the use of external assessors when it is difficult to appoint a panel without an independent element.

Equal Opportunities Policies

4.64   We referred briefly in Chapter 3 (paragraph 3.27) to the evidence presented to us on the adverse effects of excessively rigid application of equal opportunities policies. We are well aware that some employers, notably some local authorities, will argue that what we are proposing runs contrary to their interpretation of equal opportunities policies. The Committee takes very seriously the sound application of equal opportunities policies. However, these were never intended to override the best interests of children, as Volume 4 of the Guidance on the Children Act 1989 makes clear, "Those responsible for recruiting staff to children's homes should seek to ensure that the composition of the staff group reflects the racial, cultural and linguistic background of the children being cared for."; "Similarly there should be a proper balance of male and female staff ....." (paragraphs 1.36 and 1.37 of Volume 4). Section 5(2d) of the Race Relations Act 1976 and Section 7(2)(e) of the Sex Discrimination Act 1975 can be used to ensure that staff of the appropriate gender or ethnic background are appointed in homes.

4.65   It is also no part of an effective equal opportunities policy to introduce such rigidities into the selection processes that employers place themselves in a position whereby they are prevented from obtaining all relevant information about a candidate before making an appointment. This is particularly the case with staff in children's homes who have substantial periods of unsupervised access to vulnerable children. These positions of trust require employers to probe thoroughly into candidates' backgrounds, personalities, attitudes and track records. Providing all the selection procedures are the same for all applicants for a post they are not discriminatory. If information is available that raises doubts about a candidate, it is negligent and contrary to the interests of children for an employer not to probe further into their suitability.

4.66   We know that some local authorities, have particular concerns over the use of informal interviews and they believe that these are inconsistent with equal opportunities policies. However, in our view these policies present no barrier to the use of informal interviews or the conveying of information from them to those involved in deciding the appointment of candidates, as long as this is balanced with the information obtained from all the other staff selection tools. Moreover, against a background in which more than a half of all local authorities have acknowledged having no policies in place to ensure gender and ethnic mix in the staffing of children's homes, we believe they are poorly placed to limit their selection processes in the name of equal opportunities.

4.67   A picture has emerged of some employing authorities applying equal opportunities processes in ways which unreasonably constrain the process of interviewing (eg set questions and no follow-up; no informal discussions; providing limited information about candidates to interviewers). This can only increase the risk of unsuitable appointments, and is contrary to the best interests of children. Instead the aim should be for the potential employer to build up as full a profile as possible before interview. The National Children's Bureau commented that, in local authorities, there is a tendency for interview procedures to become standardised across the whole council, with no possibility of adjustment to take account of the requirements of residential care for children. Where this is the case we think it should stop. We do not consider that - properly applied - any of the selection techniques and processes we describe in the rest of this chapter will in any way breach equal opportunities legislation.

Concluding Remarks

4.68   We recognise that we are proposing far more rigorous and thorough selection procedures for the staffing of children's homes; and that some of these changes will conflict with established arrangements in many places. We are unapologetic about this because the vulnerability and needs of children and young people in residential care totally justifies more stringent selection procedures. Our recommendations will have resource implications also for employing authorities, both in terms of time and financial resources. Some extra costs are unavoidable if children are to be protected.

4.69   Careful planning should ensure that the full selection process, from the visit to the home to the final interview, should not take more than one day in the case of care staff, and 1½ - 2 days in the case of heads of homes. Disruption to the day-to-day running of the home should of course be minimised.

4.70   We recognise that it will be difficult for many private homes and smaller voluntary organisations to implement many of the procedures on their own. It will be possible to run a few pilot projects to test the feasibility of employers from all sectors acting in consortia to develop these selection procedures collectively; and also to pilot assessment centres as a regional resource. We hope that the Department of Health and employers organisations will encourage such joint ventures.

4.71   We recognise that some further work needs to be undertaken on some aspects of some selection techniques. However, we consider that employers should move quickly to adopt a wider range of techniques for appointing staff in children's homes, particularly heads of homes. Table 4.2 summarises which techniques we consider should be required and which should be optional for heads of homes posts and for care staff. We believe this greater stringency will make children's homes safer places.

TABLE 4.2

Selection Technique	Heads of Homes	Other Care Staff
Application Form	Required	Required
Written Exercise (as part of application form)	Required	Required
Visit to Home	Required	Required
Group Exercise	Optional	Optional
Aptitude Test	Required	Optional
Personality Profiling	Required	Optional
Preliminary Interview	Required	Required
References	Required	Required
Final interview	Required	Required

Recommendation 24

Employers should be required to use a wider range of selection techniques (as set out in Table 4.2) for the appointment of care staff and heads of children's homes.

ANNEX 4A - APPLICATION FORMS

Application forms for posts in children's homes should be designed to collect information relevant to the post to be filled as defined in the job description and person specification.

The style and graphics that employers use in application forms is clearly related to the culture of the organisation. But the nature of the responsibilities of people working in children's homes means that there must be minimum collection of data to ensure that employers have applicants' full employment history, receive full and relevant references and can make necessary police and other checks.

Information to be Sought From Applicants in Application Forms

Personal Details

Name

Full name, including maiden name. Ask if applicant has changed name since the age of 18.

Address

Including home and work phone numbers, and changes of address over the previous three years (Note: this will aid police checking procedures)

Age

Age *and* date of birth.

Full Employment History

Details of <u>all</u> employment including, for each job:

- Name and address of employer

- Dates employed

- Position held

- Duties and achievements

- Salary

- Reason for leaving

And for <u>current</u> employer:

- Period of notice required

Local Government Probationary Period

Candidates should state in which local authority they completed their local government probationary period (if applicable), and the date of completion of the probationary period.

Education, Training and Qualifications

Schools attended and courses taken, with dates and locations. If qualifications held, level and grade achieved.

Other Experience

All time since leaving full-time education should be accounted for. Full details should be given for any period not accounted for by <u>full-time</u> employment, education or training. This would include for example unemployment, voluntary work, raising a family, part-time work or education.

References

Candidates should be asked to provide the name of one referee if they wish to do so. This referee should <u>not</u> be a current or previous employer.

Applicants should be informed that references will always be taken from the current employer, and may not only be sought from the named referee, but also from <u>any</u> of the previous employers.

(**Note:** It is important not only to reserve the right to take up all employment references, but to inform candidates of this. This will help prevent bogus employment histories being provided.)

Supporting Statement

To invite applicants to explain how they see their experience, skills and knowledge meeting the requirements of the person specification for the post.

Written Exercise

Applicants should be asked to complete a brief written exercise, on a topic selected by the employer, reflecting some aspect of residential child care.

Exemption under the Rehabilitation of Offenders Act

Candidates should be advised that the post for which they are applying is exempt under the Rehabilitation of Offenders Act and that all criminal convictions must be stated, with dates.

Applicants must be asked to sign that the information they have provided on their criminal convictions is a true statement. There should be a statement making clear that failure to disclose any criminal conviction will disqualify the candidate from the appointment and, if appointed, may render the individual liable to immediate dismissal without notice.

Other Information

Driver's Licence

Applicants should be asked if they hold a current driver's licence.

Canvassing

A statement indicating that the applicant will be disqualified if they directly or indirectly canvas with regard to their appointment.

Acknowledgement

Indicate if application forms are acknowledged.

Monitoring

- Equal opportunities monitoring.

- Where applicant saw post advertised.

CHAPTER 5:   APPOINTMENT OF STAFF

Stern daughter of the voice of God!
O Duty! if that name thou love
Who art a light to guide, a rod
To check the erring and reprove.

William Wordsworth, Ode to Duty, 1807

Introduction

5.1   Employers have a duty when making appointments to children's homes to do their utmost to check on those with potential to err. They must be on their guard and not assume that the appointment of staff ends with the selection of appropriate candidates. If safe appointments are to be made in children's homes, there are a number of checks to be undertaken before appointments are offered to the best candidates to emerge from the selection process. At present these are verification of birth certificates and educational/professional qualifications; police checks for criminal convictions; and Central Government lists of staff who have been dismissed for misdemeanours and unprofessional behaviour while working with children. In the future there may be a national list of approved practitioners to be checked: we discuss later in the chapter the current proposal for a General Social Services Council that might become the custodian of such a national list (paragraphs 5.28 - 5.30). We have already discussed references, which in our view should be seen as part of the selection process because they provide part of the information that affects the decision to select one candidate in preference to another, although they are an essential part of the vetting process as well.

5.2   Even the most rigorous selection and appointment process is not totally foolproof. That is why there is a long-established system of probationary periods for new entrants to a job. Probationary periods are not just of value to employers. They also provide an opportunity to induct new staff into an organisation and start training them for the job they have to do. (We discuss training issues in Chapter 7.) Staff may discover during the probationary period that they are not suited to a particular type of work, after all. We see these periods as an important part of the appointment process and later on make some proposals for improving their effectiveness as far as children's homes are concerned.

5.3   To ensure that appointments are not offered before all necessary checks have been made, well-run organisations will have designated a person as the 'Appointing Officer'. Before discussing the range of checks and aspects of probation, we want to begin this chapter about the final stage of the appointment of staff by considering the role of the designated appointing officer.

The Designated Appointing Officer

Definition

5.4   The person responsible for making the final decision on appointments is the designated appointing officer. In general we consider that this should be the organisational 'grandparent' (ie, the line manager of the line manager of the post in question). It is the responsibility of a designated appointing officer to ensure that appointments are not offered before all the appropriate certificates, police and Central Government checks have been completed, although the detailed checking may well be undertaken by an employer's Personnel staff. There may be very exceptional circumstances where an appointment must be offered before checks are completed, for example where a post would otherwise be left unfilled for a very long time, to the detriment of the home and the children looked after. In these circumstances the appointment should be made totally conditional on the satisfactory completion of all checks; and this should be made absolutely clear to the appointee in writing. The appointee should have no unsupervised access to children until all the checks have been completed satisfactorily; and the designated appointing officer should have no hesitation in withdrawing an appointment offer if doubts emerge in the checking process.

Monitoring role

5.5   Designated appointing officers will have a wider role than simply taking decisions on which candidates should be appointed. As they will invariably be involved with the line management of the post this should not impose any major burdens on them. They should be involved in the selection process from the time that a vacancy is identified, and monitor the procedure as it progresses. Once the appointment has been made the designated appointing officer should monitor the performance of the officer during the probationary period (see paragraphs 5.35 - 5.40 below).

Checking certificates

5.6   People have brought to our attention various instances of job applicants pretending to be another person or falsely claiming particular professional qualifications or levels of educational attainment. Apart from anything else such behaviour would suggest that a person was not trustworthy enough to work in an unsupervised way with children. We would urge that employers, through their designated appointing officers, check birth certificates and validate that successful job applicants have the educational and professional qualifications they claim. Any evidence of false pretences should be grounds for immediate termination of employment if this has commenced, and for placing a name on the Central Government lists (see paragraphs 5.22 - 5.27 below). The application form should inform candidates of this, and warn them that, should any of the information which they have provided - and which by signing the application form they have declared to be true - subsequently turn out to be false, they will be liable to summary dismissal.

Employment contracts

5.7   From our evidence, survey and visits some people have encouraged the movement of staff between homes as a means of preventing staleness, assisting staff development and checking bad practice. Movement between homes can be made more difficult if staff have contracts which require them to work in a specific home rather than in any home operated by an employer. (A more widely-drawn contract would need to safeguard the position of the employee in terms of consultation, due notice and reimbursement of costs incurred on transferring to another home.) We know that many local authorities already use contracts that are more widely-drawn. As a matter of good practice, and because it is in the best interests of children and staff we consider that, where an employer runs more than one home, contracts for staff should relate their appointment to any home operated by that employer, subject to any safeguards we have indicated for employees. Staff who move from one home to another should be retrained as necessary to ensure that they have the appropriate skills to enable them to provide continuity of care within the new home, in accordance with the home's statement of purpose and objectives.

Recommendation 25

Employers should only offer appointments after completing police checks; checks against Central Government lists (and any lists of approved practitioners that may be established in future); and verification of birth certificates and educational/professional qualifications; and should allow no unsupervised access to children before completion of all checks.

Recommendation 26

Employers should designate people at a level above the manager of the appointee as "designated appointing officers" who should be take final responsibility for all appointments; oversee all stages of the appointment process; and ensure that all checks are made.

Police Checks

Utility of checks

5.8   Local authorities now see police checks as an important part of establishing the suitability of a person who will have "substantial access" to children. In 1986 Government guidance (Circulars HOC(86)44, DES 4/86, LAC(86)10, WOC(86)28, revised and updated in 1988) was issued introducing for the first time access to police checks for local authorities, although voluntary and private children's homes were excluded. The police now carry out around 500,000 checks a year on people working with children, although only a small proportion of these relate to people working in children's homes.

5.9   Although checking whether a candidate has a criminal record is a useful safeguard for posts in children's homes, it is important to recognise their limitations in terms of child protection. Home Office statistics suggest that only an estimated 4% of all offences committed result in a criminal conviction, so police checks are going to reveal only a very small proportion of child abusers. We were told by the Home Office that about 10% of checks on criminal records reveal a criminal conviction. The knowledge that police checks are undertaken may serve to deter some abusers from applying for jobs in children's homes. Application forms should therefore always include a statement to the effect that the post is exempt from the provisions of the Rehabilitation of Offenders Act, and that all criminal convictions must be stated, with dates. Candidates should also be told that a check will be made with the police for previous convictions (see Annex 4A at the end of Chapter 4). In these circumstances we consider that police checks should continue for all people offered jobs in children's homes, provided that employers do not see them as a substitute for sound recruitment, selection and appointment procedures. However, there are several problem areas that need addressing.

Delays

5.10   One of the greatest difficulties reported to the Committee by employers is that of delays in police checks. The picture from our survey and from visits to local authorities and homes is that there is a huge variation across the country in response times to requests for police checks. More than half of those responding to our survey reported that the average time for completion of police checks was more than four weeks. This difficulty is particularly acute in London Boroughs, where delays of more than four weeks occur in over 75% of cases. Some respondents expressed great frustration at this, noting that in many cases potentially good recruits were lost. A small minority cut corners and make appointments before receipt of police checks, arguing as one person put it, that "delaying would cause organisational chaos".

5.11   We have taken evidence from the Home Office on the subject of delays. Their information confirms that there are problems, although where checks are confined to the force conducting them, the majority of police forces reply within two weeks. The problems arise where one police force has to approach another for a check to be completed. Here the Home Office acknowledge that delays of three weeks or more occur in a significant number of cases. The worst cases are from one to two months in the Metropolitan Police, Thames Valley, Bedfordshire, Suffolk and Nottingham, although at a late stage in our work we were told that efforts were being made to clear backlogs and speed up checks.

5.12   Although we have considerable sympathy for the Police over the extra burden of checking imposed on them in recent years, we do not regard the present position as acceptable. Some staff take up post without satisfactory completion of checks, or successful staff are lost because the checks take so long. We recognise that the disclosure of criminal records is at the discretion of the Chief Officers of Police and we welcome the way that the police have co-operated with Government guidance on this issue in order to protect the vulnerable. We appreciate also that it is a time-consuming business matching the names of applicants to criminal records, some of which are held at local police stations and some of which are held on micro-fiche at New Scotland Yard. We realise that the whole process of checking should be speeded up when the whole national collection of criminal records is computerised - on present plans by the end of 1995. Also the police have been asked to cope with five times as many police checks as was originally estimated in 1985. Nevertheless, the fact remains that many police forces seem to have been able to organise their resources so that they can reply speedily to requests for criminal records checks, while a minority of forces provide a much less acceptable service. In our view all police forces should look towards conducting their checks on criminal records for people selected to work in children's homes within three weeks at the latest; and within 10 working days where there is no need to check outside the home force.

5.13   We consider that the Home Office has a responsibility to identify where delays are unacceptable; and to promulgate the examples of good practice which occur in the most efficient forces. We recognise that blame cannot be attached solely to the police, who are facing competing claims on their resources and priorities. Further guidance to local authorities on the correct procedure for requesting checks would help to prevent the frequent return of incorrectly completed forms. We have taken note of the suggestion by the Association of Chief Police Officers in their evidence that the criminal records of employees could be periodically rechecked, for crimes committed since appointment. We believe that if the police have the resources for such a system they should use them first to speed up the present checking arrangements. In short we consider that it is the responsibility of the Government to ensure that <u>all</u> police forces give appropriate priority to conducting checks on criminal records for people selected to work in children's homes.

Prioritising checks for children's homes

5.14   We think that posts in residential child care are qualitatively different from most other jobs which involve working with children. Staff in these homes may not only have substantial unsupervised access to children, but will have access for longer periods of time to some of the most damaged and vulnerable children in society. We believe that there is a strong case for treating requests for checks on these staff as a priority over other requests; and that some form of 'fast track' system could be used. This would involve only a relatively small number of checks annually, and would not impede substantially checks on other staff. We know that the Association of Chief Police Officers have reservations about such a scheme in case local authorities use it to accelerate checks on other staff. However we believe that such misuse could be easily detected because the number of staff in children's homes is small. Also, if employers confined checks to people they intend to appoint - rather than shortlisted candidates as is often the case - this would reduce the burden on the police. We consider that with goodwill on all sides it should be possible to develop a system for 'fast-tracking' police checks for children's home staff - possibly by using different coloured forms - so that police forces gave these checks sufficient priority to meet the timetable we propose at the end of paragraph 5.12.

Private and voluntary homes

5.15   Local authorities have relatively easy access to police record systems for the purposes of checking on job applicants. It is equally essential that employers running private or voluntary homes should be able to undertake police checks on the same basis. Both the Association of Chief Police Officers and the Association of County Councils recommended in their evidence that the independent sector be brought into line with the statutory sector. We recognise that police forces would neither be able nor wish to deal with the multiplicity of organisations who might request checks. However, the success of the pilot scheme operated by the National Council for Voluntary Child Care Organisations (NCVCCO) acting as a focal point for checks by its member organisations could be built upon. Consideration should be given to extending the benefits of this project to voluntary organisations who are neither nationally-based nor members of NCVCCO. There is no equivalent organisation who could undertake a similar role on behalf of private sector homes, but we believe that nominated officers in local authorities would be the appropriate conduit for requests for police checks. This is already current practice in some local authorities. There are about 350 homes in the independent sector, and our soundings suggest that police would be able and willing to cope with the small extra workload involved, providing proper procedures were agreed and adhered to. We appreciate that the Government has indicated that there should be no extension of police checks until the computerisation of criminal records has been completed, but we consider that a small exemption should be made in respect of staff joining private and voluntary children's homes in view of the risks involved.

Agency staff

5.16   Evidence presented to us suggests a very muddled and unsatisfactory situation over police checks on staff in children's homes employed from agencies. Agencies are not allowed to obtain police checks themselves. About 15% of local authorities replying to our survey said they made no background checks for agency staff. The figure was slightly lower in the private sector, but higher - at around 25% - for voluntary homes. Although several respondents said they required agencies to undertake police checks, we are not sure how safe this is because police forces do not accept applications for checks from private organisations such as employment agencies. Moreover the 1988 guidance to local authorities makes it clear that they are expected to conduct checks on agency staff. The situation would appear to be that a proportion of staff in children's homes from agencies never have any checks made on whether they have a criminal record. We accept that the police want to limit the sources for applications for checks; and we consider that it must be the responsibility of the owners of the homes to ensure that police checks are made on any staff obtained from agencies. Providing that the arrangements for private and voluntary homes in paragraph 5.15 are introduced there should be no difficulties in these sectors. There is no excuse for local authorities not making these checks now and they will have to be more diligent in the future.

Information covered by police checks

5.17   From our evidence and visits there seems to be some confusion about precisely what information the police checks cover. The 1988 Circular from Central Government Departments is quite clear:

"The police will reply either showing that there is no trace of the person on the details supplied, or giving full details including cautions, bind-over orders and other relevant information"

"Other relevant information would include factual information which the police would be prepared to present as evidence in court, or details of acquittals or decisions not to prosecute where the circumstances of the case give cause for concern"

We believe some of the uncertainty may arise from different local customs and practices among police forces about what is disclosed. We saw some good examples of police forces using their local intelligence systems sensitively to pass on information casting doubt on the suitability of a would-be employee to work with children. This reflected the good working relationship and trust between police and social services that is essential for child protection. We would not want to see this lost in an over-zealous pursuit of standardisation.

5.18   We know that when criminal records are computerised, information about cautions will also be held on the national computer system. Although final decisions have yet to be taken on what other local police information will be held nationally, it would seem to us likely that local police forces will continue in future to have sensitive but relevant information that needs to be passed on to employers about applicants for jobs in children's homes. We believe that it would not be in the best interests of children to do anything to jeopardise the flow of this information. This may mean that not all of it can be put in writing to employers - even though this is desirable - and employers may have to continue to accept the passage of telephone information to a nominated officer. We think that it would be helpful if the Home Office, when they revise the 1988 Circular, reiterated the information to be provided as a result of police checks; recommended the use of written information where possible; and encouraged local forces to be as forthcoming as possible. We appreciate that these issues may also be discussed in the consultation paper on disclosure of information from police records that the Government has promised.

Recommendation 27

Employers should not make appointments before completing police checks, but should confine requests to those candidates which they intend to appoint, rather than all shortlisted candidates; and local authorities should ensure liaison between Chief Constables and Directors of Social Services to reduce delays in conducting police checks for appointments to children's homes.

Recommendation 28

Police forces should continue to complete checks on staff applying for posts in children's homes through nominated officers in local authorities; should wherever possible provide written confirmation of the information given to nominated officers when the modernisation of the police computer system has been completed in 1995; and should complete checks within three weeks at the latest and within ten working days where there is no need to check outside the home force.

Recommendation 29

All police forces should check staff to work in voluntary and private homes through the nominated officers in local authorities or the National Council for Voluntary Child Care Organisations, and in accordance with a procedure acceptable to the police.

Recommendation 30

The Home Office should take steps to reduce the unacceptable delays in some police forces and promulgate examples of good practice; should consider introducing a 'fast track' system for requests for checks on staff appointed to work in children's homes; and in revising guidance should clarify what police information other than convictions should be made available to employers, and the form of that information.

Crown Prosecution Service Information

5.19   The present arrangements for the disclosure of any criminal background exclude the Crown Prosecution Service. However, an Efficiency Scrutiny into the National Collection of Criminal Records carried out by the Home Office in 1991 recommended that:

> *"It should be open to the Crown Prosecution Service, following an acquittal or decision to discontinue proceedings for any charge involving serious violence or sexual assault on a person less than 16 years old, to recommend that the fact of the charge and acquittal or abandonment of proceedings should be retained on the record, instead of the record of pending proceedings being removed (and the whole record being removed where there were no previous convictions)."*

The Scrutiny Report considered that the retention of the information on a person's record should be made where the Crown Prosecution Service thought it likely, on the balance of probabilities, and on the evidence available, that a person's behaviour suggested that he or she would be a threat to the safety of children. Because of our overriding concern with the safety of children we thought it essential to consider this issue and consult the Crown Prosecution Service about it.

5.20   We recognise that this issue will be dealt with in the forthcoming Government Consultation Paper on the disclosure of criminal records. We are also aware that the Crown Prosecution Service is opposed to - and will continue to oppose - the recommendation on two main grounds. First it could be construed as a breach of a person's civil liberties that would, as they put it, "taint" a person's reputation where there had been no conviction. Secondly it would be inappropriate for an independent prosecution service to be seen to be involved "in any way in the selection and retention of sensitive information for vetting purposes". We accept that there is considerable force in the arguments of the Crown Prosecution Service, and we would not want to disregard them.

5.21   However we consider that there is an overriding public interest argument where the safety of children is concerned; and we would ask the Government and the Crown Prosecution Service to consider this matter further. To some extent the information that the Crown Prosecution Service is concerned about is probably being made available to employers now. The police would know when an acquittal had been made and they would usually - if not always - be notified by the Crown Prosecution Service of the reasons for their discontinuance of a case. What nobody knows for certain is the extent to which this information is held on local police criminal intelligence systems and the extent to which local police forces pass it on to employers when conducting police checks. The Home Office believes that this often happens but cannot be certain. Given that information originating from the Crown Prosecution Service is already in some cases being passed on to employers we find the Crown Prosecution Service position a little purist. Instead we would suggest to the Government that a position that responds to Crown Prosecution Service sensibilities and meets the needs of child protection would be for the Crown Prosecution Service to notify the police of all the cases described in the 1991 Home Office Scrutiny Report: this would be no more than a courtesy given that the police will have provided the basis for the prosecution in the first place. The Home Office might then encourage the police to retain this information on local criminal information systems and make it available to employers when conducting police checks.

Recommendation 31

The Crown Prosecution Service should make available to the police information suggesting that individuals should not work with children, who in turn could inform employing authorities through the medium of police checks.

Central Government Lists and Inter-Agency Checks

5.22   Two lists are held by Central Government Departments. The Department of Health operates a Consultancy Service, which holds details of staff who have been dismissed for misdemeanours and unprofessional behaviour whilst working with children; who have voluntarily left their employment as a result of similar circumstances; or who have committed criminal offences whilst working with children; as well as information from the police on convictions of those who have worked with children. The Department for Education operates List 99, a list of people who have been convicted of certain offences whilst employed in teaching. The origins and purposes of the Consultancy Service predates 1939, when the nucleus of the database was limited to particulars of persons considered by the Home Office to be unsuitable for employment in approved schools. List 99 began about 70 years ago. An important distinction to be made between the two lists is that the Department of Health Consultancy Service is informal, whilst the Secretary of State for Education has a statutory responsibility for List 99, as well as the power to prohibit specified persons from being employed in education.

5.23   These lists can be consulted now by local authorities, voluntary organisations, private child care organisations and employment agencies. The Department of Health holds an up-to-date copy of List 99, so when someone accesses the Consultancy Service they are also effectively accessing the information held by the Department for Education. During the 1980s use of the Department of Health Consultancy Service has increased between 4- and 5-fold; and around 54,000 checks were made by employers in 1991. However as the number of checks has increased the proportion of positives has reduced: in 1990 only six positives were found although over 52,000 checks were made. Thus these lists are hardly rooting out large numbers of would-be abusers for employers in the residential child care sector, although the greater publicity around their existence may deter abusers from applying for jobs with children.

5.24   A significant contributory factor to reduced positive checks may be the behaviour of employers themselves. The lists are only as good as the employers make them by informing the Government Departments of employees who have been dismissed or leave for misdemeanours and unprofessional behaviour while working with children. Our survey shows that only about half of local authorities - and a slightly higher proportion of voluntary and private homes - claim that they "always" or "usually" alert other potential employers about staff leaving their employment about whom there may be concerns. These responses suggest to us that a significant number of employers have not been notifying the Department of Health of people to be placed on their list. We hope that this will change as a result of the Children's Homes Regulations 1991 which require those responsible for homes in all sectors to inform the Consultancy Service of the conduct of staff which indicates that they are not suitable persons to be employed in work involving children. Not only is it the law now that employers should notify the Department of Health, but it is in their own best interests. We would hope that the Social Services Inspectorate make the use of Government lists a priority in future inspections.

Consistency of information

5.25   It is difficult ensuring the consistency of information passed to the Consultancy Service by employers. The Association of Directors of Social Services (ADSS) commented in their evidence that the current system is flawed, in that its information relates only to persons convicted of an offence whilst employed in Social Services work; and it does not require employers in the private and voluntary sectors to provide comprehensive information on previous convictions or concerns. The Department of Health should issue guidance pointing out the responsibility of all employers to pass on information about unacceptable behaviour; making it clear to all employers the types and characteristics of behaviour which are deemed unacceptable and therefore notifiable; and clarifying the format in which this information should be passed on. New guidance would provide an opportunity to give added publicity to the Consultancy Service.

5.26   The contribution that the Central Government Lists can make to the appointment of suitable staff to children's homes is always going to be limited. As with police checks they are no substitute for good selection and appointment procedures. However they do provide a mechanism through which prospective employers can be put in touch with people who may have adverse information - outside the police system - about those they are considering as employees. Until the changes we have recommended are introduced they are also the main way of giving voluntary and private employers access to limited police and other information of an adverse nature. We consider therefore that the Central Government lists should continue to be maintained by the Government Departments, although their quality should be improved by the measures we propose in paragraph 5.25. We have looked at whether a non-governmental agency should maintain these lists, but consider that this would make employers less likely to notify information. We conclude that Government Departments should continue to maintain these lists, unless the Government chooses to integrate them into a National Criminal Records Service or other body at some future stage.

Requirement to consult

5.27   Although the Children's Homes Regulations 1991 now require employers to notify the Secretary of State for Health of misconduct which indicates that a person is not suitable for working with children, the requirement to consult the service is in guidance only. Our survey reveals that many employers do not use the Central Government lists. The Consultancy service is used by about half the employers in the local authority and voluntary sectors but by less than one-third of private homes. There is some use of List 99, but users are heavily outnumbered by non-users. Clearly the Government guidance is not being followed by large numbers of employers. We recommend therefore that the requirement on employers to consult both the Consultancy Service and List 99 be put on a statutory basis, by incorporating it in Regulations. This will help also to reinforce the importance of notifying Government Departments of adverse information on staff.

Recommendation 32

The Department of Health should issue guidance, clarifying the categories of behaviour which should be notified to the Consultancy Service and the information which should be provided, and publicising the existence and value of the service.

Recommendation 33

Employers should be required by Regulation to consult the Department of Health's Consultancy Service and the Department for Education's List 99 in respect of any person they intend to appoint to a children's home.

National List of Approved Practitioners

5.28   For several decades now there has been discussion of establishing an independent regulatory body for social workers that would hold a list of approved practitioners. If such a list existed then this would make the job of vetting would-be employees easier for employers. However it would be no guarantee against abusers obtaining employment in a children's home because some of those convicted of abuse in institutions have been qualified professionals who would have been on any national list of approved practitioners.

5.29   In 1990 Professor Roy Parker produced a report, "Safeguarding Standards" which concluded that there was now a compelling case for a regulatory body that covered all social services staff, not just social workers. While we have been at work an Action Group - with representatives of all the major interest groups and chaired by Sir Peter Barclay - has produced several consultation papers on the establishment of a General Social Services Council. Such a Council would be responsible for "setting, promoting and improving standards of practice, conduct and training in the personal social services".   All those registered with the Council would be subject to a code of conduct, breaches of which would lead to deregistration. The consultation papers are now under consideration by interested parties and the Action Group will make proposals to Government by the end of 1992.

5.30   Our Terms of Reference prevent us from commenting on groups other than children and young people in children's homes. As far as this group is concerned we consider that there is a strong case for establishing a system of registration and regulation in terms of regaining and retaining the confidence of the public. This would make it possible to ensure that those working in children's homes were subject to a national code of conduct and would only be permitted to continue to work in homes if they had a "licence to practise". It would be possible to link the "licence to practise" to either particular qualifications or the adherence to a Personal Development Contract of the kind we recommend in Chapter 7 with an approved employer. This would be a safeguard for children, the public and employers. We have not sought to work out the approval arrangements in detail but we hope that the Government will consider this approach alongside the proposal for a General Social Services Council.

Recommendation 34

The Government should consider the introduction of arrangements for giving a "licence to practise" to care staff working in children's homes and for withholding or withdrawing such licences when agreed conditions were not fulfilled.

Probationary Appointments

Purpose of probation

5.31   From the evidence presented to us there is a wide variety of interpretations of the purpose of probationary appointments. As a consequence there is confusion about how probation should be used, and practice varies greatly across the country. In our view probation is not a system for sacking incompetent staff, but a way of assessing whether a candidate demonstrates the right qualities for the job for which he or she was recruited. It also provides a means of monitoring the effectiveness of the employer's recruitment and selection procedures. Failure to complete successfully the probationary period will often indicate that an individual is not suited to a particular post, rather than possessing wider deficiencies.

Use of probation

5.32   Because of the view that failure of probation inevitably leads to dismissal, employers are extremely apprehensive about failing a member of staff. Our survey shows that in 97% of local authorities no head of home has failed probation since 31 March 1989, This is likely to be because they have previously worked in a local authority, and hence had no probationary period to fail (see paragraph 5.33). This would not however explain the situation in the private and voluntary sectors, where the figures are slightly lower (93% and 88% respectively), but of the same order. The figures for other care staff reflect this pattern. We think we have demonstrated that the current selection and appointment procedures are not so rigorous as to produce success of such a high order. Instead, these figures suggest to us that current probationary systems act as a barrier to removing unsuitable staff from particular children's homes when they cannot be dismissed under normal disciplinary or inefficiency procedures, but where they are shown to be inappropriate for the post to which they have been appointed. The standard of probation depends on the competency of the assessor; and it seems to us that insufficient attention has been paid to ensuring that assessors are aware of the importance of the probationary period.

5.33   The problem is underlined in local authorities by the national conditions of service. At present, those already working for a local authority do not have to undergo a probation period when moving into residential child care from any other area of local authority work, although we understand that some local authorities do impose their own probationary requirements outside the national terms and conditions. Only some 14% of authorities report that all staff in children's homes must complete some form of probation no matter what their background.

Length of probation period

5.34   There is a wide variation in the length of probation periods. Eighty-nine percent of local authorities have a six month probationary period. Within the independent sector the period is sometimes longer. Sixteen percent of voluntary organisations have a 12 month probationary period; and one private home reports having a probationary period of 24 months. We consider that it is in the best interests of children that the probationary period should be not less than 12 months for all appointments to children's homes, regardless of the background of the person appointed. We recognise that, in the case of employees moving from one local authority post to another or within a local authority, this will necessitate changes to the national terms and conditions by the National Joint Council.

Assessment of probation

5.35   The fact that very few people fail the probationary period raises doubts about the rigour applied in the assessment. More structured use of the probationary period must be made with regular assessments, properly documented. A substantial minority of employing authorities (13% of local authorities, 22% of voluntary organisations and 15% of private homes) report having no formal appraisal at the end of the probation period. The probation period should be closely linked to the formal induction and initial training processes for new members of staff and the use of Personal Development Contracts (see Chapter 7). Probation thus becomes part of an individual's personal development in the first year of appointment, and it is vital that there be regular assessment and monitoring of progress. The end of the probationary period should hold no surprises for the member of staff. Regular formal assessment should ensure that at all stages of the probation period the individual is aware of progress and of his or her shortcomings, and advised on how problems are to be tackled. This may be as much in the interests of the employee as the employer, as it gives the employee an opportunity to reappraise at an early stage whether he or she should be seeking another appointment.

5.36   We consider that there should be one formal assessment within six weeks of appointment; and a second within six months of appointment. At this latter the member of staff and the immediate line manager should agree what further development is needed for the successful completion of probation, and there should be time for the appropriate action to be taken before the end of the twelve month period. The final formal assessment should take place at 12 months. Employers should have no misgivings about extending the probationary period where the development of the member of staff to enable them to satisfy the requirements is properly planned. A probationary period should not be extended more than once, and no probationary period should ever last more than two years.

Recording of assessments

5.37   The results of all formal assessments within the probation period should be agreed by the member of staff and the immediate line manager, and recorded. The method of recording should allow for any disagreements to be registered. The outcome should be seen by the designated appointing officer, who will thus be able to monitor the appointment. The final assessment after a year should involve the member of staff, immediate line manager and designated appointing officer. If probation is successfully completed, the member of staff should be given written certification that he or she has successfully completed probation. This should record what induction and training has taken place, and the requirements of the probation period. This certification should not be seen as a 'licence to practise', but as a record that the individual has satisfied line management that he or she is competent to work with children in that particular home.

5.38   These changes in the system of probation are intended to ensure that all employing authorities are operating according to the principles of best practice which we have observed during our inquiry. It is important that probation is seen as a component of a total package of induction training, development and assessment during the first year of appointment. There are clearly links with other aspects of training, in particular the Personal Development Contract, of which the certification that an individual has successfully completed the probationary period could form a part.

Staff who fail probation

5.39   Given these more rigorous procedures in relation to probation, we recognise that there is likely to be an increase in the number of appointees who fail probation and will not be able to continue to work in the home to which they were appointed. This should be offset to a large extent by the more rigorous recruitment and selection procedures which ought to filter out many applicants who may have gone on to fail probation. However, there will undoubtedly be a number who, for a variety of reasons, fail probation. If they are unsuitable for work in residential child care as a whole employing authorities should feel under no obligation to re-employ these staff in another children's home. If they are simply felt to be unsuitable for work in a specific home the possibility of redeployment to a more suitable home should be considered (with appropriate supervision and training), although they will of course need to begin a new probationary period.

5.40   Exactly how these situations should be handled must be left to the discretion of the employing authorities. However, we anticipate that the numbers involved will be very small. In all cases the overriding principle is that the welfare of the child must be the foremost concern of the employer; and staff who have shown themselves to be unsuitable for work in residential child care have no right to remain employed in that field.

Recommendation 35

The Local Authority Associations should negotiate amendments to the National Terms and Conditions so that probationary periods of 12 months become standard practice for <u>all</u> new appointments to children's homes irrespective of whether a person comes from within the same employing authority or another local authority.

Recommendation 36

Employers should ensure that the performance of individuals is rigorously monitored and documented by the immediate line manager during probationary periods with formal assessments within the first six weeks, within six months, and a final appraisal at 12 months, with a certificate that the person has satisfactorily completed probation; and that assessments are seen by the designated appointing officer.

Traineeships

5.41   Traineeship is a further development of which we are aware. This involves employing people new to residential child care on an initial one year contract, during which period they work under close supervision, with an option to take that person on permanently at the end of the year. It is a useful way of ensuring that appointees moving in from other areas of employment do not remain in post if they are unsuitable simply because of the difficulties in dismissing them. We recommend that consideration should be given to establishing pilot projects to determine whether this system can be applied across the whole sector.

Recommendation 37

The Department of Health and Local Authority Associations should consider establishing a number of carefully monitored pilot projects whereby new entrants to work in children's residential care could be regarded as trainees working under supervision for a defined period as an alternative to the probationary system.

Applicants from within the European Community

5.42   We note that selection and appointment arrangements are often different in other European countries. These variations will have important consequences as the free movement of labour within the European Community increases. Some respondents to our survey noted greater difficulties with obtaining references and checks on criminal records for staff from overseas. The police have made it clear that - other than in exceptional circumstances - they cannot make inquiries about the pasts of people from overseas or establish details of convictions acquired outside the United Kingdom. Although applicants from some European Community countries may be able to produce certificates of good conduct, it is difficult under current arrangements in some Community countries to undertake criminal records checks on other Community nationals who wish to work in the UK. However it will not be possible to impose restrictions on people from other countries within the European Community which disadvantage them in relation to UK nationals. We would urge the Department of Health and the Home Office to consider the implications of this for children's homes.

Recommendation 38

The Department of Health and the Home Office should consider the implications of greater mobility of labour within the European Community for the checking of staff from other EC Countries who wish to work in children's homes in the United Kingdom.

CHAPTER 6:   MANAGING HOMES

"Management....is an art not a science. Each of us approaches the problem from a different background, and each of us is dealing with a different situation, and a different culture, and from a different starting point"

John Harvey Jones 'Making it Happen', 1988

Introduction

6.1   All children's homes are different because the mixtures of staff and children are different. We accept that there will always be a great deal of individuality about the way children's homes are managed. It is no part of our purpose to propose a set of rules for managing homes that produce an excessively homogenised product and a serious loss of individuality. That would not be in the best interests of children. However if homes are to be safer places offering children a beneficial experience, we consider that it is both necessary and possible to define some elements of a management framework that is likely to be beneficial for all children's homes. This chapter discusses those elements.

6.2   To manage children's homes well and safely we consider that eight key elements need to be considered carefully by all employers. These are:

- Statements of purpose and objectives

- Sound management structures and principles

- Performance appraisal and supervision

- A clear role for the governing body

- Independent visitors

- Complaints procedures

- Contracts

- Independent inspection and monitoring

The remainder of this chapter considers these in more detail.

Statement of Purpose and Objectives

6.3　　　　A feature of other inquiries, some of the evidence presented to us and the experience of visits is that many children's homes lack any clear definition of what they are trying to achieve. This is bad in itself for children, staff and those making placements there. It is also dangerous because it makes a home vulnerable to 'capture' by those who wish to impose their own - often idiosyncratic - view of what the home should be doing. Half-understood and misapplied alleged 'therapies' are more easily introduced into homes where there is no clear statement of purpose approved by the employer and understood by the staff.

6.4　　　　There is no longer any excuse for this situation to occur. Regulation 4 of the Children's Homes Regulations 1991 makes it quite clear that those responsible for running children's homes should prepare and keep up to date a statement of the purpose and function of each home. The Regulations set out 15 items to be included in each statement, including "the purpose for which the home is established and the objectives to be attained with regard to children accommodated in the home". Volume 4 of the Guidance on the Children Act makes it clear that

> *"The overall purpose of the statement is to describe what the home sets out to do for children and the manner in which care is provided. The statement of aims and objectives is intended to be designed for those making placements, staff and parents. It is also directed at those responsible for managing the home in order that they have a clear basis for making management decisions"*

6.5　　　　We support totally the thrust and content of both the Regulations and the Department of Health guidance and would wish only to enhance their authority. However, based on our own analysis we consider that it is necessary to elaborate on the content of each home's "statement of purpose and objectives" - as we have called it. This is because this statement is the basis on which the home and its managers should be judged; it is the starting point for the recruitment, selection and training of staff; and it is the tool for monitoring the home's activities by external observers.

6.6　　　　We do not think that it is possible for the average children's home with 10 - 12 places to be all things to all children. Although the number of children going into residential care may be shrinking, their diversity is probably increasing. To illustrate this we note that one local authority was using 15 different categories to classify the primary functions of the independent sector homes in its area. It is the responsibility of those running homes to produce clear statements of purpose and objectives for their homes and not to arbitrarily deviate from it in opportunistic ways (eg., because bed occupancy is down). Where there is to be a major shift of direction, those who have placed children in the home must be informed so that they can review placements.

6.7　　　　Building on the material in Volume 4 of the Guidance on the Children Act 1989 and the Utting Report, we would like to see statements of purpose and objectives for homes cover in as precise, quantified and specific a way as possible, the following items:

- Age and sex of children for whom the home is competent to care

- Conditions, behaviours or disabilities that represent the home's primary purpose and competence (eg., substance abuse, sexual abuse, sexual abusers, physical disability, learning disability, severe behavioural disturbance)

- Care and development objectives for children

- Policy on child development, religious observance and discipline and control

- Management and staff values

- Therapeutic methods used at the home

- Physical environment the home is seeking to achieve

To some extent these items are covered in the Children's Homes Regulations and associated guidance, but there are no requirements on homes to define their purposes and objectives in such a precise form. Unless there is more precision and standardisation in the presentation of information it will be difficult to identify inconsistencies in homes' approaches and pick up early-warning signals of trouble. It will also be difficult to ensure appropriate management and staffing. We consider that there is more likely to be effective management and monitoring of children's homes if there are statements of purpose and objectives covering the items we have identified. These statements should be the starting point for job descriptions and person specifications recommended in Chapter 3 (see paragraphs 3.18 and 3.27).

6.8   We are <u>not</u> saying that homes should confine themselves to these items in preparing the statements currently required of them under the Children's Homes Regulations, which involve a wider range of information covering items such as a home's organisation, staffing, facilities and services. These are important aspects of a home's accountability, as are the statements of admissions policy required under the Children Act guidance. What we are proposing is more precision and standardisation in the main statement of a home's purpose and objectives to avoid misunderstanding and confusion. An appropriate opportunity might be taken by the Department of Health to recast the Regulations and guidance to cover matters in the way we suggest.

6.9   In very large, campus-type establishments with more than one unit we consider that each unit should have its own statement of purpose and objectives, reflecting the individual nature of each unit.

Employer approval and review

6.10   These statements should have the approval of the governing body or elected members and should be reviewed annually. Employing authorities should ensure adherence to the terms of the statement - in particular the numbers, ages, gender and behaviours of the children looked after - to ensure that homes do not attempt to take on inappropriate tasks. Where changes are made job descriptions should be altered accordingly, and staff should be made aware of this. If the objectives of the homes change substantially, requiring of the staff new skills or competencies, appropriate training should be provided to enable the staff to meet the new objectives of a home. It may be necessary to consider closing the home for a short time to enable staff to receive appropriate training. It would not be appropriate to retrain staff for <u>wholesale</u> changes while they are caring for a changing group of children.

Monitoring

6.11   Monitoring of adherence to these statements is an important task for management, to avoid homes changing by chance. We have observed that homes are frequently called upon in an emergency to look after children who would not normally be placed in that home, and often this placement becomes long-term or permanent. Not all such placements are inappropriate, but homes should not be used for this purpose unless it is a specific part of their purpose and objectives. Monitoring by management is vital to ensure not only that homes are achieving their objectives, but that those objectives are being achieved for the right children. In addition, adherence to the statement of purpose and objectives should be considered in the course of inspections.

Registering homes

6.12   Greater standardisation of statements of purpose and objectives would make it possible to consider a scheme of home categorisation and possibly registering homes by specialisation as a means of enforcing higher standards. We discuss this issue further in Chapter 9. Meanwhile we turn to the management structure and principles that need to underpin these statements.

Recommendation 39

Employers should approve, keep up-to-date and monitor a publicly available statement of purpose and objectives for each home - or in large homes each unit - covering the items specified in paragraph 6.7 as part of the obligations placed on them by the Children's Homes Regulations.

Management Structures and Principles

6.13   At present the management structure within which homes are managed varies widely: in local authorities according to geography and the size of the residential child care sector; and in the independent sector according to the local or national structure of the organisation, the number of homes operated and main users of the facilities. We do not consider that it is practicable to identify a single structure as a model but there are a number of considerations that need to be addressed by organisations in determining sound management structures within which children's homes operate. We have tried to set out some principles which should guide employer's thinking in determining their own management structures.

Grouping of homes

6.14 Although the size of children's homes varies considerably - from the largest at around 120 to smaller homes looking after as few as four or five children - the trend is towards smaller homes. Units of 10 to 12 places are becoming the norm. This will undoubtedly have considerable implications for the management of homes which, combined with the overall reduction in numbers of homes, suggests that management structures will need a degree of flexibility to accommodate change. Structures must be able to meet the demands which fewer, smaller homes will impose. A small home may produce staffing difficulties when there is sickness or limit the scope for training opportunities. It may be difficult to ensure sufficient breadth of opportunity and experience for staff in a small home. A small home may be seen by some managers as less of a management challenge; and lots of ungrouped small homes provides fewer career opportunities for those from a residential background.

6.15 In general we think that it is easier to reconcile the smaller size of individual homes with management and staffing needs by grouping smaller homes under a single manager. This would enable employing authorities to ensure adequate flexibility of staff deployment, satisfactory training arrangements, proper supervision, high quality managers and wider experience for staff. It will also help to overcome problems of isolation of staff in smaller homes which are at present managed as a single unit, as managers can ensure frequent contact between groups of staff. Clearly this will only be possible in local authorities or in larger private or voluntary organisations which are regionally rather than nationally based, or which have a large provision within a given geographical area.

6.16 Where the grouping of smaller homes is not practicable, there may be scope for linking children's homes in a management structure with other service responses to children. Possible examples of these are family centres providing outreach work to children in the community; specialist fostering services; some intermediate treatment centres. All these services help children of a similar age and sometimes of a similar background to those in children's homes and such linkages provide scope for staff to move between services and extend their knowledge and experience. There may well be merit in linking these services to children's homes managerially even where there are enough homes to form a workable grouping.

Linking homes to fieldwork

6.17 There are complex arguments within local authorities about whether children's homes should be linked managerially to those field social workers who are responsible for assessing the needs of a child in care. Although some employers have linked fieldwork and residential care in a single structure, there are some potential dangers to which we would draw attention because of potential conflict of interest. Theoretically at least, a child's field social worker has assessed the child's needs; placed the child in a particular home in accordance with an agreed plan for the child's future; and will see the child regularly to monitor progress. Thus the social worker and his or her line management can play a key role in ensuring standards of care within a home. This will be crucial where children are placed in homes in the independent sector, and management structures may be less strong than in local authorities, or where the home is geographically remote from the placing authority. There becomes a potential for conflict of interest for a senior manager if field social workers criticise practices within a particular home. This can be avoided if field social workers and heads of homes do not report to the same line manager. Separation of management responsibility in this way will ensure that there are more safeguards for the child.

6.18   We recognise that in the real world it does not always work this way. Sometimes the field social workers are conspicuous in the homes by their absence; and the key worker in the home takes on the role of the field social worker. Regrettably it is occasionally the case that a child does not have a field social worker at all. We are also aware that in some places there are long-standing arrangements whereby fieldwork and residential work are managed within the same structure. Nevertheless, we consider that as a matter of management principle it is better to manage fieldwork services separately from residential care in order to avoid conflict of managerial interest and enhance safeguards for children.

Flatter management structures

6.19   Several inquiries have revealed an excessively large number of management levels between the individual home and the head of the organisation. This can make it extremely difficult, for example, for Directors of Social Services in large authorities to know accurately about problems in individual homes. Staff need to have access to senior managers; and they should not perceive the management superstructure as there to prevent messages getting through to their employer. It is clear from our visits that some staff in children's homes do not see the management structure above them as supportive or relevant to their needs. Overall we believe that the more layers of management there are between the head of home and the chief officer of the organisation, the less effective management becomes because responsibility and accountability become diffused. We consider that organisations need to review their structures to ensure that management levels between homes and the head of the organisation have a role to play that contributes significantly to the quality of care in the home. Where it does not, it should be eliminated. In general the principle should be that the fewer the layers of management (ie, the flatter the management structure), the more flexible and responsive the management framework will be to the needs of the individual children's home.

Managers of heads of homes

6.20   We have observed during the Inquiry that where the manager of a head of home does not have experience of residential care their credibility with the home's staff can be diminished. This may make it difficult for them to take decisive action in a home if things start going wrong. We are also aware of many instances where a head of home has shown outstanding ability in that post, but has not shown similar abilities when promoted to manage a group of homes. Experience of residential child care is desirable wherever possible. However, there is no doubt in our minds that the line managers of heads of homes should be recruited primarily for their management competence. Proper recruitment and selection processes should ensure that these managers have the appropriate experience to carry out their management role. Where they lack experience of residential child care, steps should be taken to ensure that they gain appropriate experience as part of their induction.

Accountability

6.21   Management structures should not blur lines of accountability for any staff in children's homes. If they do then it becomes almost impossible to hold anyone to account when things go wrong and this cannot be in the best interests of children. We have already mentioned the single line of accountability for the head of home, but it is equally true that the management lines of accountability should be fixed, and known to all staff. Each member of staff should know at all times the limit of his or her responsibility, in respect of children, their colleagues and their managers. The lines of accountability should be clear and, most importantly, written down in job descriptions (see Chapter 3). Staff should have a clear statement setting out a number of issues, including who they should report to; with whom they can discuss problems or other issues; and their supervisory responsibilities. This will ensure that all staff are aware of their position in the hierarchy of the organisation, and are clear about their duties.

Delegation of authority

6.22   We agree entirely with the statement in the Howe Report, "The Quality of Care", that homes should be managed on the principle of 'subsidiarity' - namely that responsibilities should be devolved "to the lowest level consistent with the maintenance of good standards". This enables the decision-making process to be responsive to local needs, and places responsibility for management nearer to those who are responsible for service delivery. Checks and balances need to be built into the decision-making processes and management of homes, and we discuss these later in this chapter. Checks and balances should not undermine the principle that management responsibilities should be devolved to the lowest possible tier within an organisation. In particular we consider that responsibility for budgets should be held at the level of the individual home or (within a very large home) the unit. We note that there is a trend towards this within larger employing authorities, and believe that this trend should be encouraged. Heads of homes we have met who already have budgetary responsibility have welcomed this extra responsibility, and there is no evidence that they have misused it, provided they are held to account through proper supervision and appraisal (see paragraphs 6.24 - 6.34 below).

6.23   A key issue that has been raised with us is the importance of being able to use the resources of the home flexibly as the needs of the children in it change. Placing unnecessary restrictions on homes because of out-dated procedures and misguided notions of financial control can only make the jobs of heads of homes more difficult. In our view heads of homes should be given the greatest flexibility possible to move resources within budgets, although they must always operate within the parent organisation's policies and work programmes. As a corollary to the devolution of financial authority, responsibility for training and staff development should also be at the level of the individual home; and heads of homes should be empowered to acquire training which is responsive to the needs of the staff in their home. This is essential if our proposals on work-based training in Chapter 7 are to work effectively.

Recommendation 40

Employers should review the management structures within which their children's homes operate to assess their consistency with the principles set out in this report, ensuring where possible that the management of homes is not linked to the management of field social work because of potential conflicts of interest.

Recommendation 41

Employers should consider grouping smaller homes under a single manager, or with other related services where this is not feasible; should ensure wherever possible that the person to whom heads of homes report has experience of residential care; and should provide each home or unit with its own budget and the maximum delegated authority for heads of homes to redeploy resources within approved policies, work programmes and budgets.

Supervision

6.24   Working on a daily basis with children who are hurt, disturbed and angry can be a debilitating experience. Without regular and effective supervision care workers can become worn down as they find there is nobody with whom they can talk through their own reactions and responses to the behaviour with which they are confronted. Their own anger and frustration can turn in on themselves and the result is burn-out and less effective care for children. Standards can drop and inappropriate staff behaviour can develop unchecked. Regular supervision and performance appraisal has a vital role to play in maintaining standards and morale in children's homes. Staff must be able to discuss constructively problems and challenges they are facing in their work. Managers should use supervision as a way of discussing the performance of an individual member of staff, and encouraging their development. For supervision to be valuable, it must be seen as a two-way process from which both parties can gain.

6.25   Earlier Inquiries such as Leeways, Kincora and Pindown have all emphasised the importance of good supervision and appraisal arrangements as a defence against inappropriate conduct by staff. However the picture from our survey is far from encouraging. Formal appraisal systems exist in only 30% of local authorities for heads of homes and 18% of authorities for care staff. We are aware of large authorities where there is little or no appraisal. Moreover there is significant variation between different types of authority. Although over half the Counties have appraisal systems for heads of homes and about a third have them for care staff, these figures drop dramatically in the Metropolitan Boroughs to under 10% and 5% respectively. In the independent sector over half the organisations reported having an appraisal system for heads of homes and care staff. We find it extraordinary that in the 1990s, and after all that has been said about the importance of appraisal, such a high proportion of staff in homes are not subject to any formal appraisal. We do not believe that supervision without some element of appraisal can ever be effective in maintaining and raising standards. A major change of attitude is required.

6.26   There is some slightly better news on supervision of care staff by heads of homes, which takes place fortnightly to monthly in nearly all cases and weekly in nearly half of private homes and a quarter of voluntary homes. However interpretation of the term "formal supervision" may vary between homes, and it is clear that much supervision is informal. One respondent drew attention to the "vicious circle in which staff require supervision by more senior practitioners who are not trained to provide it".

Frequency of supervision

6.27   Supervision should be regular and planned. Time should be made available to enable supervision sessions to take place at predetermined and agreed intervals. In many homes staff felt that the level and frequency of supervision was much lower than they would have wished, as they are unable to spare the time from their day to day tasks for formal supervision. Many employing authorities report that the bulk of supervision in children's homes is 'informal'. By this we can only assume that they mean it is unplanned, ad hoc and irregular. Formal management supervision should take place between a member of staff and his or her line manager <u>at least</u> fortnightly - as already happens in some places. Outcomes should be agreed and recorded by both parties. The manager at the next level should regularly monitor the recording of supervision sessions, and check that the action agreed has been taken.

Content of supervision

6.28   There can be two elements to supervision: professional support and oversight; and management of performance. Where care staff have no management responsibilities, then clearly supervision will be concerned more with individual case issues that need to be dealt with. Even then staff performance can still be assessed by a supervisor. However, it is essential that when a job has both management and professional elements, the supervisor should be capable of dealing with both elements, and able to raise and resolve issues of poor performance in either area.

Staff concerns

6.29   Supervision presents an opportunity for staff to raise with their line manager concerns which they might have about a particular child or the actions of another member of staff. It may not always be possible or easy to do this. We have recommended elsewhere that systems be established to ensure that staff are able to go outside the line management structure or the employing authority if they consider this to be necessary (see

Chapter 8). However, staff must understand that, in the first instance, they should discuss these issues with their line manager during supervision providing of course that their concerns are not about the actions of the line manager. The recording of agreed outcomes, and monitoring of those outcomes by more senior management should ensure that staff will not suffer repercussions from their line managers if they raise uncomfortable issues.

Development

6.30   Supervision sessions should be used by staff and line managers to consider development issues. The main channel for this will be the Personal Development Contract (see Chapter 7). Supervision sessions should be used as a chance to review the agreements contained in the Personal Development Contract, and if necessary to consider whether any changes are necessary.

Recommendation 42

The Government should require employers to ensure that regular supervision of all staff by line managers takes place at least fortnightly and appropriate remedial or developmental action is agreed, recorded and taken as a result.

Recommendation 43

Employers should ensure that supervision is seen as the normal means by which staff are able to raise with their line manager any concerns about the welfare or treatment of a child; but that staff have access to advice about a child outside the line management chain and are able to raise any concerns through an independent staff support service.

Recommendation 44

Line managers should take the initiative in supervision sessions in raising developmental issues with staff and should ensure that Personal Development Contracts are used effectively to develop staff in ways consistent with a homes objectives.

Performance Appraisal

6.31   Proper performance appraisal is essential to ensure that each member of staff is contributing appropriately to the achieving of a home's objectives. Unfortunately this is simply not done in most employing authorities. There are no formal appraisal systems for heads of home in 70% of local authorities, 48% of voluntary homes and 36% of private homes. The situation is worse for other care staff in all sectors. We recognise that, particularly in the local authority sector, there is a reluctance on the part of staff to see appraisal as anything other than a critical process. However, it should be seen as a constructive two-way process that gives staff an opportunity to discuss their own long term development and to assess their future career. Appraisal is as much about what the organisation should do for the individual as it is about what the individual should do for the organisation. We are strongly of the view that it is not in the best interests of children or staff to continue to resist appraisal, and that changes must be made quickly.

6.32   Formal appraisal should take place annually, the first event occurring one year after the final appraisal at the end of the probation period (see Chapter 5). It should take the form of a meeting between the member of staff and his or her line manager, to an agenda agreed in advance by both parties. The appraisal interview should contain no surprises for either party. All issues and concerns should have been raised in the course of the regular formal supervision sessions. The appraisal should be a summing up of those issues, and any action taken or to be taken.

6.33   The outcome of the formal appraisal session should be recorded. This should include a note of the discussion, of action agreed for the following year - in particular of training needs to be met as part of the Personal Development Contract - and of any disagreements. Both parties should sign the record, which should be seen by the next line manager and placed on the member of staff's personal file. We would urge all employers to begin consultations with their staff quickly, and bring such arrangements into operation within a year.

Training

6.34   It is clear that many managers need training in the role of supervision and how to conduct appraisal sessions. We would hope that Central Government and employers' interests would take the lead in ensuring that good quality training material is widely available to help bring about much needed change in this area.

Recommendation 45

The Government should require employers to introduce within a year arrangements whereby all staff have their performance formally appraised annually by their line manager; and an employee's personal file should contain a record of the appraisal showing the level of performance achieved and the agreed training needs to be met within the next 12 months as part of the individual's Personal Development Contract.

Recommendation 46

Government and employers should ensure that training material on supervision and appraisal is available to all managers.

The Role of Governing Bodies and Elected Members

Tasks

6.35   Governing bodies and elected members have to oversee the homes for which they have ultimate responsibility, without doing the job of their managers. It is essential in our view that they should not be involved in the day-to-day management of children's homes. We recognise that the trend nationally is towards local authority elected members taking less of a part in management decisions. In our view, the tasks which properly fall to governing bodies and elected members include:

- agreeing the strategic aims of residential child care, by making decisions on what is required of the sector, and its place within the strategy of the organisation;

- approving the statement of purpose and objectives for individual homes, and reviewing and modifying them as necessary;

- securing and allocating the necessary resources to do the job they have approved;

- monitoring performance, by obtaining information about the performance of individual homes and taking remedial action where necessary though their managers.

In order that governors and members are able to fulfil their role in setting strategic goals for residential child care elected members will need to take an interest in homes and responsibility for ensuring that they are properly managed, but without interfering in the care plans of individual children or undermining the day-to-day supervisory and managerial activities of local managers.

Monitoring the performance of homes

6.36   Members and governors have the final responsibility for the performance of children's homes. It is therefore important that they receive information about each home in order to monitor the standard of care which is being provided, and to ensure that where these standards fall below acceptable levels, appropriate remedial action is taken. They should also monitor the situation to ensure that problems are rectified. Elected members and governing bodies should receive annual reports on the performance of each home for which they are responsible. In order to monitor properly the performance of individual children's homes, it will be necessary to develop agreed annual operating targets. In addition management and employers should define criteria by which managers and members can judge performance.

Monitoring physical standards

6.37   The monitoring role of governors and members should include the physical standards of homes. The governing body has a responsibility to ensure that these standards are maintained to a satisfactory level. Reasonable physical standards are essential to good care. The success of a child's placement will be adversely affected if the fabric, decor and furnishings of buildings are allowed to deteriorate. Placing budgets at unit level should enable minor repairs to be undertaken quickly. Repairs and maintenance of more major items should be subject to annual review. Children should be involved in such matters as decoration, and consulted about changes to the physical environment, much as they would in a family setting. However, this should not be used as 'doing things on the cheap' and should only happen when reasonable standards and quality can be assured. We noted on visits to children's homes in the Netherlands that children were involved in all aspects of the physical upkeep of homes, including in one case helping to design an extension to the home, and helping out with the building work. Devolving budgets to individual homes should encourage staff to take responsibility for maintaining the physical environment of the home to a good standard.

Visiting homes

6.38   Elected members of local authorities, and members of boards of trustees for voluntary homes and, where appropriate, the management board of private homes have a role in visiting children's homes. Currently this is undertaken under Regulation 22 of the Children's Homes Regulations 1991, and we recommend that such visits continue. We note that many elected members are unwilling to carry out this role as they are expected to do so without reimbursement of costs, and in their own time . We recommend therefore that, in order to ensure that designated members are able to visit children's homes in their area, this should be regarded as an approved official duty so that they can receive an attendance allowance and out-of-pocket expenses for each visit. Evidence presented to us suggests that the standard of information gained on visits to children's homes by local authority members is variable; and we consider that the Department of Health and the Local Authority Associations should produce guidance, similar to that for other visitors (see paragraph 6.43 below) outlining the purpose of the visits, what should be looked for, and how and to whom reports should be made.

Unprofessional practice

6.39   Governing bodies and elected members have an overriding responsibility for ensuring that children in their homes are properly cared for and that children's welfare is protected at all times. Thus they have a responsibility for ensuring that evidence of malpractice, or unprofessional behaviour is properly investigated. The monitoring role, along with their role in visiting homes and talking to children (see above) should ensure that

99

they are made aware of any allegations, and can monitor the subsequent investigation. As the corporate parents of children in care they have a responsibility not to let matters rest until their concerns have been allayed. Where they are not convinced by a chief officer or head of home's reassurances they should not hesitate to have matters fully discussed within the governing body or appropriate committee of the local authority. In small private homes this is a key role for inspection and registration authorities.

Budgets

6.40   Governors and elected members have an especial responsibility to ensure that the budgets for homes are realistic for doing the job that they have asked staff to do. If the children admitted to a home increase in difficulty and the task of providing care becomes more complex then the governing body has a responsibility to either provide the additional resources required or, if these are not available, to reappraise a home's future. To allow homes to stagger on inadequately resourced is not in the best interests of children, is unfair to staff and is a recipe for trouble.

Recommendation 47

Governing bodies and elected members should approve the statement of purpose and objectives for homes; and review and modify them as necessary from time to time; allocate the necessary resources; monitor that the physical standards of the home and its quality of care are satisfactory by means that they have determined; and ensure that they receive a report on the overall performance of homes once a year.

Recommendation 48

Governing bodies and elected members should recognise that they have an over-riding responsibility for the welfare and protection of children in their care; should regard it as their duty to have fully investigated any evidence of malpractice or behaviour that puts children at risk of abuse and to take appropriate action to protect children; and as part of these responsibilities should continue to visit homes.

Recommendation 49

The Department of Health and the Local Authority Associations should prepare guidance for elected members of local authorities and governing bodies on the purpose of visits to children's homes, the information to be collected, the format of their reports and the systems for reporting back information; and the Government should regard such visits as approved duty for the payment of attendance allowances and expenses.

Independent Visits to Children's Homes

Openness of homes

6.41   The nature of children's homes requires that they should always be regarded as potentially 'closed' institutions that require a variety of known and documented procedures to ensure the welfare and protection of children within them, however good the management arrangements. The more rigorous recruitment and selection procedures which we are recommending will help to prevent mismanagement, malpractice and abuse. However, there will always be a need for regular checks on the work of the home; and its procedures should be open to monitoring, well documented, and familiar to children, staff and management. External visiting is an important part of these "checks and balances" but it is important to remember that children's homes are primarily <u>homes</u>. Children should not be subjected to endless visits from strangers concerned for their welfare. The balance between these two requirements will be difficult to achieve, but the first stage must be to ensure that all visits are planned, have a purpose, and that the children are aware of and involved with them.

6.42   Properly planned visits to homes can play an important role in ensuring that the day to day operation of the home is seen by someone outside the line management structure responsible for the home. There are already a number of systems in place for visiting homes. These include:

- independent local authority inspection and registration units;

- the Social Services Inspectorate (in the case of voluntary homes);

- the requirement in the Children's Homes Regulations 1991 that someone who is not employed in the home should visit and report monthly to the responsible body;

- Independent Visitors appointed under paragraph 17 of Schedule 2 to the Children Act 1989.

These can all provide a valuable picture of the home. However, we believe that there is scope for extending the scope of these checks in a way which is more child-focused, more frequent, and which reports in a more formal and systematic way.

Independent visitors

6.43   Broadly, Independent Visitors are appointed to visit children who are being looked after by a local authority but are not being contacted or visited by their parents on a regular basis. Their role is to "visit, advise and befriend" the child. We believe that there is a place for Independent Visitors in providing a valuable link between the community and children's homes. Independent Visitors could take on a role with individual children in homes which is not at present carried out by any of the other visitors shown above. We recommend that the Department of Health establish a number of pilot projects to consider how the role of Independent Visitors could be extended to more children in residential care. Guidance on the conduct of visitors to homes should also be prepared, outlining the tasks to be undertaken; the parameters within which visitors are operating; and the nature and scope of reports.

Recommendation 50

The Department of Health should establish several pilot projects extending the role of Panels of Independent Visitors established under the Children Act 1989 to enable Independent Visitors to visit children's homes; and should prepare national guidelines for the conduct of independent people visiting homes that clarify the parameters within which they are operating.

Complaints Procedures

6.44   An essential part of effective management arrangements for children's homes are robust and accessible complaints procedures that provide for the thorough and speedy investigation of:

- Complaints and allegations by children against staff and other children

- Concerns by staff about the behaviour of other staff or superiors towards children.

We consider the right of children to have concerns and complaints fairly and impartially considered and investigated to be integral to the proper management of children's homes. However we recognise from the evidence presented to us and from the comments made on our visits that many staff consider themselves excessively vulnerable to unjustified complaints about their actions. It is essential to the good management of homes that staff are treated fairly - and seen to be treated fairly - when complaints are made against them. We believe that this can be achieved if a child's right to complain is balanced by a parallel right of staff to receive support independent of line management when under pressure as a result of a complaint, and by adherence to written procedures for investigating complaints that avoid unfair damage to the reputations of staff.

6.45   Much has been written already about complaints procedures; and in 1991 the Department of Health published guidance on complaints procedures in Social Services Departments called "The Right to Complain". We have not seen it as within our remit to review all this material in detail or to involve ourselves in long-established grievance procedures that are concerned primarily with individual staff dissatisfactions with their employers. Instead we have concentrated on complaints and concerns about individual members of staff that relate to the safety and protection of children. We wish to confine ourselves to some points of emphasis about how these types of complaints should be handled, rather than make detailed recommendations about complaints procedures. In large part we think that our survey suggests that the battle has been won to give children and staff the right to voice complaints independently of a home's management, with a reasonable prospect of independent investigation. However this is not true everywhere and without vigilance there could be backsliding.

Independence and information

6.46   Our survey shows that almost all local authorities have arrangements whereby children can make complaints outside the line management of the home. In over 80% of cases this can be done privately (eg., by the use of Freephone facilities, tear-off slips to the Director of Social Services), or by direct access to the head of the independent inspection unit or Children's Rights Officer. The proportion of homes in other sectors with such practices is broadly similar. In nearly two-thirds of local authorities - and most notably in Counties - children are made aware of complaints procedures through leaflets either before or on arrival. In only about 50% of independent sector homes are leaflets used and they rely much more on oral methods which are used by only about a quarter of local authorities. It is reassuring to see so much progress in this area but the task is now to ensure that all homes produce leaflets for children and introduce arrangements whereby they can complain independently of the line management of the home. In this latter regard homes need to comply with the requirements in the Children's Homes Regulations 1991 that all homes instal a pay telephone to enable them to make external calls in confidence. They should also follow the guidance on complaints procedures that all children be given the telephone number of someone independent outside of the home whom he or she can contact if they have problems.

Advocacy

6.47   Some employers are now using outside agencies to provide an independent advocacy service for children. Nearly 25% of Social Services Departments replied to our survey saying that children could have an advocate of their choice, and about 60% said that they could "to some extent". Over a third of independent sector homes said that this independent advocacy service was available. Many respondents made it clear that independent advocacy services were under development. We wish to encourage such developments, and note the joint project between Childline and a London Borough to provide access to a helpline service for children in the Borough. We consider that such schemes should be developed in other areas.

Children's rights services

6.48   We have noted the development of Children's Rights Service in a number of local authorities. Such a service will provide another valuable check on the conduct of children's homes; and further means by which children are able to have their concerns voiced.

Children in independent sector homes

6.49   The Children's Legal Centre have recommended that every child in a private or voluntary sector home should be able to choose whether to make his or her complaint through the complaints procedure in the home or through that of the placing local authority. We sympathise with this view, and in addition feel that the child should also have the option of using that of the local authority in which the home is situated.

Notification of other agencies

6.50   Where a serious complaint about a member or members of staff is found to be justified after the appropriate investigations have been made, the local authority responsible for running the home (or within whose area the an independent sector home is located) should notify all local authorities or other agencies who have children placed in the home of the nature of the complaint, the staff involved and the outcome. This would ensure that placing agencies are aware of all the circumstances within which children for whom they are responsible are being looked after. Local inspection and registration units should also be notified.

Staff awareness of procedures

6.51   Staff should be aware of the complaints procedures, what they involve and how they affect them. In many employing authorities this is already the case, and we note that many authorities have held seminars to explain to staff the procedures involved, and what the implications are for staff. The information provided should address what constitutes a complaint; how complaints are made; who can make them; who will investigate; timetables; and the right of staff to be heard. We have observed that when staff are properly aware of these issues they tend to perceive the complaints procedure as less threatening.

Complaints by staff

6.52   Evidence suggests that a procedure enabling staff to voice their concerns about the actions of other staff in the home or more senior management is essential. Staff have expressed to us their difficulty in making known their views about professional issues arising in homes. These may be about the way another member of staff is treating children in the home; the management regime; allegations of abuse by other staff; or the inappropriate use of therapies. Normally the line manager will be the appropriate person to whom such concerns should be made known, but this will not always be possible: The line manager may be the subject of the complaint; there may be some element of collusion between line management and the member of staff concerned; or the line manager may be unresponsive or unsympathetic. We have had our attention drawn to several cases where a member of staff has felt that they had to resign before they could express their concerns about their experiences.

6.53   We are aware from our survey that many employers - over two thirds - have given care staff guidance on the circumstances in which they should make a formal complaint. We consider that this should be done everywhere. It is also reassuring that our survey reveals that the proportion of local authorities in which care officers can make complaints to more senior officers outside the home and outside the line management structure is 80% and 65% respectively. In addition, care officers have access to private and confidential counselling support outside the line management structure in about two-thirds of authorities (see the section on Staff Care at paragraphs 8.30 - 8.33), and in private homes this proportion is over 80%. These are very encouraging developments in producing a climate of legitimate "whistle blowing" by staff when they see children being mistreated or abused.

6.54   However employers cannot rest on their laurels. Staff in all children's homes must be able to raise concerns outside the line management structure, in the confidence that genuine complaints will not have repercussions for them in their day to day work or their later careers. This is particularly important where their concerns are about their line manager, or the line manager has been unresponsive to a member of staff's concerns. The complaints procedures established under the Children Act 1989 allow a number of people to make complaints. Among these are "such other person as the authority consider has a sufficient interest in the child's welfare to warrant his representations being considered by them" (section 26(3)(e)). We believe that staff working in children's homes should always be considered as having a "sufficient interest in the child's welfare" to allow them to make use of the complaints procedure. As with children, all staff using the system must be confident that it is impartial and confidential, and should be supported at all stages of the procedure.

Recommendation 51

Employers should provide children with easily understood guidance on how children can raise concerns and complaints and in particular how this may be done initially without the knowledge and involvement of the person complained of.

Recommendation 52

Employers should ensure that all children in residential care have access to a telephone helpline on which they can raise concerns without being overheard and have the support of their own advocates when pursuing serious complaints against staff.

Recommendation 53

Employers should accept that staff in residential homes for children should be able to raise significant concerns outside their normal line management when they consider the line manager has been unresponsive or is the subject of concern; they should enable staff to make use of complaints procedures established by legislation.

Recommendation 54

Employers should have published procedures that make it clear to staff how complaints will be taken up and investigated, by whom and within what timescale; should inform placing agencies and inspection/registration units of serious substantiated complaints; and should involve the police when conduct of an apparently criminal nature is alleged.

Contracts

6.55   Contracts are an important means of ensuring the accountability of the managers of children's homes, and in monitoring the performance of a home and the outcomes of placements. In almost all cases contracts will be between a local authority (as the placing agency) and the management of a home, whether in the local authority, private or voluntary sector. When a local authority places a child in a private or voluntary home this always involves the creation of a contract between the local authority (the <u>purchaser</u>) and the owner or manager of the homes (the <u>provider</u>). When the home is provided by the local authority itself, a non-legal framework is more appropriate - usually referred to as a Service Level Agreement. However, the terms of a formal contract and a Service Level Agreement should be similar, and the approach to relationships between field social workers and the home is likely to be the same, whichever type of home the child is placed in.

6.56   In local government generally and the care field in particular there has been a great interest in recent years in exploiting the advantages of clearer contractual relationships in the provision of services. This interest has come from several directions:

- the impact of competition generally on local government as a means of securing and demonstrating value for money

- the impact of the purchaser/provider split in Health Services and the development of community care for the elderly, the mentally ill and disabled people

- the development of more explicit child care plans when a field social worker arranges appropriate services chosen from a variety of sources, including residential care.

A clear contract is at the heart of good social work practice for developing secure futures for children. We see contracts as part of good management in children's homes, and wish to encourage their development.

Contracts for individual placements

6.57   The starting point for contracts is the individual child. For each individual placement there should be a clear agreement or contract between a field social worker and the home. This should include a timetable for the placement; specification of the services to be provided for the child; who will provide the service; the required outcome of the placement; what external inputs will be available; arrangements for monitoring the placement; costs; arrangements for external visits from social workers, family etc; service inputs, including staff time, qualifications of staff and facilities provided; and arrangements for handling complaints.

General contracts

6.58   As well as individual contracts, we also see a need for more general contracts between homes and placing authorities. For agreed payments the purchaser will be able to arrange the care of a defined number of children in a particular home. Such contracts are likely to have benefits even in local authorities which have not formally adopted a purchaser/provider split for their children's services. They can ensure that there is an obligation to honour the statement of purpose and objectives of the home, in that the home should not contract to provide any services which are not within the remit of the statement. They can provide also for verifiable objectives for the outcomes of placements. Homes can be held liable for their performance and conduct in a much more legally binding way and this can only help to improve standards. We consider that this is the direction in which local authorities should move in their relationships with particular homes. Homes that could not meet the more exacting standards of contracting would need to consider their future.

Reviewing contracts

6.59   All contracts should be reviewed regularly. Where the contract is for a single placement, the review of the contract should take place at the same time as the child's case review, as provided for in the Review of Children's Cases Regulations 1991. This will mean that the child and his or her parents will wherever possible be involved with the review of the contract. Any changes to the contract should flow from the changing needs of the child, as determined at the review.   Where the contract is for the provision of a general service (as at paragraph 6.58 above), the review should take place at the time of the annual review of the home's statement of purpose and objectives. Thus any changes in the home's objectives should be discussed with the purchaser, who should have an input into the process. If the home's objectives no longer meet the needs of the purchaser, they would have an option not to renew the contract.

Monitoring and quality of care

6.60   We believe that contracting arrangements will provide more scope for rigorous monitoring of quality. Apart from statutory inspection of children's homes by independent local authority inspection units or the Social Services Inspectorate (which we discuss in paragraph 6.63 below) our contractual model provides three elements of monitoring:

- The field social worker retains responsibility for the overall care and development of the child and has a statutory duty to review the appropriateness of care arrangements (including residential care) at regular intervals.

- The purchasing local authority will want to satisfy itself that the provider continues to provide services which the local authority needs and to a quality which is acceptable to the local authority in meeting individual children's needs. Feed back from field social workers will be essential to this end.

- The owner or manager of the children's home will want to ensure that the head of the home is so managing the home as to deliver the quality requirements of the purchaser and the field social worker.

However, all contracts should be consistent with national and local standards for inspection and registration (discussed at paragraph 6.63 below). Published inspection and registration standards will feed into the contracting process and ensure that the outcomes of placements are not below the minimum required standards.

> **Recommendation 55**
>
> When children are placed in residential care, the placing agency should have a clear written agreement (contract) with the home on the nature, duration, cost and anticipated outcomes of the care to be provided in accordance with the home's statement of purpose and objectives; should ensure contracts are consistent with national and local standards for inspection and registration; and should jointly review agreements/contracts at regular intervals, with the involvement of the child and parents.

Independent Inspection and Monitoring

6.61   An important safeguard for children's homes ought to be the new independent inspection and registration arrangements that were brought into effect by the Children Act in October 1991. From then on local authorities were required to have an 'arms-length' unit (ie., independent of the home's line management) for inspecting their own and private children's homes. Voluntary homes would continue to be inspected by the Social Services Inspectorate, in part because many do not wish to be covered by these new arrangements. Private homes had never been subject to any independent inspection prior to October 1991. We decided to find out how those new arrangements were working in our survey, because they are an important aspect of managing children's homes.

6.62   Our survey was conducted about six months after the new arrangements came into force. The proportion of pre-arranged, unannounced and night visits by independent inspectors reported by homes was as follows:

<u>TABLE 6.1</u>

	Local authority homes	Voluntary homes	Private homes
Pre-arranged Visits	87%	63%	81%
Unannounced Visits	88%	67%	64%
Night Visits	81%	45%	49%

Thus there is a significant proportion of private and voluntary homes not receiving visits by independent inspectors, while over 10% of local authority homes had not been visited at the time of the survey. This caused us some concern, given that local authorities claim that independent inspection of homes will be made no less than six-monthly. Moreover, less than a quarter of authorities reported that they have mechanisms or checks to ensure that their policy requirements regarding inspection are being carried out. We recognise that it is still early days for the new inspection arrangements, but given the publicity given to concerns about children's homes, we consider that the performance should have been better. It is worth restating therefore what it is reasonable to expect from independent inspection.

6.63   As they are responsible for the inspection of their own homes and the registration and inspection of private children's homes within their area, local authorities must take the lead in establishing standards for inspection. These should of course be framed within any national standards - and we say more about this in Chapter 9. Standards need to include such issues as:

- statement of purpose and objectives

- physical state of repair of building;

- amenities available;

- privacy and individualisation;

- rewards and sanctions used;

- control procedures used;

- treatment and care policies;

- staffing levels;

- experience, qualifications and training of staff;

- frequency and nature of supervision and appraisal).

- children's rights and complaints procedures.

It is essential that local authorities should publish their standards, and ensure that they are made available to all homes for which they have inspection and/or registration responsibilities. Reports must be made available to homes quickly after inspections.

Frequency of inspection

6.64   Local authorities should also make clear to homes to be inspected how often they will visit annually (including unannounced as well as announced visits); and should make explicit what form these visits will take. For pre-arranged visits they should include the time of the visits, who they would want to meet, what facilities they require, any records which should be made available and any other matters. This information should be published with the information on standards. Inspection units should also make clear to homes the arrangements for pursuing unsatisfactory reports. This should include timetables for dealing with particular problems, arrangements for monitoring action, follow up visits, any sanctions available and the rights of individual homes to comment on reports.

Management monitoring

6.65   It is important that the line managers of homes do not see independent inspection as a justification for abdicating their own monitoring responsibilities. The main elements in monitoring processes are effective collection of information, and mechanisms for receiving that information, allocating responsibility for taking action, and ensuring that action has been taken. Senior managers should determine what information they require to monitor performance within homes, and who should be responsible for collecting the information. Responsibility for taking action should be allocated to specific points in the management structure, so that all managers are aware of their responsibilities, and senior managers should monitor the effectiveness of these actions. Reports should be passed to elected members and governing bodies so that they have an opportunity to monitor performance.

Sharing information

6.66   For the safety and well-being of the children it is essential that the three bodies who are responsible for monitoring performance - the management of the home, inspection units and those contracting for services from the home - should regularly share information, especially where the performance of a particular home has been found to be unsatisfactory. The information to be shared should include the exact nature of deficiencies; action taken to remedy a problem; timetables for completion of the action; and monitoring arrangements.

6.67   While finalising this report we became aware that the Government produced a consultation document on independent local authority inspection units, and proposing that inspection units report to the Chief Executive; and that lay members be included in inspection teams. We do not consider that these proposals would in any way affect our recommendations.

Recommendation 56

Within any national guidance, local authorities responsible for the registration and inspection of children's homes should have published standards for homes and agreed arrangements for the frequency and nature of visits by inspection units and for the pursuit of unsatisfactory reports. Inspection units should share information with contracting agencies and those responsible for managing homes.

Recommendation 57

Employers responsible for homes should have clearly defined operating targets and performance criteria for monitoring performance in homes.

Concluding Remarks

6.68   We recognise that the proposals in this chapter may represent an increase in the amount of monitoring, but we consider this to be part of effective management. Past experience in children's homes strongly suggests that it is necessary to have a range of checks and balances in the system. It is important that all those concerned with different aspects of monitoring understand their particular roles and how these relate to others. It is particularly important that children and staff know where they can go to express concerns. There should be a number of systems providing for checks on the functioning of children's homes, so that if one fails there should be a good chance of another working to protect children.

6.69   Of all the issues in this chapter, the two which must be addressed as a matter of urgency are supervision and appraisal. Whatever the reasons and fears about performance appraisal and supervision, the present system must change quickly if the care and treatment of children is to improve significantly and if staff are to have their competency improved. Supervision between a member of staff and their manager must be regular, structured and beneficial to the junior member of staff. Its emphasis should be developmental and corrective of inadequacies rather than punitive. Supervision must be reinforced by an annual appraisal of performance that records achievement and developmental needs. Inquiry after inquiry has emphasised the importance of appraisal and supervision, yet too little has been done by most employers. Senior managers must put systems in place now, or their employers should be regarded as negligent. We consider that the Government must give an unequivocal message to employers about the importance of performance appraisal and supervision.

———————————————————

CHAPTER 7: STAFF DEVELOPMENT, TRAINING AND QUALIFICATIONS

*"Training is everything. The peach was once a bitter almond;
cauliflower is nothing but cabbage with a college education"*

Mark Twain, Pudd'nhead Wilson, 1894

Introduction

7.1   It is hard to see how staff in children's homes can do their jobs without
some level of expertise. If they are not professionally qualified then training and staff
development programmes must ensure that the workforce is able to discharge the roles and
responsibilities assigned to it. Training and staff development ensure that practice does not
stagnate; and it can prevent poor practice becoming the norm, by encouraging staff to
reassess their approaches and procedures. It is the prime means of bringing new ideas and
practices into children's homes.   Training is essential to good child care practice and
ultimately the safety of children. Workplace training is particularly important because it
helps to involve staff in the work of their colleagues and the home. Ideas for improving
care can be shared and disseminated; and staff will be able to feel that they are playing a
full part in the development of the home and improving the quality of care.   Training is also
essential for attracting, recruiting and retaining high quality staff. Good staff are unlikely to
be attracted to the sector if their continuing development and the opportunity to learn new
skills cannot be guaranteed. Children's homes fall a long way short of this picture of
training and staff development.

7.2   Training has been recognised as vitally important in children's residential
care for a long time. A 1987 publication by Barr listed 50 reports between 1946 and 1985
calling for more and better training for residential staff. More recently the Utting and Howe
Reports have done the same. However, the Utting Report found that "the proportions of
residential child care staff who possess a relevant qualification is no higher than it was 10
years ago". We recognise that some improvements have been made in the past three years
through the use of the Government's Training Support programme to encourage employers
to provide more training for staff in residential care. This has ensured that most staff in
residential care have received some general child care training; some child protection
training ; and introductory training in the Children Act. Laudable though these
developments have been in providing some basic training for staff, they fall a long way

7.3   From the evidence available to us, most staff in children's homes do not have appropriate training. Many employers seem unable to offer sufficient training and development to staff. Too often expectations raised on appointment are not fulfilled in the member of staff's subsequent career. Opportunities for development are fundamental to the motivation of staff, including the motivation of prospective staff to consider working in the sector. Our Inquiry suggests that a major change of attitude by employers is required to make good the staff training deficits in the sector. At the moment a situation has been created in which the most disadvantaged and difficult children in our society are being cared for - and sometimes "treated" - by a group of care staff who overall have been given the least training to do so.

7.4   It is clear from our visits that the majority of staff in homes want to develop their skills and are hungry for more training if only their employers made it available. We set out in the rest of this chapter how we consider the issue of staff development and training should be tackled under the following headings:

- Assessment of current position

- Elements of a new training strategy for residential child care

- The role of the Personal Development Contract

- The issue of professional qualifications

- Vocational qualifications

- Induction training

- Management training

- Costs of training

Assessment of Current Position

7.5   As we have indicated in Chapter 3 there are some 11,000 care staff in children's homes. Table 3.2 shows that about 80% of care staff and 40% of heads of homes in local authority homes have no social work or other relevant qualification. In the independent sector the position is better with over 30% of care staff and over 80% of heads of homes having a social work or other relevant qualification. Thus the independent sector - on paper - has a better qualified workforce than local authorities. If one regards a social work qualification as the hallmark of a trained workforce, then the local authority homes have a slightly better qualified workforce, because the independent sector regards other qualifications as at least as relevant as a social work qualification. We discuss this issue further at paragraphs 7.27 - 7.34 below. Whatever one's perspective, the overwhelming majority of staff in children's homes have received no formal training leading to a professional qualification, even though some training has been provided through the Training Support programme in the past few years.

7.6   Using a small sample survey of 20 local authorities, the 1991 Utting Report found a similar picture on care staff but a less pessimistic picture on heads of homes. However that report had no information on the independent sector; and a subsequent trawl by the Social Services Inspectorate revealed significantly higher numbers in local authority homes requiring training. Following the Utting Report a Residential Child Care Initiative was announced, and this will use special training support funding to start training in 1992-93 over 140 heads of homes and deputies for the Diploma in Social Work. No decision has been taken on how long this initiative should run but there are at present no plans to increase training capacity beyond an intake of 140 places per year. The Department of Health estimate that over 4,000 staff in local authority children's homes - heads, deputies and other staff with potential - would be eligible to go on these courses. So if one assumes no fall-out of trained staff from homes - an unreal assumption because staff leave or retire - then it will take about 30 years on present plans to train all eligible staff outside the private sector for the Diploma in Social Work.

7.7   Making training places available is no guarantee that employers will avail themselves of the places. To support a seconded member of staff for a Diploma in Social Work course for two years; pay their tuition fees; and pay for their replacement will cost an employer about £50,000. However, for the next two years the Department of Health will contribute no more than two-thirds of the costs for a local authorityemployer. Most respondents to our survey say that unqualified staff are eligible to receive assistance from the employer to obtain professional qualifications, but many also say there are funding problems. Employers often claim that they cannot afford to cover the absence from the workforce of significant numbers of staff. This is not just an issue for long courses like the Diploma in Social Work but also for shorter courses, especially where a team of residential staff need to be trained together.

7.8   However the evidence of our survey suggests that it is not just a matter of money but of employer commitment to training the workforce in children's homes. Only about 60% of local authorities have a statement of minimum training requirements for heads of homes; and for care staff the figure plummets to 13%. For both staff groups these statements are most common in County authorities. The voluntary sector is worse than the local authority sector, but the private sector is better. We regard the widespread absence of these statements as indicating a lack of commitment to training by many employers because they have not identified what training their staff need, whether or not they can afford it.

7.9   It is clear from our visits and our survey that some employers and managers are making a real effort to identify training needs for staff in children's homes, prepare plans for meeting those needs and provide the funds to make the training happen. We are not convinced on the evidence available to us that they are the majority. The overall picture we see is a children's homes' workforce trying to cope with difficult and complex tasks for which most have not been trained and for many of whom there are no plans to provide adequate training in the foreseeable future. Even below the level of training for professional qualifications we have little sense of employers making a systematic attempt to provide training and support for their staff to develop the essential skills to undertake their pressurised work in the most effective way. New staff are sometimes exposed to difficult client contact without even rudimentary induction training and too often there is a fatalistic expectation that this is inevitable because of time and resource pressures.

7.10   Even where there is a good level of spending on training it is not always clear that the training activity is linked to the overall needs of particular homes or of the service in general. Too often we have observed training for residential child care being seen essentially as a formal qualifying process which merely fulfils the need to have some qualified staff. In most places Diploma in Social Work training is accessible to a very select few and is often seen by them as a passport out of residential care and into field social work. Such outcomes probably reinforce the reluctance to support qualifying training at the local level that we have seen in some places. That reluctance is given emphasis by the severe doubts expressed to us by many people as to whether the Diploma in Social Work as it stands provides the correct training for a children's residential care service that is largely concerned with adolescents, many of whom are emotionally disturbed. There is certainly some force in the argument that more relevant training could be given to more children's homes staff by a different use of the resources put into producing 140 qualified social workers a year for residential child care. This would require using training resources to develop the reservoir of skills and knowledge located in the experience and expertise of existing members of staff in children's homes. These skills and knowledge may not be credentialed at present, but they do represent a major training resource for helping newcomers and supporting peers; and could be of value in any systematic attempt to rethink and upgrade training in children's homes. In the next section we set out our thinking on a different approach to staff development and training, and outline the key elements of a new training strategy.

A New Training Strategy for Residential Child Care

Changing direction

7.11   Following the Utting Report considerable energy has gone into expanding the capability of the social work training establishments to convert annually about 140 heads of children's homes and their deputies into qualified social workers. It is not clear how long this initiative will last and how many of these newly-qualified professionals will actually return to work in children's homes. As far as we can see little effort has been put into addressing the training needs of the large number of other staff in children's homes not covered by this initiative. In our view a realistic training strategy should start from the other end and provide a way to respond more to the training needs of the overwhelming

116

majority of staff in children's homes. After all, this is the pool from which future heads of home are likely to emerge. We think that this approach is likely to do more in the foreseeable future for the welfare of children and the job satisfaction of most staff than producing a few more qualified social workers each year, some of whom will not stay in residential care.

7.12   We fully support the Utting Report's concern for training in residential child care to build towards a recognised professional qualification or qualifications with the status of the Diploma in Social Work. We discuss later how that can be done. However it has to be recognised that the present arrangements for acquiring professional qualifications mean that staff have to be supported away from the workplace for long periods in academic establishments; expensive tuition fees have to be paid; and considerable staff replacement costs have to be met by the employer. As we have indicated earlier at paragraph 7.7, these costs are substantial, and many employers say they cannot afford to send staff on these courses. Unless large additional resources are going to be injected to support this training model - which we think unlikely - the current approach cannot make good the existing training deficit and will leave unmet the training needs of the majority of staff. Any training strategy for children's homes which places undue emphasis on off-site training is probably doomed to failure because the resources will be concentrated on relatively few people and the training resource of experienced staff in children's homes will not be properly utilised.

Work-based training

7.13   In our view the only practical way to train a lot more staff quickly and effectively within the resources likely to be available is to concentrate more on work-based training. The evidence available to us suggests that work-based training is the best means of providing staff with directly relevant skills and competencies which they can immediately relate to their day-to-day tasks. Action-centred learning of this kind is often seen by staff as the most relevant type of training. It enables staff to learn from situations encountered in the everyday work of the home; to develop ideas for dealing with problems as a group; and to utilise the expertise and experience of their peers. We have heard from staff how much they value this type of training, but that they feel that it is not made a priority by management. We recognise that there will often be some conflict in providing work-based training, in that the task of caring for the children in the home must take precedence over the training needs of staff. This can only be overcome by ensuring that staff are <u>allowed</u> to take time out for training; by providing adequate cover while it is taking place; and by ensuring that time is allocated to this task; and by ensuring that management encourage work-based training by emphasising its value and importance.

Teaching concepts

7.14   We know that critics of our approach will argue that it inadequately provides for teaching the conceptual framework within which residential child care should be practiced, and runs the risk of isolation from the mainstream of social work activity. We consider that it is perfectly possible to teach the conceptual framework away from the workplace, but without requiring staff to be absent for long periods. Employers can provide this away-from-the-workplace training directly from in-house training facilities; buying in specialist training skills for a specific task; buying places on training courses elsewhere; providing training in consortia; or using distance learning such as that provided by the Open University. Distance learning can mean staff giving up some of their own time to enable them to take advantage of the opportunities that it provides, but managers can also enable staff to take time out of their normal working day to undertake distance learning programmes. What is required is a change of attitude away from the idea that learning and training have to take place in educational establishments to be effective.

Learning from errors

7.15 It is the nature of effective vocational training that people learn from their errors. The present climate of critical scrutiny of the residential child care sector severely inhibits the development of an atmosphere in which staff can learn creatively from errors and difficulties. There is absolutely no incentive to use everyday problems as a source of learning. However, with a strategy in which staff develop their skills in the workplace, it is imperative that staff feel able to learn from their errors, and from problems which they are facing every day. Work-based training - with its element of self-criticism and self-management - is the most appropriate way of learning from errors, and staff must be able to discuss problems with management and colleagues. For staff to learn in this way from experience in the working environment it will be important to ensure that, where possible, a climate is established which encourages the creative use of doubt or error as training materials.

The role of supervision and appraisal in training

7.16 For the training strategy we are elaborating to work there have to be regular planned supervision sessions for all staff by trained supervisors, together with periodic formal appraisal. We have already recommended in Chapter 6 (paragraphs 6.24 - 6.34) new arrangements for supervision and appraisal in all children's homes. These arrangements must also be seen as key parts of staff development and training. Staff must see supervision sessions as opportunities to raise their concerns and problems and to identify developmental and training needs. We believe that staff have to take more responsibility for identifying their own developmental and training needs rather than leaving it to managers and employers to guess. Both managers and staff have their part to play and we consider that a new mechanism is required to ensure that supervision and appraisal sessions fulfil their training as well as their managerial functions. This mechanism we have called the Personal Development Contract.

The Personal Development Contract

7.17   We see the Personal Development Contract as a way of recognising the importance of training for the development of staff and of ensuring that it is given sufficient priority by line managers. In our view the Personal Development Contract should be regarded as a means by which staff and their managers consider the training requirements of the member of staff; plan how those training needs will be met over the next year, including who will meet them; and agree a written plan for training that is signed by all parties. The Contract should be linked to the statement of purpose and objectives for the home, so that the development of staff is linked to that of the home and the organisation. We regard this Contract as a key element of a new training strategy and we wish to see one established for every care officer and manager in children's homes. We discuss in paragraphs 7.22 - 7.26 how the Personal Development Contract would work as part of an accredited and portable system of workplace-based training.

The competent workplace

7.18   The aim of this new strategy is not simply to develop and improve the skills and competencies of individual members of staff, but to ensure that each home is able to develop its capacity to carry out the functions defined in its statement of purpose and objectives. Thus the training needs of staff must be linked closely with those of the home and the organisation. Equally important is that each home must ensure that it is competent to meet the training needs of the staff. This will mean ensuring the commitment of the employer and the staff to the development of the home as a competent care unit for training staff.

Accreditation and portability

7.19   Staff understandably want training that builds towards recognised qualifications and is portable between employers. Often in-house training by employers fails to meet the accreditation and portability criteria. It is of no value to children's homes to have undertrained people reluctantly trapped in their employment because they cannot access recognised qualifications. Accreditation will not only upgrade capability but also provide recognition and improve self-esteem. Large elements of the continuous training we are suggesting can and should be dovetailed with the established structure of qualifications and should not be seen as a cost-saving, down-market alternative. However to achieve accreditation and portability the work-based and other training will have to cover competencies recognised for qualifications; to be undertaken in a structured way; and be part of a system of rigorous checks and supervision to ensure that standards remain high. In particular portability and recognition of experience gained in the workplace will depend to a large extent on compatibility with National Vocational Qualification (NVQ) requirements. Ultimately the modules of training completed by staff should build towards recognised professional qualifications at degree level and beyond. We discuss the relationship of a work-based training strategy with the structure of vocational qualifications in paragraphs 7.35 - 7.38 below.

Employer commitment to training

7.20   It will be pointless to develop the other elements of a new training strategy without a new commitment by employers to the training of staff in children's homes. Employers need to start by recognising that the nature of work in children's homes requires a properly trained workforce whose knowledge is kept up-to-date. They must then accept that everyone employed in residential child care should be given relevant training which is both recognised by the qualification-awarding bodies and valued by the staff. This training needs to be provided on a continuous basis so that there is a long term expectation that the capability of staff is constantly being upgraded. It is not a one-off experience. Employer commitment also means ensuring that sufficient resources are available for staff to undertake the relevant training set out in the Personal Development Contract to which each member of staff should be working. The range of training opportunities available to staff should be sufficient to meet a wider range of needs than secondments to Diploma in Social Work courses. Staffing levels should be high enough to ensure that management can feel confident that allowing staff to undertake training will not undermine the work of the home, and for staff to feel that undertaking training will not in any way jeopardise the well being of children in the home. This is important not only for seconded staff to acquire formal qualifications, but also to ensure that work-based training is properly recognised and that the day-to-day requirements of the job do not override training needs.

7.21   We recognise that the approach we are suggesting has resource implications, involves radical changes of attitudes and requires a better trained and more responsive management. However we hope that employers will accept that they will never resolve the problems associated with children's homes unless they invest in their staff and help them increase their skills and knowledge. Without a better trained and qualified workforce children's homes will be a perennial problem for employers. Systematic provision of training and development for staff at all levels offers the most powerful and cost effective means of recruiting and retaining staff. We would urge people to accept the strategy <u>as a whole</u>, and not simply take from it those elements which appear to be the easiest or cheapest to implement.

Recommendation 58

The Government, employers and qualification-awarding bodies should agree a new training strategy for staff in children's homes, with more emphasis on work-based training, and less on lengthy secondments to educational establishments; that uses a more formalised system of supervision and appraisal to identify staff development and training needs; that introduces a Personal Development Contract for all staff and managers in children's homes; and that secures more accreditation and portability of qualifications for supervised and assessed work-based training.

Recommendation 59

Employers should regard training as a major means of recruiting and retaining staff, and dealing with change in the home; should ensure staffing levels that enable staff to maximise supervised work-based training; should provide time, encouragement and financial assistance to enable suitable staff to obtain relevant training; and should ensure that their training programmes are structured and delivered in ways that maximise their portability through acceptability for recognition by qualification-awarding bodies

Recommendation 60

Employees should accept their responsibility to be supervised and appraised regularly and to contribute ideas for their personal development as part of their Personal Development Contract, including identifying opportunities for training and obtaining qualifications; and should take the initiative in raising with line managers their doubts about being able to cope with particular situations or young people with a view to securing appropriate guidance and training.

The Personal Development Contract

7.22   At the core of this new training strategy is what we have called the Personal Development Contract. To illustrate this new approach, examples are shown at the end of this chapter (Annexes 7A and 7B) - but more work needs to be done by employers to develop the concept. The first stage in the process of developing a Personal

Development Contract would be an assessment of the individual member of staff's skills and experience and any gaps or deficiencies, including those skills necessary for the development of both the employee <u>and</u> the home. This assessment would take place annually, usually at the time of the member of staff's annual appraisal (see paragraphs 6.31 - 6.34 on performance appraisal). This will be a forum to discuss past performance and future development; and there should be agreement on any areas of weakness, and areas of potential development. Having identified weaknesses and shortcomings, it would then be necessary to identify training needs associated with improving residential child care practice. These training needs should be agreed and recorded; and should not be limited by the perceived availability of particular training programmes or, within reason, by other resource considerations. If staff and manager agree that it is essential to develop a particular skill or competency, then the means of doing so should be found within a reasonable period of time. If the resource implications, for example, mean that it will be impossible to meet those needs, then managers should put pressure on their line management, and ultimately the employers.

7.23   The identification of training needs should be followed by identification of the sources of training provision. These will need to be agreed with whoever is responsible in the organisation for the provision of training - the training manager, the third party to the Personal Development Contract. Sources of training need not be in-house; the training manager should contract to <u>facilitate</u> rather than directly provide training. Some elements of the training plan may involve others, for example group training within the home, and much of the training is likely to be workplace-based, although involving some input from outside the home. Having agreed a training plan and sources of training, it will be necessary to agree timetables. These must of course be realistic; and the training manager will need to agree them also. However, timetables must be adhered to; and managers will need to ensure that the terms of the Personal Development Contract are given priority when allocating resources. Unless all parties stick to what is agreed the whole process will quickly become discredited.

7.24   The Personal Development Contract is a written agreement. As with any contract, it should be signed and adhered to by all parties (the member of staff, the line manager and the training manager). It should record the training needs identified; detailed plans for meeting those needs; and the timetable for action. Action taken to provide the training agreed in the Personal Development Contract must be continuously monitored and reviewed. The appropriate forum for monitoring will be the regular supervision sessions (see paragraphs 6.24 - 6.30) and any changes to the training plan should be agreed in supervision. The annual review of the Personal Development Contract should take place at the time of annual appraisal of the member of staff. Where appropriate the line manager should certify that all the action agreed in the Personal Development Contract has been undertaken and training and development objectives met. A copy should be retained by the member of staff, and one placed on the personal file of the individual.

7.25   The Personal Development Contract should help to achieve portability of training and qualifications. It will provide a member of staff who takes up another post with a record of all training undertaken, qualifications achieved and certification by line management of developmental attainment. This should ensure that the system is consistent between employers, and staff will have a permanent record of their training and development achievements. However to be effective the Personal Development Contract will have to be compatible with arrangements for verifying and recognising attainments under the new system of National Vocational Qualifications (NVQ). We discuss this at paragraphs 7.35 - 7.38 below.

7.26   We recognise that ensuring consistency in standards and in the introduction of a system of Personal Development Contracts across all sectors will almost certainly have resource implications. In the interests of ensuring that high standards are attained, we consider that the Government needs to recognise these resource implications at the outset, and assist with funding for the first few years of the scheme. Given the size of the sector, and the existence in some employing authorities of Staff Development Programmes which will provide a base on which to build, we do not believe that the extra costs will be high. We discuss in paragraphs 7.47 - 7.49 the whole issue of funding this new training strategy.

Recommendation 61

Employers should develop model Personal Development Contracts for all care staff and managers in Children's Homes and introduce a new system within two years.

Professional Qualifications

7.27   It is essential that the training strategy we have outlined provides a pathway to professional qualifications of standing. We have already mentioned the problems associated with the current arrangements for seconding people for two years to obtain a Diploma in Social Work. Many staff and managers have told us that they would have problems in accepting two year secondments for staff to follow a Diploma in Social Work course, given the needs of the home from which the member of staff is removed. Although money has been provided from the Training Support Programme to cover the cost of the training, employers are finding it extremely difficult to fund replacement costs for two years. Furthermore, the experience of Northern Ireland, where a similar scheme has been under way for a number of years, leads us to believe that, once trained, staff will continue to leave for other areas of social work. These arguments would apply with equal force to any Diploma or Degree course requiring absence from the workplace for two years and which provided immediate entry into another field of professional activity.

7.28   We have been impressed also by the strength of feeling across the residential child care sector that the current Diploma in Social Work - or the former CQSW -

is <u>not</u> necessarily the most appropriate qualification for staff working in residential child care. Many experienced people in residential child care believe that the content of the Diploma in Social Work does not provide the knowledge or skills for successful professional practice in today's or tomorrow's children's homes. Critics recognise that the generic nature of the Diploma in Social Work provides a useful common core for all social work, but consider that at present it lacks the focus on child development and group living that working in children's homes requires. Whilst welcoming the recommendation in the Utting Report that higher levels of qualified staff in children's homes are vital to improving the quality of the care provided, we are not convinced ourselves that the Diploma in Social Work is the right way forward. Staff in homes who obtain secondments naturally welcome the opportunities which this initiative has provided: some because they see it as the key to furthering their career; others because they believe it will help to improve their professional practice. No doubt others see it as a passport out of residential care into fieldwork. Those for whom secondment is only a distant prospect take a less positive view. We recognise that, following the Utting Report, the Central Council for Education and Training in Social Work (CCETSW) has been looking at these issues through the establishment of an Expert Group, which will be reporting. However this Group is confined to giving greater emphasis to the residential care content of the Diploma in Social Work; and it has to operate within the framework of the Diploma which limits the extent to which it can add on residential-relevant aspects to the curriculum and practice requirements of the Diploma. We believe a different approach is required, particularly as CCETSW already has difficulty making the present Diploma in Social Work arrangements work because of a shortfall - estimated at 1,000 places - in the practice placements required for qualification.

7.29   We think that it is important to remember that until the Utting Report was published in 1991, those working in children's homes thought that a range of professional qualifications - not just those associated with social work - were acceptable for work in children's residential care. Certainly our survey suggests that many staff in children's homes have 'other relevant professional qualifications'. As Table 3.2 has shown, far more heads of homes of private and voluntary homes and their care staff have qualifications other than in social work. In replying to our survey their employers regarded these other qualifications as just as relevant as a social work qualification. Even in local authority homes there are more care staff with other relevant qualifications than with social work qualifications. It is only among heads of homes of local authority homes that those with social work qualifications outnumber those with other relevant professional qualifications. We think that it is important not to lose the benefits of other areas of expertise in children's residential care, particularly in any redesign of qualifications.

7.30   We are aware of the different European tradition of the 'pedagogue' - a class of workers, separate from teachers and social workers, whose task is to care for and encourage the development of children. Residential child care is seen as distinct from social work in many European countries and the professional qualifications required to enter this field of work are different. In the UK child care professions have always been considered a subset of either education or social work. However, the four primary tasks of the residential child care worker are significantly different from general social work. They are: the provision of basic day-to-day child care; enabling group living; utilising and managing activities - including education - (the social task); and therapeutic work. Each of these calls for a range of skills and knowledge which, although not individually unique to residential child care, nevertheless form an area of expertise which is different from general social work. This is the reality which has been recognised elsewhere in Europe in the professional training required for working in residential child care, with 'ambulant' social workers confined to operating outside the children's home. We believe there are strong arguments for examining further the European model and learning from it in devising a professional qualification that fits residential child care.

7.31   We are convinced that residential child care today calls for a range of knowledge and skills that it will be almost impossible to encompass satisfactorily within the framework of a two-year Diploma in Social Work, however hard CCETSW tries. Also we consider that there may be valuable lessons to be learned from other fields such as psychology, paediatrics and nursing. For example, we are aware of a clinical nursing course in Child Adolescent and Family Psychiatric Nursing , many elements of which would be appropriate to residential child care staff. There are doubtless many other such courses of equal relevance. By concentrating on adapting the Diploma in Social Work we believe a crucial opportunity is being lost to design a professional qualification of standing that is truly relevant to the needs of children's homes. In our view residential child care today justifies the creation of a new professional qualification covering a wider range of disciplines than social work. However, any such qualification must be at an equivalent level to the Diploma in Social Work; and we would be strongly opposed to any new qualification which was at a lower level. Thus we are suggesting that the Government consider arranging the introduction of a new Diploma at an equivalent level to the Diploma in Social Work, the content of which would be related more closely to the developments and treatment needs of difficult adolescents. Such a qualification could also be relevant in other areas, in particular aftercare and juvenile justice.

7.32   We were not constituted to define the academic content of such a new qualification. However, it is possible to identify a number of general areas which are essential to working with young people. These include, for example, child and adolescent psychology; therapeutic and control techniques; counselling; group skills and living; child care theory; and adolescent development. There would also be a need to incorporate theoretical and practical elements from the Diploma in Social Work and other social work courses: anti-discriminatory practice; the legal framework of social care; child protection issues; management and supervision, to avoid residential child care losing important linkages with other aspects of child care. There may be scope for a shared common core of social work theory for both courses, with later specialisation leading to separate but equivalent qualifications.

7.33   We believe strongly that this new Diploma should be designed on a modular basis so that staff can build up the modules over time without impossibly lengthy absences from the workplace and can learn on the job. We have seen an example of a shorter course designed for residential work with adolescents, which reduced the time away from the workplace significantly without any loss of effectiveness. Closely supervised practice placements at the student's own place of work can ensure that the replacements costs are kept to a minimum, and that students receive an academic qualification which will address directly the needs of the individual <u>and</u> the employer. At present securing recognition of courses of this kind seems to be difficult, although they represent precisely the kind of practical approach we think needs to be encouraged. A modular approach also makes it easier for a new Diploma to draw on skills gained in other professions, such as nursing, teaching or psychology: some existing qualifications could be regarded as meeting part of the Diploma requirements. For example, the previous completion of a course in adolescent psychiatric nursing could be accredited for the purposes of a new Diploma, so that the student would not need to undertake the whole course.   Academic training should not necessarily need to be completed in a single two year block; greater flexibility would enable the course to be undertaken at the convenience of the employee and the employer.

7.34   An expert body composed of different professional disciplines and currently active residential child care practitioners would need to be established to design a new qualification and curriculum in detail. This would need to report to whichever body was to approve the course and training arrangements. If CCETSW were to be the authentication body for the new Diploma then we recognise that changes in its composition and remit are likely to be required. We consider that by designing a new more flexible Diploma with a more relevant combination of knowledge and skills, the needs of children, staff and employers will be better met than by concentrating on the approach of more Diplomas in Social Work. We also think it offers a better prospect of obtaining a more professionally-qualified workforce for children's homes than the current Diploma in Social Work strategy. We see ourselves as supporting the objective of the Utting Report in seeking better qualified staff linked to the wider realm of child care, but achieving this by an alternative means. We think it would be for others to give a title to this new Diploma, which we believe would enable a reconstituted CCETSW to be regarded as the award-recognising body.

Recommendation 62

The Government should reconsider its current policy on qualifications for heads of homes; and should consider arranging the design and introduction of a new Diploma, focused more on the group care of children and young people at an equivalent level to the Diploma in Social Work as the preferred professional qualification for staff working in children's residential care.

Recommendation 63

This new Diploma should be designed on a modular basis, drawing on the relevant skills of professions other than social work; should minimise absence from the workplace for staff undertaking it; and should be obtainable over a period longer than two years.

Vocational Qualifications

7.35   Not all staff in children's homes need to be qualified at Diploma level, and not all will aspire to such qualifications. What we are certain of is that it should be possible for all staff to undertake training at the workplace that achieves recognised vocational qualifications that build towards the new Diploma we have commended if staff wish to proceed that far and are competent to do so.

7.36   Of particular relevance to staff in children's homes are the new arrangements for National Vocational Qualifications (NVQ). NVQ provides much more opportunity for workplace training and assessed competences to lead to accredited qualifications that are recognised nationally and build towards higher qualifications. It fits entirely with our assessment of the training needs of staff in children's homes, and particularly our proposal for a Personal Development Contract for each member of staff. This Contract will make it possible to identify the NVQ units of competence each person requires.

7.37   When fully in place the NVQ system should provide considerable flexibility for staff to acquire qualifications at their own pace, and to draw more on work-based training and distance learning in doing so. In essence it will be possible for children's homes staff to move through the system as shown in the diagram on the following page:

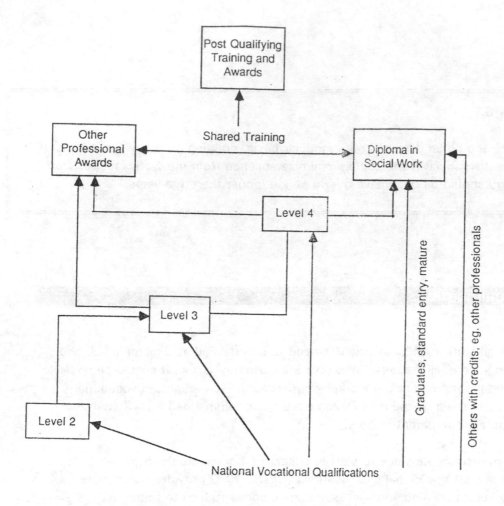

Unfortunately, the building blocks are not yet in place to enable residential child care staff to progress through this system.

7.38   NVQ pilot schemes relating to Levels 2 - 3 have been operating in residential care for the past year or so within a framework of nationally agreed standards recognised by the Care Sector Consortium. This consortium - which covers both the NHS and Social Services - is charged with producing a definition of the competencies to be achieved in the residential sector at the different NVQ levels. There are some problems over Level 4 in respect of its relationship with professional qualifications. In frustration some employers are designing their own Level 4 courses, some with a distinctive management component as distinct from professional element. We would hope that the Government will ensure that the thinking in our report is fed into the work on defining competencies and approving awards, because it is essential that the NVQ system meets the training needs of children's homes. We would also hope that the Government would give strong encouragement to the Care Sector Consortium to give a high priority to resolving outstanding differences, insofar as these are adversely affecting the recognition of awards for residential child care at all NVQ levels. There is a particular need to settle as a matter of urgency the relationship at NVQ Level 4 with other professional qualifications, but to do so in a way that is compatible with the content of any new Diploma for residential child care staff.

Recommendation 64

The Government should take steps to ensure that the new system for recognising and awarding NVQs meets the training needs of children's homes staff in the ways we have described as quickly as possible.

Induction Training

7.39   Induction training is crucial if new staff are to make a satisfactory start in caring for children when they join a home. Our survey suggests that most employers recognise that training needs to start from day one. Formal induction is provided by around three-quarters of local authorities for heads of homes and in 80% of local authorities for care staff. In the large majority of cases induction begins within two weeks. In about two-thirds of authorities the induction training is more than two days, and in about a quarter more than a working week. Comparison with the independent sector suggests that induction training is longer and there occurs more frequently in the private sector than anywhere else. In at least 75% of organisations induction includes:

- Time with managers senior to the head of home

- Guidance on departmental child care policy and procedures

- A full guide to the home's aims, structure and methods

- Requirements of the Children Act 1989

Guidance on handling violent behaviour takes place in about two-thirds of homes during induction.

7.40   Although this picture on induction training is more reassuring than most other aspects of training, our discussions with staff suggests that all too often induction of new staff is given a low priority. The day-to-day needs of the home take priority over the developmental needs of new staff. Some new staff are asked to start work immediately if they have previous experience, and induction will take place on the job. There are still about a fifth of employers providing no induction at all. This situation is in our view unacceptable and unsafe. Employers ought to provide sufficient resources to ensure that a planned period of induction can be provided for all staff. Clearly the needs of an experienced care worker moving from one employer to another will be very different from a member of staff new to the sector, but there needs in all cases to be a structured and systematic process which aims to integrate the new member of staff into the work of the home and into the team of staff with whom he or she will work.

7.41   We think it might be worth restating the right approach to induction training. The first stage of the induction process should be an assessment of the requirements of the new member of staff. The level of skill and experience will be known from the recruitment and selection process. The initial point of induction training will be an identification of gaps in knowledge and experience, and the formulation of a plan to ensure that these gaps are filled during the induction period. Thus, for example, there will be little point in automatically providing information on the Children Act to <u>all</u> new members of staff, unless all new members of staff lack knowledge of the Act. The induction process must be <u>flexible</u> and <u>personal</u>, ie., tailored to the specific needs of individuals in particular homes. In all cases it will be essential that new staff are given detailed information on the home's aims, policies and principles. There will be a need for information on the type of children looked after, their particular problems, the therapies employed, and the aims of the home in terms of outcomes. All homes will differ in these respects, and for all staff this will be the basis of their work. The way in which this information is provided will be for local decision, and indeed is likely to differ for each new member of staff.

7.42   The induction process should begin immediately a new member of staff takes up a post. The delays between starting a new job and starting induction which occur all too often imply either that new staff are working with children without having received appropriate training or, where this is not the case, that they are not doing anything. The form that induction will take should be agreed by the member of staff and the line manager immediately the member of staff takes up the post. The training required should be identified and recorded, and timetables set for achieving targets, including an agreement on when the induction period will end. Asking an experienced member of staff in these circumstances to act as a mentor to a new person can have considerable advantages.

7.43   There is a clear link between the induction process and the probation period (see paragraphs 5.31 - 5.40). One of the considerations which should determine whether a member of staff has successfully completed the probation period will be their success in achieving the goals set at the beginning of the induction period. A member of staff who has failed to achieve the targets for training which were agreed as being essential for him or her to work successfully in the home is unlikely to be considered to have successfully passed probation. The two issues are linked in such a way that they should be considered as part of a single process.

Recommendation 65

Employers should provide structured induction training to all new employees in children's homes before they have unsupervised access to children, and use this period to set goals for the successful completion of the probationary period.

Management Training

7.44   At the other end of the scale from the induction of new staff are the management and training needs of heads of homes. From the evidence available to us we would say that the heads of children's homes are undertaking a wider range of management tasks than in the past. We believe that the role of head of home is becoming more one of managing the provision of care within the home, although direct work with children should not be excluded from the role. Our visits to homes have indicated that the head of the home tends to play an increasingly diminishing part in the direct provision of care. They tend to work different hours from the rest of the staff - often more conventional office hours. With the general trend towards the devolution of responsibilities within organisations, including budgetary responsibilities, the role of the head of home has changed substantially and can be expected to change further.

7.45   In many places senior management have not recognised the changing role of the head of home. The result is that many heads of home - particularly those who have been in post for a long time - have not received appropriate training for their new roles and tasks. We consider that there needs to be much greater clarity about the management role of the head of home and the skills required to discharge this effectively in today's circumstances. We believe that there is a role here for the Local Government Management Board to help to identify the key elements of a management development programme for heads of homes which should be linked with the Management Charter Initiative. Also some employers have in place management development programmes for a wider group of managers, and these may meet the needs of heads of homes.

7.46   We do not believe that there is a single answer to meeting these management training needs. Decisions on the most appropriate management training for a particular manager will depend on the needs of the individual and the circumstances of his or her home and organisation. All we would say with absolute conviction is that all newly appointed heads of home should undertake management training of a reasonable duration not later than six months after appointment. It would also be desirable for all employers to review the management training needs of their existing heads of home.

Recommendation 66

Employers should ensure that all new heads of homes have undertaken appropriate management training no later than six months after appointment; and should review the management training needs of existing heads of homes.

> **Recommendation 67**
>
> The Local Authority Associations should commission work on the identification of the core elements of a management development programme for heads of children's homes, and if possible link this with the Management Charter Initiative.

Costs of Training

7.47   We recognise that we are proposing a greater investment in the training of managers and staff in children's homes, although we have concentrated on cost-effective approaches which minimise absences from the workplace. This extra investment we regard as essential for the well-being of the children in the homes and to remedy years of training neglect in this sector. There will be some initial extra resource implications in providing a better trained workforce. However, we believe that these would be offset to some extent by a substantial reduction in staff turnover, as a result of greater job satisfaction; reduced levels of stress in staff who are properly equipped to do the job; fewer staff failing to perform adequately in the job; better child care, which may save money at later stages of the child's development; and fewer claims for compensation. There will however be start-up costs and some extra continuing costs. Better and more thorough supervision arrangements and replacement costs for staff who are undergoing training will have resource implications also. We consider that the Government and employers will have to accept that if they want safer and better-run children's homes - and improved standards of child care - then more money will have to be spent on training. However within the total social services sector, children's homes are only a very small part and the cost of improving training for children's homes staff is likely to form a very small proportion of the total social services training budget

7.48   We doubt, on past experience, if simply exhorting employers to do better in training will deliver the changes we regard as essential for improving care in children's homes. We believe that the Government has a role to play in targeting money on training for children's homes, although it would be desirable for employers to demonstrate their commitment by funding part of the extra training effort. The Government already has in place a mechanism for targeting money on training - the Specific Grant underpinning the Training Support programme - which provides local authorities with 70% of the funds for approved training programmes, with employers funding the remaining 30%. We appreciate that funding for this programme has not been allocated beyond 1994-95, and that the Government faces a difficult public expenditure climate. However we consider that the special circumstances of children's homes would justify continuing the Training Support Programme for a few more years , but targeted specifically on children's homes training.

7.49   If assistance is to be given to local authorities for securing a better-trained workforce in children's homes, it would be wrong to overlook the needs of staff in voluntary and private homes. We can see that there might be objections in principle to direct Government subsidy to private homes. However we consider that collaboration over training between all three sectors is essential. We believe the best approach might be for places to be provided on joint training programmes for all three sectors, but with the independent sector employers contributing to the programme costs in the same proportion as local authorities. This would achieve collaboration and a measure of cost-relief for independent sector employers.

Recommendation 68

The Government and employers should accept that a better-trained workforce in children's homes is likely to require extra expenditure by them on training, supervision and replacement costs.

Recommendation 69

The Government should give clear financial recognition to the importance of training as a means of improving the quality of care in children's homes by continuing a targeted Training Support Programme for several years with a specific grant meeting part of the cost borne by employers; and should encourage joint training programmes for staff in all sectors in order to raise standards everywhere.

PERSONAL DEVELOPMENT CONTRACT
- CARE STAFF

For: _____

Date: _____

There are four parties to this Personal Development Contract:

<u>The staff member</u>

Name: _____
Signature _____

<u>The head of home</u>

Name: _____
Signature _____

<u>The training department</u>

Name: _____
Signature _____

<u>The head of home's manager</u>

Name: _____
Signature _____

BEFORE COMPLETING THIS DOCUMENT, PLEASE REFER TO
THE GUIDANCE NOTES AT THE END

1 WHAT	2 HOW	3 WHEN BY	4 RESULT	5 REVIEW	6 COMMENTS
List here the skills/knowledge areas you want to develop in priority order	State how you plan to develop these skills/knowledge	Date(s)	How will you know when you have acquired these skills/knowledge?	Agreed review procedures and dates	

GUIDANCE NOTES

Column 1   Insert here one, two or three skills/knowledge areas that
            have been identified and jointly agreed as basic to your role
            (at two months), and (after one year) as necessary to qualify
            you as an officer in charge.

Column 2   Insert the chosen development options that you intend to
            use. Seek help from any colleague you feel is proficient in
            the identified skill area, or anyone who can help you to
            identify ways to meet your objectives.

Column 3   Insert a challenging but realistic target date for the
            attainment of the objective.

Column 4   Indicate how you will know when you have achieved the
            objective. How will others know when you have achieved
            your target? What will be different?

Column 5   Insert dates for your regular review meetings with your
            homes' manager and your officer in charge. Such meetings
            should cover progress to date, obstacles, new opportunities
            etc.

Column 6   Jointly consider what, if anything, should follow the
            attainment of developmental objectives. How can these
            improvements be best transferred and utilised in the work
            situation? What next?

PERSONAL DEVELOPMENT CONTRACT

- Head of home

For: _____

Date: _____

There are three parties to this Personal Development Contract:

<u>The head of home</u>

Name: _____
Signature _____

<u>The head of home's manager</u>

Name: _____
Signature _____

<u>The training department</u>

Name: _____
Signature _____

BEFORE COMPLETING THIS DOCUMENT, PLEASE REFER TO
THE GUIDANCE NOTES AT THE END

PERSONAL DEVELOPMENT PLAN

IDENTIFYING NEEDS	SELECTED LEARNING APPROACH	PROJECTED RESULTS	TIMESCALES
What do I want to Achieve?	What learning methods will best meet my needs?	What will be the effect of my applying learning experience and activities?	When will I be able to apply my learning?

GUIDANCE NOTES (1)

THE BENEFITS

Adopting a planned approach will help you to create opportunities for the kind of development you want to pursue, as well as taking advantage of experiences as they occur.

By developing yourself, you make your contribution to the effectiveness of the Home and being leader of a team equipped with the skills required to fulfil its objectives.

Progression should be continuous, taking advantage of opportunities to learn as they arise, in whatever form, not limited by or timetabled to the availability of courses.

You should explore alternative ways of meeting your development needs. Recognising that, while your employer provides a range of learning resources and support, you can also create and manage your own learning.

DEVELOPING THE PLAN

You should have ownership of the plan and generate the content. Your manager should assist to ensure the plan is a balance of personal needs and activities, not just a list of technical knowledge and skill requirements. The plan should therefore cover three areas:

Performance Improvement Needs - These will focus on skill and knowledge areas identified on an ongoing basis and required in order to perform your job to the agreed standards. In order to meet the current and future challenges of the home, these will require regular reviewing and updating.

Personal Development Needs - These should be identified to enhance existing skill and knowledge areas. This will help maximise you potential and growth now and in the future.

Additional Learning Opportunities - We are constantly confronted by new learning experience both in and out of work. It is important to recognise these and take every opportunity to reflect upon and learn from each one. Whilst not planned, such opportunities can be equally valuable in helping you to meet the needs you have identified.

GUIDANCE NOTES (2)

<u>IDENTIFYING YOUR NEEDS</u>

You may wish to consider the following questions before developing and discussing your plan:

What are my main strengths and limitations?	What are my six most important personal goals over the next 12 months?
What opportunities are there for me in the future?	What do I need to learn to enable me to achieve them?
What can give me more information on these opportunities?	How, when and where am I going to learn it?
What have I achieved in the last three months that I am most satisfied by?	What do I most want to change?
What didn't I achieve? Why?	How am I going to change?
What would I like to be doing in two years time?	What resources are available to me?

CHAPTER 8: SPECIALIST SERVICES AND SUPPORT FOR STAFF

*"Well, my heads full of questions
My temperature's risin' fast
Well, I'm lookin' for some answers
But I don't know who to ask"*

Bob Dylan, Mixed Up Confusion, 1968

Introduction

8.1   We were asked to look at support for staff in our terms of reference, and we have found this to be an important, difficult and often controversial issue. This chapter considers the specialist support provided for children's homes, both in terms of direct work with children and in supporting staff in their work with children. It also examines some of the difficult issues around controlling children in homes and the treatment and support for staff when allegations are made against them - sometimes mistakenly. Children in residential care are no different from any other children in that they need regular access to education and health services. However, as we have shown in Chapter 2, possibly as many as 70% of children in residential care are said to have significant levels of emotional or behavioural disturbance; and up to one third are said to have been sexually abused. This would suggest that staff are likely to need ready access to specialist types of education and health services which are tailored to the needs of children in residential care: child and adolescent psychology; educational psychology; psychotherapy; psychiatry; counselling.

8.2   Direct clinical work with children needs to be coupled with support for staff in their work with children. This is particularly appropriate where a home has very disturbed children and is providing therapeutic treatment for the children. Here professional support is needed to train and advise staff. Staff themselves also need personal support if they are to cope with some of the most difficult and demanding children in our society.

Assessment of Current Position

Use of therapeutic methods and techniques

8.3   Respondents to our survey were asked to indicate whether therapeutic methods and techniques were used in their homes. We received a relatively small number of replies, although of those homes which did respond the most frequently occurring methods claimed were those for behaviour modification. However, of this small number acknowledging the use of such techniques about a fifth have no access to external professional support. Although the evidence is not conclusive, we are left with an uncomfortable sense that there are homes attempting to practice therapeutic techniques without the necessary professional skills and competence. This was the position identified in the Pindown Report. It is possible that the Leicestershire Inquiry being conducted by Andrew Kirkwood QC may reveal a similar situation with regard to what was described as 'regression therapy'. We find this position extremely worrying.

Need for psychiatric and psychological support

8.4   The Pindown Report found that "No psychiatric, psychological or educational advice of any kind was obtained before or after Pindown was brought into existence." Were this advice to have been sought, and had there been proper oversight of the regimes, it is unlikely that Pindown would have been instigated or continued for so long. Utting reports that "strong representations were made to me about the difficulty of securing psychological and psychiatric support in dealing with some extremely troubled young people." The picture to emerge from our visits is that too often staff in children's homes are left to cope with abused, disturbed and violent young people without access to the specialist psychiatric and psychological services that are needed. We have visited homes where children are receiving little or no education because no places could be found for them in local schools.

8.5   In our survey we asked employers about the availability of specialist advice. Their replies show considerable variation around the country and significant differences between sectors. In answering the question "Is specialist advice readily available in those homes which have a specialist therapeutic role", employers replied as follows:

<u>TABLE 8.1</u>

	Local authority homes	Voluntary homes	Private homes
Yes	51.0%	78.9%	70.0%
To some extent	28.6%	10.5%	26.0%
No	20.4%	10.5%	4.0%

Thus a much smaller proportion of local authority homes can say unequivocally that specialist advice is readily available. In all sectors some homes say they have no access at all.

8.6   When asked specifically about access to help from psychotherapists, psychiatrists and psychologists, and the frequency of access, replies for those homes claiming a specialist therapeutic role again show a patchy picture:

TABLE 8.2

	Local authority homes	Voluntary homes	Private homes
Access monthly or more frequently	40.8%	63.0%	61.3%
Access less frequently than monthly	54.9%	29.6%	32.3%
No access at all	4.2%	7.4%	6.5%

Thus there are some homes with little or no access to a psychologist, psychotherapist or psychiatrist. Given the characteristics of the residents in the homes we regard access of a frequency greater than monthly as far from ready access. By our standards about half the homes do not have ready and frequent access to the type of specialist support and advice most likely to be needed.

8.7   The picture which has emerged from evidence, our visits and from the survey is not encouraging; and reflects that set out in the Utting Report. There is good practice around the country, but in many places the levels of professional input and support to children's homes are inadequate. Where links with external professionals are established, the standard of work of the home and the outcomes for children are greatly improved. The National Society for the Prevention of Cruelty to Children (NSPCC) noted in their evidence that professional support and consultation from outside the home is invaluable in enabling staff to improve the care and development of children. If the specialist help needed by many of the children in residential care is not provided, the children's development is impaired, their frustration and anger increases and the care and control problems of staff are exacerbated.

8.8   With an estimated two-thirds of children in children's homes having behavioral problems, there clearly needs to be a much higher level of NHS support to homes to enable staff to care for and treat these children properly. Unfortunately that high level of support does not appear to be provided in many areas. The service is inadequate for a number of reasons. One of these is the low priority which an already stretched health service gives residential child care. Children's homes are perceived as at least providing a level of care which could not be provided, for example, in a family setting. The placement of children in residential care seems to produce a belief that the problems of behaviourally disturbed children are somehow 'contained', and the health services can attend to other priorities.

8.9   We appreciate that there is a general shortage of appropriately qualified staff nationally. The Department of Health has informed us that there are about 340 (whole-time equivalent) consultants in child and adolescent psychiatry in Great Britain; and around 300 clinical psychologists working with children for all or a substantial part of their time. There are 174 psychotherapists, of whom about 80% work in the four South East Regional Health Authorities: five Regions have no access to child

145

psychotherapists. Clearly these are problems which must be addressed by the National Health Service rather than local authorities. There are similar problems about children gaining access to the approximately 1,300 (full-time equivalent) educational psychologists in this country. The Department of Health also noted the frequent lack of agreement between health authorities and local authorities over the most appropriate way to deliver services: whether there should be direct clinical contact between the professional and the child; or whether professionals should provide support for staff who are dealing with the child. Whatever the problems of supply and demand of scarce professional skills, action has to be taken to improve the level of specialist support that the NHS gives children's homes.

Education service

8.10   Similarly with education. Children in residential care have the same entitlement to education - and access to educational psychologists - as any other group of children. The Pindown Report noted that, for children in residential care "educational needs and achievement have tended to take second place to social and family needs", and recommended that there needed to be a much sharper national focus on these issues. We have found that too often these children - many of whom need special help as a result of their behavioural problems, or previous non-attendance at school - are receiving little or no education. We visited homes where children of school age were not in school during the day either because they had been suspended or because no place could be found for them in local schools. We recognise that because of their particular problems, children in homes can be disruptive for schools, or will play truant.

8.11   In their evidence, the Social Care Association noted the consequences of the move away from the direct provision of education in Community Homes with Education, and that "many young people 'deposited' in small children's homes were excluded from schools and left to languish in the homes. The current round of changes in education and the introduction of local management arrangements is likely to exacerbate these difficulties." During the course of our Inquiry we have detected concerns that children from children's homes may have an increasingly difficult time with the development of local management and grant-maintained schools. These developments reduce the scope for Local Education Authorities to influence decisions on admissions to individual schools. We are not arguing against local management of schools or against grant-maintained schools, but these developments do not absolve Local Education Authorities from the need to provide a satisfactory educational service for children in residential care.

8.12   The position was well put by the Department for Education in their evidence to us:

> *"Most of the youngsters in children's homes....are children with difficulties, often arising from other problematic features in their lives. Such children are less appealing to schools, do markedly less well in public examinations and may pose more discipline problems. There is unlikely to be any financial incentive for schools to admit or retain them but....schools cannot refuse to admit them if they have places available"*

This is not the most optimistic view of the future educational prospects for children in residential care. We can understand why the Utting Report recommended that the Department of Health "should discuss with the Department of Education the feasibility of guidance to education authorities about the educational needs of children being looked after." We believe that a little more than a Circular may be needed and we make some specific recommendations later.

8.13 People who have expressed concern to us would have had fewer anxieties if the alternative to mainstream schooling looked attractive. Some children in residential care are educated already in the children's home itself. The Department for Education estimate that about 100 homes provide education in this way. However, a study of 28 establishments between 1988 and 1990 conducted by Her Majesty's Inspectors of Schools (HMI) is not encouraging. The homes varied in size but mainly catered for boys aged 14 - 16 with considerable personal and social problems which had often resulted in disrupted educational histories and difficult behaviour. The main findings on the 28 homes inspected were as follows:

"In 11 establishments the curriculum is satisfactory or better in most respects but many pupils spend too much time on a narrow range of subjects.

Over half the lessons observed were satisfactory or better but there is a marked polarisation between establishments: in four establishments all the lessons observed were unsatisfactory. In the majority of lessons teachers established good relations with their pupils, often in very difficult circumstances. Many handled difficult and distressed behaviour skilfully but concern with pupils' personal difficulties too often led to low expectations of their educational achievements. Standards of achievement varied markedly between establishments but were generally low.

The quality and range of education in these establishments is more influenced by the accommodation provided than in ordinary schools. Accommodation in 15 of the establishments had some serious defects which constrained the curriculum provided.

In general, the establishments were staffed by suitably qualified and dedicated staff but small establishments with few teachers faced great difficulties in trying to develop a broad curriculum.

Local authorities need to offer greater professional guidance on curricular matters and ensure that staff have fuller opportunities for in-service training and career development. A greater measure of co-operation between local authority departments is necessary if the educational experience of young people in these establishments is to be enhanced."

This is far from a glittering end-of-term report for many of those local authorities who have a responsibility for the education of the young people in their care. No evidence has been presented to us to suggest that matters have improved since the HMI report.

Legal Responsibilities of Authorities

8.14   Our concern has to be with the welfare of children in residential care and the specialist support needed by staff in the homes. Inadequate support adversely affects children's welfare. We have examined carefully therefore the legal responsibilities and powers of the various agencies to provide and invoke specialist support for children's homes as a basis for making proposals for change.

Education

8.15   Local Education Authorities have certain responsibilities in respect of all pupils in their area whether or not they are being educated in LEA-maintained schools. In particular they are under a duty, when they have issued a statement of special educational needs under section 7 of the Education Act 1981, to ensure the provision specified, whether the child is in residential care or otherwise. We therefore consider that Local Education Authorities are under an obligation to provide the full range of services to children in residential care to no worse a standard than if they were in mainstream schools. This obligation also covers the services of an educational psychologist where needed. The Department for Education accept that this is a fair statement of the position.

National Health Service

8.16   The Department of Health accept that under current legislation children in children's homes have the same entitlement to NHS services as other children; but that as they have considerable health deficits, these should be addressed pro-actively by health authorities. NHS support should be available to provide a balanced assessment and to widen the range of therapeutic interventions.

8.17   Social Services Departments have a means of ensuring that both health and education authorities face up to their responsibilities to children in residential care. They have a duty (under section 22(3) of the Children Act 1989) to safeguard and promote the welfare of children they are looking after and to make such use of services available for children cared for by their own parents as appears to the local authority to be reasonable. Additionally, under section 27 of the Act, where it appears to a local authority that any health authority, NHS Trust or education authority could, by taking any specified action, help in the exercise of the local authority's functions under Part III of the Act (Local Authority Support for Children and Families), the local authority may request the help of the authority or Trust, specifying the action in question. The authority or Trust is required to comply with the request if it is compatible with their own statutory or other duty and obligations and does not unduly prejudice the discharge of their functions. We recognise that there may be some scope for differences of view between education and social services, but it is the job of a local authority with responsibility for both services to resolve those differences. Overall, we consider that this legislative position gives Social Services Departments the authority to pursue more actively health and education services to ensure they meet the needs of children in residential care. The Department of Health accepts that this is an accurate reflection of the current legal position.

Improving Specialist Support to Homes

8.18 Given the legal position we have outlined, we would like to see a dual approach:

- Clear and up-to-date guidance to health and education authorities on their obligations to children in residential care.

- Sharper identification of the health and educational needs of children in homes, and firm presentation of those needs to the responsible authorities.

8.19 Arrangements for joint working between health authorities and local authorities are set out in a Circular issued in 1974 (HRC (74)19). We believe that this guidance should be restated and explained to both health authorities and local authorities in so far as it relates to children's homes. We welcome the fact that the guidance to be issued to health authorities on the Secretary of State's priorities for 1993/94 will include the need for services required for the implementation of the Children Act 1989 to be provided. We understand that these services will include "...the provision of psychological and psychiatric support in children's residential care". We are glad to see this recognition that priority should be given to the needs of these children, and we would urge the Department of Health to monitor implementation of these policies by health authorities.

8.20 We would hope that the Department for Education follows the lead of the Department of Health and reminds Local Education Authorities of their obligations to children in children's homes. A reminder of the unsatisfactory situation revealed by HMI would not come amiss. It would also be desirable to remind local authorities that, as they have both education and social services responsibilities, it is their duty to provide a satisfactory education service for the children whom they are looking after.

8.21 However, it is no use reminding health and local authorities of their responsibilities if children's needs are not clearly presented. We know that some Social Services Departments, in the absence of local services, may have given up presenting individual children's needs to the responsible authorities. We can understand their attitude but consider that such a despairing approach must be abandoned. The fact that around 70% of children in residential care have behavioural difficulties, and that this proportion has been increasing for some time without a parallel increase in specialist support services leads us to conclude that there needs to be a systematic audit of the requirements of those children and of the staff caring for them. We recommend that such an audit should be undertaken within the next twelve months.

8.22 We consider that those responsible for managing homes should look at the needs of individual children in the homes. They should determine what type of professional input each child needs - both clinical and educational. They should look at the level of input required and, most importantly, who should provide the service - ie, whether there is a need for individual clinical services or if, with the appropriate specialist support, residential staff will be able to provide the necessary help. There will be a need for professional advice in the course of the audit: staff will not always be best placed or able to determine the clinical or educational needs of individual children. Employers should identify the extent to which these needs are being met, and whether existing arrangements are adequate to meet the needs of the children. The outcome of the audit should be discussed with those who will be asked to provide the service, normally the local health and education authorities; and steps should be taken to agree plans to rectify deficiencies. In the course of this exercise, employers should also determine the most appropriate format for providing support for staff: whether by training or consultation; and whether this should be provided for groups of staff or individually. We say more about staff in paragraphs 8.25 - 8.29.

8.23   The statement of purpose and objectives to which each home will be required to adhere should precisely define the professional interventions which will be used; and how the needs of staff will be met. This will mean that when a child is admitted to a home, a thorough assessment of his or her needs should be undertaken, identifying the specialist professional support which will be needed. Arrangements must then be made to provide this support. It is likely to be harmful to a child to admit him or her to a home and not provide the professional support needed. It is also grossly unfair to the home's staff.

8.24   The specialist support services needed by a child should be provided at no charge by the health authority or education service (except where a local health or education service recharges an authority in the area from which a child originates). Some of these authorities appear to be unclear as to the services which they are required to provide at no charge. We believe that this can be addressed in part by a clear statement from the Government of what is expected of them in the guidance we have proposed.

Recommendation 70

The Government should issue new guidance to health and local education authorities on the services and support they are expected to provide without payment to those responsible for running children's homes and relate this to Regional Health Authority priorities and the need to work collaboratively with Social Services Departments in improving support to children's homes.

Recommendation 71

Within the next 12 months all employers should audit services in children's homes, distinguishing between the needs of staff and children and between individual and group work; should identify whether or not there are adequate arrangements for providing specialist support to children and staff and should plan how to rectify identified deficiencies in collaboration with their local health and education authorities.

Recommendation 72

Health authorities should ensure that adequate specialist services such as clinical psychology are available to meet the identified needs of children in residential care; and Local Education Authorities should take steps to meet more fully the identified educational needs of children in residential care, including the provision of educational psychology services.

Support for Staff

8.25   As we have discussed in Chapter 1, children's homes should have a therapeutic and developmental role. A number of children's homes are using - or claim to be using - therapeutic techniques. Our concerns are that some of the regimes in homes using therapeutic techniques may not be appropriate; they may have been established to test a 'pet' theory of a senior member of staff (as described in the Pindown Report); they may not be adequately supervised or monitored by suitably qualified people; and they may be undertaken without adequate training of staff. Normalisation and rehabilitation should be the basis for all therapies used in children's homes. Therapies and any psychotherapeutic techniques must have credibility and validity among the wider psychiatric and psychological community; and no-one should be allowed to undertake them without comprehensive training and specialist supervision. All therapies should be age-appropriate, and based on the needs of the child rather than the home. Such an approach, however, requires homes to have ready access to psychiatric, psychological and psychotherapy professionals to train, supervise and support the home's staff.

8.26   Often the most cost effective and appropriate role for professional specialists is that of supporting staff in children's homes who are working directly with children. This view reflects that expressed by Christopher Beedell and Roger Clough in their evidence, that "the best [professionals] recognise that some continuing relationship with the home is the proper context in which to offer their expertise". The British Psychological Society noted the range of support and guidance which psychologists visiting homes can offer:

- Specialist contributions on a range of issues, for example bullying; sexualised behaviour by young people; promoting social independence; withdrawal; sleeping and eating disorders.

- Service training on specialised topics: managing difficult behaviour; observation and assessment skills; alternatives to punishment; stress reduction; management skills.

- Helping managers develop quality standards and indicators.

We consider that there is scope for using the professional NHS or educational specialists to train, advise and support staff in homes. This should have immense benefits in terms of cost, in that staff will be able to deliver services which would otherwise require a great deal of input from outside the home; external professionals will be able to monitor the performance of staff in delivering treatment to children and the effectiveness of therapeutic regimes; and the status of staff will be enhanced as they take on a more professional role with respect to children.

8.27   We recognise that the approach we are suggesting could raise some difficult 'boundary' issues between the NHS and social services. Training homes staff in new skills will often be a way of reducing the obligation of the NHS or Local Education Authority to undertake direct work with individual children by using scarce professional skills more effectively. It would be easy for a financially-strapped health authority to argue that this is really staff training that enables a home to ensure that its staff can cope with the clientele it has accepted. This would be an unnecessarily narrow and unconstructive approach by health authorities, many of whom have neglected children in residential care for many years. We believe the acid test has to be that, if the children in a home require therapeutic regimes in the spheres of child psychiatry, psychotherapy or clinical psychology, then it is the responsibility of the health authority to supply that service free of charge to the children. However it should be a matter of negotiation locally as to what is the most effective way of helping the greatest number of children, whether by training homes staff in methodology and techniques, working with individual children or group work. We consider that the local audits we have recommended should enable health and local authorities to reach agreement on what is needed in particular homes and how the NHS will respond to the needs.

8.28   However it will be equally important for those responsible for children's homes not to exploit NHS goodwill. This is particularly the case with psychological services. The focus of support can often be much more on staff development and coping mechanisms than with the needs of individual children. The role of psychologists can cover training staff in child development; origins and management of behaviour problems; the management of challenging behaviour, and other areas. Sometimes psychologists can provide counselling to individual staff or groups of staff, or chair staff groups. These activities are essentially staff training and development, and in our view they are the responsibility of the employing authorities running homes. A good employer would pay for the training and support needed by their staff to do their job, and home owners should accept the financial responsibility for buying psychological services that have a primary focus of staff training, development and support.

8.29   We noted that a few local authorities have employed psychologists to provide staff training and support in their Social Services Department. This is the kind of responsible attitude we would like to see encouraged, providing the NHS meets that part of the costs concerned with direct work with individual children (or alternative ways of undertaking that direct work). In our view, there should be nothing odd about local authorities employing or seconding psychologists to Social Services Departments. As Beedell and Clough pointed out in their evidence, "in the rest of Europe employment of these professionals as part of social services for children would be taken for granted". Given the difficulties many staff are experiencing coping with the type of children in homes today, we consider that many more employers will need to buy in the services of psychologists to train and support the staff in children's homes. They should do this in consultation with their health or education authority locally, but where that authority declines to help, the welfare of children and staff must be the paramount concern of employers. In those circumstances they should be free to look at alternative means of providing support. This could be by direct employment; by secondment from another agency; or by arranging for specialist services to be provided through a consultancy agreement.

Recommendation 73

Employers should accept responsibility for funding any psychology services required primarily for the purposes of staff training, development and support and should arrange such services in consultation with the local health authority or, in the case of educational psychology services, with the local education authority following their audit of specialist services required by children's homes.

Staff Care

8.30   Social Services Departments can often be so preoccupied with caring for others that they neglect to care for their own staff. On the evidence presented to us many staff in homes need much more personal support - as distinct from specialist support on how to do their job - at times of personal crisis. Managing stress is an important consideration when working in children's homes. Many staff feel that it is the main cause of their disenchantment with the job, and only rarely did they tell us that they felt as though they had any support or help in dealing with it. Staff in children's homes are also the victims of threatening or violent behaviour - sometimes on a regular basis. Some worry that they provoked the behaviour by mishandling a volatile situation. Others can have their confidence destroyed by a violent assault. Most of us would need help if we were regularly exposed to verbal abuse or physical violence, as can be the lot of some staff in children's homes.

8.31   Some local authorities have responded to this by developing a stress counselling service for Social Services staff, including children's homes staff. Some have a similar service for victims of threatening or violent behaviour. It is possible to combine both services. The evidence is that this is an extremely valuable way for an employing authority to provide support to staff. Such a service must be outside of the line management of the home. Some authorities have used independent organisations to provide the service, others have provided an independent service in a consortium with other authorities. Counsellors may be directly employed, seconded, charged for by the outside agency providing the service, or employed on a sessional basis with the local authority organising the provision of the service to staff. All of these systems have been found to work. The key criteria are that the service should be confidential and perceived by staff as being independent of line management. For these staff care services to be effective we believe that they should not be narrowly defined and should be easily accessible. To illustrate the approach we commend, we have included at the end of the chapter (Annex 8A) as an example of good practice the general principles of a staff care service we encountered during the Inquiry.

8.32   We appreciate that many smaller employers in the independent sector will not be able to operate a scheme of this kind themselves. However it should be possible for them to identify locally others who could provide such a service. We see nothing wrong in them buying into a service that could be provided by a nearby local authority for their own staff.

8.33   A particular point made to us by staff is that when a complaint has been made they may find themselves subject to disciplinary proceedings, when they themselves have invoked grievance procedures. Often investigations under these procedures are carried out in parallel with other investigations (for example external complaints or child protection investigations). We believe that every effort should be made to make these procedures compatible; and to ensure that information gained in the course of one type of investigation should be made available to other investigations of the same incident(s).

Recommendation 74

Employers should ensure easy access to independent Staff Care schemes for providing support to staff in children's homes that they can access independently of line management to discuss any concerns and receive advice and counselling.

Recommendation 75

All employers should have written staff grievance and disciplinary procedures that are consistent with local child protection and complaints procedures.

Care and Control Issues

8.34   To care for children it is sometimes necessary to control them, both in an ordinary domestic setting and in a children's home. Even in a well-run, caring children's home there will be many occasions when the authority of staff is severely tested or rejected and a young person engages in disruptive or violent behaviour. On some occasions the behaviour may constitute a serious threat to the safety of the young person or to other children, or to staff. Sometimes there will be an attempt to abscond in circumstances that staff might reasonably regard as likely to lead to a young person harming themselves (eg., to engage in substance abuse or prostitution) or to commit a criminal act. The reality of life in today's children's homes is that these events can occur much more frequently than the public or senior managers might expect.

8.35   Throughout our Inquiry staff and others have raised with us the issue of control, and how staff are expected to behave. Since the Pindown Report staff feel that they have been told all the things they must not do, but given little help on how they are expected to deal with some of the most difficult children in society. If children run away the staff are criticised, but if they stop absconding staff are accused of exercising undue restraint. Many staff feel powerless to deal with children who physically threaten them, or who defy their authority. They lack the economic, emotional and other sanctions that a parent has with their own child. Staff have pointed out to us that guidance and regulations prohibit most sanctions - a situation which they accept and agree with - but that there is little or no guidance on how to deal with young people who threaten them physically. On many occasions we were informed of situations where staff have been forced to defend themselves against attack by a young person, and having done so, have found that the child has made a complaint against them. As a result staff have become wary of using any form of physical restraint, and feel unable to attempt to restrain children who are behaving violently. If they are to do their job conscientiously and protect themselves and other children, we consider that staff in children's homes need to be given much clearer guidance and training on the physical control of children; on the restriction of children's liberty; and on the circumstances in which they can touch or hold children.

8.36   Staff in homes are well aware of the possibilities for allegations to be made against them, whether in a situation of physical danger, or when working with individual young people who may make vexatious allegations against them. There are particular problems now because of the high proportion of children in homes - around a third - who have been sexually abused, and may have developed inappropriate patterns of sexual behaviour, and attitudes to sexual activity. Some homes have considered these issues carefully, and established working practices which take account of potential difficulties, but others need to do so. These issues can only properly be addressed through the development of sound and sensible practice which, although protecting staff from mischievous allegations, allows them to continue to work properly with young people. This might be as simple as adjusting rotas so that there are always at least two people on duty - especially at night - and that they are of opposite sex. Guiding staff on how to avoid placing themselves in a position of 'danger' should accompany guidance on control issues

8.37   We are aware that issues of control and restrictions on liberty are to some extent covered in the Children's Homes Regulations 1991 and the Children (Secure Accommodation) Regulations 1991 and associated guidance. However it is clear from representations made to us that the current guidance does not go far enough in helping staff to cope with the many situations in which they find themselves. We recognise the difficulty of writing detailed guidance in this area, but we welcome the fact that the Department of Health is to act on the Utting Report recommendation and is preparing new guidance. We hope that it will cover the holding and touching issues we have mentioned as well as the physical control and restriction of liberty aspects. Moreover, it will need to advise staff how they can maintain good order when they have highly disturbed and violent children in a home. Clearer advice is needed on those circumstances in which the prospects of self-harm might justify restraint. Staff also need advice on how they should explain to children the need for some inhibition on their behaviour in the context of group living.

8.38   Written guidance for staff will need to be reinforced by authoritative training material from the Social Services Inspectorate related to real situations if staff are to be given the help and reassurance they need. We cannot emphasise too much how strongly staff feel that they have been left to cope with an impossible situation and with insufficient guidance and support. We would urge employing authorities therefore to ensure that this guidance is made available to all staff in children's homes, and that adequate training is provided to enable staff to cope more effectively with the difficult issues they are confronted with on control and physical contact with children.

8.39   We recognise that these are issues which may well be tested in the courts, because there are some who consider that the Children Act, and in particular the Children's Homes Regulations 1991 and associated guidance, prevents some of the action currently taken by staff (eg., to prevent children absconding from a home). We hope that employers will give appropriate support to staff involved in any legal challenges. — *And this is not meant to be a joke!*

Recommendation 76

The Government should issue full guidance for staff on the issues of control, restraint and physical contact with children in residential care; keep this up-to-date; and reinforce it by ensuring the provision of authoritative training ,material that allows staff to apply the guidance in real situations.

Suspension of Staff

8.40   One of the most emotive issues for staff is that of suspension from duty when an allegation about them has been made that requires investigation. Our survey shows that over the past years local authorities have used suspension much more frequently than final warnings or dismissal. Eight percent or more of staff have been suspended in over 6% of local authorities, whereas only 2% of local authorities have given final warnings to 8% or more of their staff, and none have dismissed such a proportion. We have dealt with disciplinary issues in Chapter 6 on Managing Homes but we want to consider some aspects of suspension which clearly affect staff morale and conduct.

8.41   When allegations are made against a member of staff, employers have to balance two considerations: the need to protect children and the need to ensure that staff are treated fairly. These are difficult to reconcile given the prevalent perception of staff that suspension from duty implies at least a measure of guilt on behalf of the individual. These concerns are particularly important in children's homes, where staff are more vulnerable to allegations than in any other setting, and some of the allegations are untrue, or a reflection of the child's emotional state. Officially employers see suspension from duty following an allegation as a neutral act, carrying no implication of guilt and allowing an investigation to take place in an unprejudiced way. Removing the member of staff from the home where the allegation has been made allows proper investigation of the facts and ensures that, were the allegations to be justified, the member of staff has no opportunity to repeat his actions. However, staff do not see suspension in this way - particularly as in many local authorities suspension from duty can also be used as a disciplinary measure. It is difficult to remove the stigma of punishment from the act of suspension, particularly for the member of staff concerned. It is seen as 'punishment without trial', and staff who are suspended and subsequently cleared over the allegation are treated as guilty by implication during the period of suspension, and frequently after they have returned to work. There can be enormous disruption in a home following an allegation and suspension: there may be adverse effects on the behaviour of the children and their treatment; and other staff may become suspicious of children and their colleagues.

8.42   There is no doubt in our minds that the foremost concern of the employing authority must always be the welfare of the child. This would appear to imply that a member of staff should always be removed from a home immediately an allegation is made. However, other factors must be considered, in particular the seriousness of the allegation and the effect of suspension on the lives of other children in the home. The British Psychological Society commented that "This associated disruption needs to be addressed, particularly in cases of dismissal or suspension, within the establishment and the wider social links, in both the short and the long term". Options other than immediate suspension should be considered; and the decision to suspend should depend on the seriousness of the allegation. Before any decision can be taken there must be some form of preliminary examination of the facts of the case. In our view there should be a brief preliminary inquiry, to decide whether there is a case to answer rather than whether the member of staff might be guilty; and this should be undertaken by the line manager of the member of staff. The line manager should look at the facts and the circumstances surrounding the allegation and take a decision speedily - taking into account the interests of other children in the home and other staff - on whether immediate suspension is appropriate.

Criteria

8.43   We consider that staff should only be suspended where one of several criteria are satisfied. These include where an allegation has been made which, if proven, would lead to dismissal or prosecution. Failure to suspend in such cases could lead to difficulties at, for example, an industrial tribunal were the member of staff not immediately suspended prior to dismissal. If a member of staff were to be convicted of an offence against children following an allegation, and he or she were not immediately suspended the employing authority could face allegations that they had been negligent of the welfare of children in their care. Suspension should always occur where a child could be placed in danger if the member of staff were not removed from duty. Suspension should also occur where it is necessary to allow a full and proper investigation and the taking of statements. Managers need to consider whether any of these criteria are met before rushing to immediate suspension. Moreover, if the circumstances make this possible, consideration should also be given to transferring staff to other work while an investigation takes place, as an alternative to suspension.

8.44   To conclude, we believe that suspension is an issue which must be treated more sensitively. Staff must have a full understanding of the implications of being suspended from duty. To achieve this there must be fully documented procedures, of which staff and children are aware, setting out the criteria for suspension of staff, the processes which must be undergone before a member of staff is suspended, the timetable for dealing with allegations, and what will happen after the investigation has been completed. This information should be provided on entry to the service, and staff should be notified of any changes or amendments.

Help for Staff

8.45   Staff should not be left isolated during suspension, bearing in mind that it is not a punishment. If appropriate, they should be kept aware of developments in their workplace so that if they return to work the time on suspension will not have been wasted. They should be able to have the support of trades unions or professional associations. There should be a manager from outside their own line management structure assigned to oversee and assist in this task. They should have access to counselling services, and this may be a role which can be taken by the stress counselling service discussed above (paragraph 8.31). A timetable should be set at the start of the investigation which aims to complete the process as quickly as possible, and the suspended member of staff should be informed of the timetable, and any changes to it. The British Psychological Society have commented that in traumatic cases independent counselling and assistance could be provided to young people (individually or in groups), staff and management, and we believe that this could be extended to the member of staff who has been suspended.

8.46   Where a member of staff who has been cleared of an allegation returns to work, he or she may feel isolated and out of touch. There may be new children, staff or managers, and it will important to support their return to work. The aim should be to ensure that the return to work is as untraumatic as possible following what will inevitably have been an extremely stressful period. As part of this process of assimilation back into the workplace explanations need to be given to children on what has taken place.

Recommendation 77

Staff should only be suspended from duty where a preliminary inquiry and careful assessment by the line manager, taking into account the interests of children and other staff suggests that a complaint could lead to dismissal or prosecution; or where a child could be endangered without suspension.

Recommendation 78

Staff should be informed on appointment of the policy and procedures on discipline and suspension from duty; should be able to receive assistance from professional associations or trades unions in any investigations of their conduct or disciplinary proceedings; and on return to work after suspension should be fully supported by management and colleagues, with appropriate retraining if necessary.

ANNEX 8A

GENERAL PRINCIPLES OF A STAFF CARE SCHEME

- Each member of staff has a personal responsibility of care for other employees.

- Each manager has particular responsibility for ensuring that positive staff care is promoted in the team or unit they manage.

- All staff should have equal access to Staff Care services.

- Staff Care services should be well publicised so that all staff are aware of their existence, their purpose and how to access them.

- All staff with work-related problems, or other problems which affect their work, should have access to welfare and counselling services without the need to disclose this to the division.

- Managers, in discussion with the staff they manage, should review working practices and conditions at regular intervals in order to reduce, as far as possible, factors which could give rise to stress or physical illness.

- Staff should be able to expect that staff care needs will be addressed by their manager and, if necessary, by appropriately trained staff or externally contracted specialists.

- Staff Care services should be able especially to assist staff who are:

  - experiencing uncertainty or change
  - victims of assault or threatening behaviour
  - experiencing personal problems that affect their work
  - finding working relationships with colleagues are difficult
  - subject to discrimination or harassment
  - involved in disciplinary or grievance procedures
  - having difficulties working with colleagues as a result of attention having been drawn to bad practices
  - experiencing stress from the nature or volume of their work

162

CHAPTER 9: THE POLICY AND PLANNING FRAMEWORK FOR CHILDREN'S HOMES

"Choosing each stone, and poising every weight,
Trying the measures of the breadth and height;
Here pulling down, and there erecting new,
Founding a firm state by proportions true"

Andrew Marvell, c.1650

Introduction

9.1   Throughout this report we have concentrated very much on the position of individual homes and employers. The overwhelming majority of our recommendations relate to what individual employers should be doing to improve the recruitment, selection, appointment and training of staff and the way they manage their homes. However homes and employers cannot operate in isolation. They function in a national and regional context; and they are affected by national legislation, guidance and policies. There are things that individual employers cannot control, such as qualification-awarding arrangements. Few - if any - local authorities have within their boundaries the full range of residential care that will be required to meet the needs of every child for whom they have responsibility. We consider that the policy framework within which homes and employers operate has an important influence on the quality of care for children. We have some concerns about some elements of the framework which we set out in this chapter.

Policy Framework and Guidance

9.2   Until recently there was little that could be described as a 'national policy' on children's residential care. It is not surprising therefore that homes have developed in different ways and adopted widely varying practices. The results of this laissez-faire approach have become clear to us during our Inquiry. We welcome the fact that the Government has recognised the need to provide a national policy framework to which individual homes and employers can relate by producing Volume 4 of the Children Act Guidance which is concerned with residential child care.   Our Inquiry followed too closely on the issuing of this Guidance for us to gauge its impact, although we saw encouraging signs in some places that employers were trying to address the issues it raises. In our view there is a need for Government to do more, as we explain in the following paragraphs.

9.3   We believe that in the past the Government has collected insufficient information about the children's homes sector to take remedial action when there were undesirable developments. We hope that they will build on the survey we commissioned from Price Waterhouse and collect on a regular basis more information about children's homes in order to produce well-informed guidance.

9.4   We consider that as employers tackle the issues in the Children Act Guidance, the amount of information about children's homes will increase. For example the statements of purpose and functions for homes that employers are required to produce under the 1991 Children's Homes Regulations will provide for the first time a nation-wide source of information about homes, providing they are monitored. We would urge the Government to use its resources - particularly the Social Services Inspectorate - to monitor change and to obtain up-to-date information about the management, staffing, condition, and activities of children's homes in a more systematic way than in the past. This will enable the Department of Health to review the guidance in Volume 4 and adapt it as necessary to reflect the changing needs and circumstances of children's homes. However, guidance must also retain reasonable flexibility for employers and heads of homes to develop residential child care in ways which meet the very individual needs of each child and which children and staff recognise as 'home', and not just another institution much like any other.

9.5   In our view the current policy guidance in some areas needs amplification. If the Government accepts our recommendations on the recruitment, selection and appointment of staff, we consider that a new Code of Employment Practice for Residential Child Care will be required to apply the changes consistently. We are not convinced that the issues we have raised over managing homes have been adequately considered by many employers; and we can see a need for new guidance here. The Government needs to give guidance to health and education authorities on the specialist services they need to provide to support children's homes; and changes are needed in the guidance relating to police checks and the Department of Health Consultancy Service. As legislation and case law changes, Government guidance will need further revision.

9.6   In essence we are saying that the Government has to give a policy lead to employers about the value, nature and range of children's homes, and their role within children's services generally. It has to do this more assertively than in the past. To improve its ability to exercise this leadership role it needs to be better informed; and this involves collecting information about children's homes on a more systematic and regular basis. The Government needs then to use the information to maintain in an up-to-date and relevant state the policy guidance it provides to employers. It needs also to monitor regularly the application of policy guidance by making greater use of the inspection capability of the Social Services Inspectorate. The recent reorganisation of the Social Services Inspectorate to separate its inspection functions from its other roles should assist this process.

Recommendation 79

The Government should give a clear lead on the importance, purpose and nature of residential care for children through the issue of well-informed guidance which should be kept up-to-date through the regular collection of information from employers and systematic monitoring of their activities by the Social Services Inspectorate; and should commission the preparation of a new Code of Employment Practice.

Standards and Enforcement

9.7   The 1991 Children's Homes Regulations are the closest thing to national standards for children's homes. We believe that as more information becomes available on children's homes, this should be collected nationally and more comprehensive national standards for children's homes should be developed. These standards would need to incorporate many of the areas in which we have made recommendations (eg, supervision and appraisal, selection of staff, specialist support services, staff care). This would enable employers and Government to monitor changes to see whether standards were rising or falling; and to take remedial action where necessary.

9.8   We recognise that the inspection and registration of most children's homes is barely a year old; and that this is insufficient time on which to make judgements about the new arrangements. We acknowledge that we have seen examples of registration authorities trying to define standards as a basis for their inspections. However, the pattern of distribution of children's homes is geographically very uneven, as we have discussed in paragraph 2.13. Even in the largest authorities there is unlikely to be a full range of children's homes; and in the smaller ones - many of which have a population of fewer than 200,000 - there may only be a very small number of homes. Yet each local authority is expected to define the standards to be applied to the homes in its area, even if it has little direct experience of particular types of home.

9.9   One of the continuing but extremely difficult areas of concern for us throughout the Inquiry has been that of homes and staff acting outside their field of competence. By this we mean children's homes admitting children with conditions for which the home is not equipped to cope. Because children's homes are seen as places of last resort they can be subjected to pressure by placing agencies to accept placements. At a time when the sector is shrinking and occupancy levels drop, homes managers of homes would be less than human if they did not overcome their misgivings and sometimes accept children in order to improve the occupancy figures. Whatever the pressures and whatever the justification, placing children in homes that are not competent to cope with them is bad for the children.

9.10   We believe that the days are past when people can regard one children's home as much like another, although we think that this simplistic view is still held in a few places. We have tried to demonstrate both the diversity of children and children's homes;

and to emphasise how important it is to construct statements of purpose and objectives for individual homes that accurately reflect their care and treatment objectives. As homes become smaller it becomes increasingly difficult for them to look after a wide range of children within a small unit. This produces a pressure for the specialisation of homes in order to make them competent and safe places. We believe that the specialisation of homes is becoming an important issue that the Government needs to consider.

9.11   The children's homes sector is small but very diverse. It would seem to us that a more rational framework for its inspection and registration would be national definition of standards according to the different types of children in residential care and the local enforcement of those standards by local inspection and registration units. We can understand why, during the passage of the Children Act, it was not possible to undertake the definition of national standards. However, now that more information about homes will become available, we think that the issue could be revisited, with advantage to children and placing agencies. We would invite the Government to consider establishing a mechanism for defining national standards for different groups of children in residential care as a basis for enforcement by local authority inspection and registration units.

9.12   We believe that an appropriate model for defining national standards for children's residential care is the 1984 'Home Life' document on residential care generally. This has been regarded predominantly as a code of good practice and standards for the residential care of elderly people and we believe that the time has come to prepare a specialist code for children and young people. In framing such a code it would be possible to address the issue of specialisation of homes that we have identified so that the standards of care reflect more precisely the needs of different groups of children. It would be important to ensure adherence to such a Code, and the Government would need to consider how this could best be done.

Recommendation 80

The Government should commission the preparation of a Code of Practice defining the national standards of residential care for different groups of children and young people, that should be followed by all employers and inspection and registration units.

Planning

9.13   There has been a considerable reduction in the local authority and voluntary sector provision of children's residential care over recent years and an increase in private sector provision. However these changes have often been unplanned and opportunistic and have not taken place on an even basis geographically. As we indicated in Chapter 2, whether or not a child ends up in residential care may be as much to do with where he or she lives as whether a children's home best meets their needs. Most local authorities are too small to have a full range of homes within their boundaries. Moreover, there is no national directory of homes that placing agencies can draw upon for placing outside their territory. Many placing decisions owe as much to grapevine, tradition and anecdote as to any strong base of factual information about homes. We believe that this situation would be improved if there was a national directory of children's homes and it was kept up-to-date.

9.14   We are aware that regional planning in the child care field has had a chequered history. However we believe that allowing the market in residential child care to change in a totally unplanned way is unacceptable. It produces the maximum uncertainty for managers, staff and children. Changes too often appear as sudden and cataclysmic and produce understandably angry reactions from staff and children. A sense of powerlessness is engendered in homes, and morale can be seriously affected by uncertainty. The London Boroughs have attempted to tackle these issues by producing collectively 'A Strategy for Residential Child Care in London 1991 - 2000'. We believe that other child care authorities should similarly look ahead, identify changing needs and produce a plan for ensuring that future needs can be met. This will enable employers to make changes to existing service provision in an orderly way and gives greater certainty and clarity to staff and managers. It will also provide a sounder basis for the letting of contracts to particular homes and so help reduce uncertainty.

9.15   Orderly change is being achieved in adult services by the production of Community Care Plans. In many parts of the country these have assisted inter-agency working and co-operation and joint planning between the public and independent sectors. In our view, Community Care Plans present a useful model for children's services, as the Utting Report recognised. We consider that the Government should encourage the preparation of local children's services plans on a basis of full co-operation and consultation by all the bodies involved - Social Services Departments, the voluntary and private sectors, and education and health authorities.

9.16   Local children's services plans should be produced by every Social Services Department. They should be needs-led in the sense of identifying present and forecast needs for all aspects of child care, including field work; adoption and fostering; day care; juvenile justice; child protection; working with children in need and residential care. The plans should identify the resources which are to be used or purchased in order to meet forecast needs. In relation to residential child care there should be a requirement to consult with neighbouring authorities and the voluntary and private sectors in considering how to meet those needs in respect of which the authority has identified it cannot be self-sufficient. The plans should include firm commitments - backed up by legal contracts - to purchase places in children's homes from other local authorities and the private and voluntary sectors. In this way, security will be delivered both to the Social Services Department that their needs can and will be met, and to the providers of residential child care that they have guaranteed resources to support the provision they are making. The plans should also indicate the extent of services required from health and education authorities and the arrangements to be made for meeting those requirements.

9.17   In many parts of the country we believe that the preparation of these plans will require local authorities and other agencies to work together in some kind of forum or consortium to plan how future needs for the residential care of children are to be met. We believe that the Department of Health should encourage these fora or consortia so that the best use is made of resources.

Recommendation 81

The Government should commission the compilation of a National Directory of children's homes, to assist agencies when making out-of-area placements; and make arrangements to keep the Directory up-to-date.

Recommendation 82

The Government should require local authorities to produce needs-led children's services plans where necessary jointly with neighbouring authorities, and in consultation with the voluntary and private sectors, and education and health authorities.

Concluding Remarks

9.18   We have considered the issues in this chapter because they are relevant to the safety and welfare of children, and are inextricably linked to the main areas of our remit. It would be wrong to concentrate only on tackling the problem areas in individual homes or with particular employers because the sector as a whole might still fail to make the necessary progress as a result of policy and planning deficiencies. We urge the Government to address the policy standards and planning issues we have raised in this chapter and to provide leadership to those at the local level in tackling the problems of children's homes.

CHAPTER 10: OUR FINDINGS AND PROPOSALS FOR CHANGE

Introduction

10.1   We believe that there is a serious situation in many children's homes. Some have called it a crisis. We have tried to produce an analysis of the problems and to propose some practical responses. The time has passed for rhetoric and debate. It is now for employers and their senior managers - assisted by Government - to tackle methodically the problems in their own backyards. They need to think positively and not allow themselves to be overwhelmed by the difficulties of changing attitudes and reordering management and resource priorities. If employers and senior managers fail to tackle the problems we have identified within a reasonable timescale there will be more neglected and abused children, more frustrated and ill-prepared staff and more scandals.

10.2   In this chapter we summarise our findings and proposals for change, before outlining an implementation strategy. That strategy allocates responsibilities and focuses on the key issues. In tackling those key issues we hope that people will draw upon the many detailed recommendations we have made throughout the report, and which are summarised at the end of this chapter.

Our Findings

Characteristics of children's homes and staff

10.3   A surprising aspect of children's homes is how little is known about them nationally. We commissioned therefore a national survey of homes in an attempt to move away from anecdote and prejudice as a basis for policy development and management action. The survey has revealed shrinking local authority and voluntary sectors of residential care for children, and an expanding private sector. Growth is taking place in the sector about which least is known. Until October 1991 there was no requirement to inspect or register private children's homes; and until our survey no-one knew how many homes there were in the sector. The reduction in the number of local authority homes in London is dramatic: London Boroughs had over 40% more places three years ago. Thus the children's homes sector is undergoing great changes, often in an unplanned way. This is very unsettling for staff and makes it more difficult to secure management commitment to change.

10.4   On average there are nine or ten children in each children's home. The average age of the children in homes is 14, and about 90% of children's homes look after boys and girls. About two-thirds of all the children in homes are considered to be suffering from emotional or behavioural difficulties. This is unsurprising given that about one-third of the children in homes are reported to have been sexually abused. Some children's homes today have high proportions of sexually abused and behaviourally disturbed children with many substance abusers and victims of serious violence within their own families.

10.5   These children are being looked after by largely unqualified and sometimes untrained staff. However, the staff are not particularly young or inexperienced. The average age of heads of homes is about 40 and that of care staff is over 30. On average staff and managers have worked in homes for about four years. Nevertheless the position on staff training and development is a considerable indictment of employers and senior management. In about 20% of local authorities there is not even any formal induction for these staff. Over 80% of local authorities appear to have no statement of the minimum training requirements for care staff, so they have not worked out what training the staff ought to have. Thus some of the most troubled and demanding children in our society are being looked after in children's homes by a largely unqualified and often untrained workforce.

Selection and appointment of staff

10.6   A range of information could be obtained about the suitability of candidates for posts in children's homes. Some of these sources of information are little used; some are neglected altogether; and some are invested with misplaced trust. In most employing authorities things get off to a bad start with application forms whose design makes them of limited usefulness in selecting staff. About the only thing on which all employers agree in the selection of staff is that they should interview in panels. We have found that many employers have a touching faith in the ability of a 30 to 40 minute interview to serve as the best means of selecting care staff for children's homes. This is despite the fact that interviews are known to produce a satisfaction score in terms of subsequent job performance of about 14 people in every 100 - somewhat worse odds than tossing a coin.

10.7   Our survey shows little current enthusiasm among employers for the use of selection techniques that would provide a more rounded picture of candidates and their suitability for work in children's homes. In selecting people there is little systematic attempt by many employers to find out anything about the way candidates relate to children; any incidents in their own pasts which might give rise to concerns; or the stability of their own sexual relationships and their ability to cope with often highly sexualised teenagers.

10.8   We have serious concerns about the way references and checks are handled. It is clear that some employers take little account of references from previous employers in making appointments. Ten percent of heads of homes and a third of care workers take up posts before references are received. Ten percent of voluntary and private homes employ staff on whom no police checks have been made for criminal convictions. There are reported delays by the police in carrying out checks of up to three months in some parts of the country, particularly London, so some staff have unsupervised access to children before police checks are made. Excuses have been offered to us to explain this situation, but we believe that the selection and appointment arrangements in many places are not designed to produce safe appointments.

10.9   We are also concerned at the use of commercial agencies for recruiting heads of homes and other care staff. This is because of the high cost of agency staff; shortcomings in carrying out police and other checks; and the fact that governing bodies are not involved in the selection of heads of homes.

Supervision and appraisal

10.10   It is not enough simply to select and appoint the right staff. They have to be supervised and appraised. Inquiry report after inquiry report has drawn attention to the importance of supervision and appraisal as a defence against inappropriate conduct by staff. Yet our survey and visits show that the advice has generally gone unheeded nationally. Formal appraisal systems exist in only 30% of local authorities for heads of home and 18% of authorities for care staff. These figures drop below 10% and 5% respectively in the Metropolitan Councils. The picture on appraisal is much better in the independent sector. As a Committee we find it surprising that after all that has been said about the importance of appraisal, so few staff are being appraised. Although there are supervision arrangements in place in most homes the frequency varies considerably - from weekly to monthly - for care staff. For untrained staff working with disturbed adolescents, monthly supervision is hardly a satisfactory position. Moreover, many employers report that the bulk of the supervision is "informal". We have tended to interpret this as meaning that the supervision is unplanned and irregular.

Developing and supporting staff

10.11   We consider that the present position on training and staff development is dire, although we recognise that there have been some improvements in the past year or two. Eighty percent of care staff and 40% of heads of homes are regarded by their employers as having no relevant qualification (see table 3.2). Even if one accepts that the Diploma in Social Work is the most appropriate qualification for residential child care - which we do not - then on present plans it will take over 30 years to train the eligible staff to obtain this qualification. The present training strategy seems more geared to helping able staff to obtain qualifications that enable them to leave than to providing practical training for the majority of staff in homes looking after children.

10.12   However good the staff training programmes become the nature of the children in residential care today strongly suggests a need for specialist support services. If nearly 70% of children are in homes because of their emotional and behavioural difficulties and around a third are thought to have been sexually abused, it would be reasonable to expect that children and staff should have regular and easy access to psychologists, psychotherapists and psychiatrists. This is not the current position. Only about 40% of local authority homes have access to these specialist services monthly or more frequently. Some have no access at all. Some homes who claim to have specialist therapeutic roles say they have no access to these specialist support services. It is clear that in some parts of the country the NHS has largely abandoned providing specialist support to children's homes and local authority staff have given up asking for help.

10.13   There is a need in many places to pay more attention to caring for staff. Working in children's homes is stressful. Staff are often the victims of threatening or violent behaviour. They are dealing with some very difficult young people but know that if they misjudge volatile and unpleasant situations they may be disciplined. In discussions with staff, only rarely have we been told that they felt supported by employers at times of personal difficulties. Sometimes one is left with a sense of employers being so preoccupied with caring for others that they forget their own staff. In only a minority of places are there good staff care schemes providing support and counselling to staff at times of personal crisis and accessible independently of line management.

Management arrangements

10.14   We have already mentioned deficiencies in appraisal and supervision. In some places the management structures above home level also need attention to provide more effective supervision and support. There seems to be a shortage of authoritative managers with residential care experience to manage groups of homes. Many staff in children's homes see the employing authorities and senior managers as remote figures removed from their problems. We are left with a distinct sense that some employers have not faced up to their own responsibilities as governing bodies for the safety and welfare of children in their homes.

10.15   There is still some way to go in some places before one can be satisfied that effective inspection and registration arrangements are in place. The voice of the child is still very muted in some places, not only in the running of the homes but in being able to make heard their cries for help. Attention needs to be given in some places to ensuring that more effective checks and balances are in place that will prevent children's homes becoming closed institutions cut off from the outside world. This means paying more attention to issues such as complaints procedures, independent visitors, and helplines and advocacy schemes for children.

10.16   In some homes the education services provided to children are most unsatisfactory, and this has an adverse affect on their development. In many parts of the country the responsible management has failed to secure the specialist psychological, psychotherapeutic and psychiatric help that many children in homes require or to ensure that specialist support services of this kind are available to staff. This unsatisfactory situation has arisen because some health and education authorities have failed to provide the services they should to children in residential care.

Policy and planning framework

10.17   In most parts of the country the residential child care sector is shrinking, sometimes in an unplanned way and in some places very rapidly. Until the Department of Health produced in 1991 the Volume 4 guidance on the Children Act there was no national policy framework to which homes, employers and managers could relate. There are gaps in the national information about children's homes. This hinders the preparation of comprehensive guidance; the development of national standards; and the monitoring of change.

Summary of concerns

10.18   On the evidence presented to us we would summarise our concerns as follows:

- An increasing number of difficult children to care for in homes.

- Low esteem of homes and staff and consequent staff morale and recruitment problems.

- A lack of sustained attention to children's residential care by employers and senior management in Social Services Departments.

- Non-existent or inadequate arrangements for staff appraisal and supervision in many places, and other poor management practices .

- Deficient and sometimes unsafe employment practices, with a need for a more systematic and rigorous approach to the recruitment, selection and appointment of staff.

- Inadequate knowledge and training to enable staff to cope with the children in their care.

- A shortage of specialist support services from the NHS for the children and staff in homes and deficiencies in the educational services provided for children in residential care.

- Inadequate definition of policy and standards at the national level; and an absence of adequate joint planning arrangements at the local level.

Proposals for Change

10.19   There is good news as well. Dotted around the country are examples of good practice in all sectors - public, voluntary and private. These beacons of good practice shine with varying degrees of light and recognition, but they are there for those who want to see them.   There are also homes and employers who recognise the need for change and are investing effort and resources in bringing about improvements. These areas of good practice and change now need to become more widespread.

10.20   Although there are some good homes and some employers determined to improve their homes, there are too many inadequate homes in too many parts of the country. Too many staff are left inadequately trained, supervised and managed to deal with some of the most difficult children and young people in our society. The evidence presented to us shows that the children's homes of today have high proportions of sexually abused and behaviourally disturbed children in them.   The management, training of staff, employment practices and investment in many homes needs to be improved to care for the mix of children being looked after.

10.21   Although we have many concerns we have also a high regard for many of the staff in children's homes. Many staff do a remarkable job in trying circumstances for very little thanks or reward. We believe that all staff need to be given a reasonable chance to succeed rather than being set up to fail. This will require a concerted and sustained effort by employers and managers to tackle some of the major problem areas - low self-esteem; deficiencies in supervision and appraisal; poor employment practices, especially in relation to the selection of staff; and patchy management that too often loses interest or fails to respond to problems. A sense of resolve is needed by managers to bring about improvements, but so is a clear plan of campaign. In the next two sections we summarise the key aspects of an implementation strategy both for employers and the Government.

Responsibilities of employers

10.22   There are no easy solutions for children's homes. Employers and their senior managers have to apply themselves to a range of issues. They have to pay continuing attention to the sector and ensure that the changes they approve actually happen. The history of children's homes is that they get forgotten and senior management loses interest. Sustained management attention is required over a period of years.

10.23   In our view there are ten key aspects on which employers and their senior managers should be concentrating attention in the near future. These key aspects are:

• Producing - in consultation with neighbouring authorities, the independent sector and health and education authorities - published children's services plans which identify needs and the means of meeting them; and supporting these plans with firm arrangements or contracts for children's residential care between the local authority as commissioner of services and all providers of services. (See Chapter 9 recommendation 82)

• Reviewing the management arrangements for homes to ensure adequate supervision and appraisal of staff in homes by competent managers above the home level; the preparation of statements of purpose and objectives for all homes; acceptance of full responsibility and accountability of governing bodies for the safety and welfare of children in homes; the effective operation of inspection and registration arrangements in accordance with Department of Health Guidance; and clear contracting arrangements for obtaining places in residential care that safeguard the position of individual children and provide greater certainty to the owners and managers of homes. (See Chapter 6 recommendations 39 to 41, 47 to 49 and 55 to 57.)

• Reviewing - and changing where necessary - the arrangements for handling complaints and providing independent visitors, helplines and advocacy schemes for children to ensure that there is a robust system of checks and balances.

174

These arrangements should ensure that the voice of the child is heard and that individual homes do not become closed institutions, cut off from the community. (See Chapter 6 recommendations 50 to 54.)

- Introducing within 12 months a system of structured fortnightly supervision and annual documented performance appraisals for all staff in children's homes; and ensuring that supervision and appraisal is conducted by trained and competent personnel. See Chapter 6 recommendations 42 to 46.)

- Introducing within two years a system of Personal Development Contracts for all staff in children's homes linked to NVQ and relying more on supervised work-based training with distance learning than on lengthy secondments to educational establishments. More immediately there should be guaranteed induction training for all new staff and management training for all new heads of homes within six months of appointment. (See Chapter 7 recommendations 58 to 68)

- Changing immediately recruitment procedures for staff in children's homes so that all vacancies are advertised externally and all applicants are sent job descriptions and person specifications related to the statement of purpose and objectives for the home, along with application forms designed specifically for children's homes. Reviewing the use made of agencies to ensure safe appointments and value for money. (See Chapter 3 recommendations 2 to 7.)

- Replacing quickly the existing arrangements for selecting staff to work in children's homes with a wider range of selection techniques that produce a more rounded picture of the suitability of applicants. For selecting heads of homes these techniques should include visits to homes; written exercises; group exercises; aptitude tests; personality profiling; preliminary interviews concentrating particularly on sensitive personal issues; full employment histories and the right to approach any current or previous employer; and a formal interview that would resolve any outstanding areas of doubt and concern. A narrower range of selection techniques could be used for care staff - with group exercises, aptitude tests and personality profiling being optional for the time being; but the range of techniques would be much more extensive than most employers use now. These changes may require some employers reviewing carefully their application of equal opportunities policies to ensure that these do not lead to them making unsafe appointments. (See Chapter 4 recommendations 9 to 24.)

- Introducing immediately more rigorous checking arrangements for applicants for posts. These will include obtaining more comprehensive employment histories from previous or current employers; completing police checks and checks with the Department of Health Consultancy Service before offering appointments; and monitoring the period of probation in a more systematic way before confirming appointments. A designated appointing officer should oversee appointments to ensure that all checks are made; and informal approaches should be made to previous or current employers to probe employment histories. (See Chapter 5 recommendations 25 to 27, 33 and 36.)

- Conducting within 12 months an audit with education and health services to identify any deficiencies in the education services for children in residential care and the specialist support services from the NHS - psychology, psychotherapy and psychiatry; and planning with those services how to improve the education and health services to better meet the needs of children in residential care. These planning reviews should address how to provide specialist support to staff as well as to individual children. (See Chapter 8 recommendations 71 and 73.)

- Reviewing the present arrangements for providing support to staff outside line management and taking steps to ensure that all staff in children's homes have access to independent counselling and support services. (See Chapter 8 recommendations 7 and 75.)

10.24   Although action needs to be taken quickly, to achieve significant change will require sustained effort by employers. We consider that local authorities will need to make children's homes a major priority for at least the next three years and judge the performance of their senior managers during this period on how well they devise and execute plans for improving the quality of care and practice in children's homes. Children's homes in the voluntary and private sectors will need to be fully included in programmes of change and employers in these sectors will need to make similar efforts.

10.25   We consider that we have set out a practical implementation strategy for change and improvement in children's homes. We hope that employers will pursue it, drawing upon the detailed recommendations which are summarised after this chapter. Too many children's homes have been forgotten for too long - until there is a scandal. They have few champions. They need continued attention from those in positions of authority who can bring about change. However they will need some help from the Government.

The role of Government

10.26   The primary responsibility for implementing change rests with the employers - individually and collectively - but the Government has a part to play. It defines the policy and planning framework within which children's homes operate; it should create a climate of good practice; it has a capacity to influence training and qualifications that is denied individual employers; it has a monitoring capability in the form of the Social Services Inspectorate; and it can use funding mechanisms to target resources and pump-prime desirable initiatives.

10.27   The Government has to give a clear lead to employers on the need for change in children's homes by taking the initiative in six key areas. These are:

- Giving a clearer lead to employers on the importance, purpose and nature of residential care for children through the issue of new guidance; the regular collection and publication of more information about the operation and conditions of children's homes; the systematic monitoring of the activities of employers through the Social Services Inspectorate; and within two years to conduct a public awareness campaign, and to promote the positive aspects of

176

working in children's homes. (See Chapter 3 recommendation 1 and Chapter 9 recommendation 79.)

● Producing a new Code of Employment Practice for children's homes, covering recruitment, selection and appointment of staff; preparing a new Code of Good Practice as a statement of national standards that could provide a clearer basis for monitoring, inspection and registration; and commissioning a National Directory of children's homes to assist the placement of children in homes that will meet their individual needs. (See Chapter 9 recommendation 81.)

● Preparing new guidance on particular issues set out in this report: ie, reducing delays in police checks; the proper use of the Department of Health Consultancy Service; the role of elected members in managing homes; the responsibilities of health and education authorities to provide specialist services and support to children's homes; and staff approaches to care and control within homes.

● Encouraging the production of needs-led local children's services plans that identify the volume, purpose and scope of residential care required for children in any area; and that provide greater certainty to local managers of residential care for children. (See Chapter 9 recommendation 82.)

● Taking the lead in the development of a new training strategy for staff in children's homes along the lines we have proposed, giving greater emphasis to work-based training. This will require reconsideration of the appropriate professional qualification for working in children's residential care; speeding up the application to children's homes of the NVQ system; and extending the period of the Training Support Programme to partly fund improved training in children's homes. (See Chapter 7 recommendations 68 and 69.)

● Ensuring health and education authorities give sufficient priority to the needs of children's homes and their staff for specialist health and education services. (See Chapter 8 recommendation 70.)

● Working with employers and possibly pump-priming innovative developments in the sphere of residential care for children. Particular projects proposed in this report that require attention are the further evaluation of certain selection techniques - the use of group exercises, personality profiling and aptitude tests; the use of traineeship schemes and advance recruitment for staff working in children's homes; the development of training material for appraisal and supervision; and a pilot project on independent visitors to children's homes. (See recommendations 1, 12, 14, 15, 34, 37, 46 and 50.)

A Development Action Group

10.28   We have in mind the establishment by the Government of a small Development Action Group for no more than three years. In our view this would indicate the Government's commitment to reform by establishing a new body overseeing the development and implementation of change in children's homes.

10.29   We are only too aware that various reports have been published on children's residential care without producing the necessary change and improvement nationally. It is clear from the results of our survey that, looking at the country as a whole, insufficient action has been taken on the findings of other inquiries. We are deeply concerned about the position of children and staff in children's homes and would like our recommendations to fare somewhat better than some of our predecessors. If a programme of desirable change in children's homes is to be implemented within the near future, we consider that the Government and employers will need help. We would suggest that this help comes from a new Development Action Group.

10.30   We see this new Group having two main roles: public watchdog ensuring improvements take place; and development agent facilitating the change process. Within these roles we consider that the Development Action Group should have the following main functions:

- Assisting Government and representatives of employers in the preparation of an action programme.

- Commissioning particular projects that formed part of the agreed action programme.

- Facilitating cooperation between different interests and helping to resolve areas of difficulty.

- Monitoring progress on implementation of the action programme agreed by Government.

- Preparing annual progress reports.

10.31   We envisage the Development Action Group consisting of six to eight independent people who will carry conviction in the worlds of social services and residential child care but who will not be seen as representatives of any particular interests. It should work to a remit agreed by the Government and report directly to the Secretary of State for Health. The Group's annual reports on progress should be in the public domain and should identify areas where progress is slow. Our expectation is that the combination of independent observers and public scrutiny would do much to prompt speedy change.

10.32   The Development Action Group would require a small secretariat from the Department of Health to enable it to maintain an information database. It should be able to make visits and to carry out surveys to check progress. It would be able to commission and oversee projects such as a national Directory of Homes and a 'Home

Life' Code of Practice. It would be available to give advice to employers and disseminate good practice through its secretariat.

10.33 We hope that the Government will recognise that some 'engine for change' is required and will support the establishment of a new Secretary of State's Development Action Group for Children's Homes for a limited period of time. The Government has found it necessary recently to appoint a Community Care Support Force to assist local authorities and others with the implementation of Community Care changes. This precedent illustrates how change in social policy areas can often be facilitated by an authoritative group that is separate from Government and employers. We are convinced that children's homes need a change agent of this kind.

Recommendation 83

The Government should establish for three years a small independent Development Action Group, reporting direct to the Secretary of State for Health to monitor and facilitate a programme of change for children's homes agreed by the Government.

Resources

10.34 A common reaction to a report such as ours is to assume that nothing can be done without additional resources being made available. We are not convinced that this is so, although we recognise that our recommendations do have resource implications for Government and employers. We are aware that in the current economic climate it will be difficult to find additional public expenditure for children's homes. That is why we consider it important to relate the resource implications of our recommendations to the wider context of total expenditure on the Personal Social Services and local government activities as a whole.

10.35 In summary the recommendations that are likely to produce additional costs for employers are as follows:-

- Additional activity by personnel staff and line managers as a result of improved recruitment, selection and appointment procedures.

- More management time devoted to supervision and appraisal.

- Some improvements in complaints arrangements, advocacy services and helplines and independent visitors.

- Additional time spent by staff on work-based training and by trainers and by managers supervising and assessing that training.

- Refurbishment of homes.

10.36   In our view the first three of these items could be funded largely by redeploying existing Social Services and local government resources as a result of giving a higher priority to children's residential care and improving efficiency. We say this for the following reasons:-

- The total annual expenditure on the Personal Social Services (PSS) is now about £5 billion. There is force in the argument that children's homes have never been an expenditure priority; may have served as a source of funds for other services after closure; and on the whole have lost out in the competition for resources. Some of the deficiencies we have identified could be put right if children's homes were given higher priority within the total PSS expenditure.

- Producing local children's services plans may reveal some scope for redeploying resources to improve children's homes. It is not evident that all the resources currently being spent on children's services are necessarily being spent in the areas of highest priority, given the absence of thorough planning and evaluation of children's services in particular localities. Furthermore, improved efficiency and rationalisation within the sector will provide further scope for financing change. Thus proper planning and prioritisation may provide scope for redeploying resources on children's homes.

- The improved employment practices we have recommended will save money eventually with the employment of more appropriate staff, and the avoidance of staff wastage and the costs of investigations into malpractice. In the short term they will involve additional activities by personnel staff and extra training resources and will require a shift of some resources from other Departments into Social Services to improve personnel practices and training in children's homes. Such changes in priorities are the very stuff of corporate decision-making that should be at the heart of local government.

In short, we consider that with sufficient will there is some scope for local authorities redeploying resources to improve children's homes from within the residential child care sector, from other areas of Social Services and from their other activities. This will require corporate working by local authorities, making children's homes a top priority, and effective local planning. We accept that our changes will have resource implications for small independent homes and that this will affect the fees they charge local authorities for placements, but the unit costs of local authority homes will be affected also.

10.37   The training and refurbishment items in paragraph 10.35 are different. Our training proposals represent much better value for money than the existing strategy of expensive secondments away from the workplace and loss of staff from residential care after qualification. Nevertheless, they also reflect a considerable increase in the volume of staff to be trained and in the short term this will increase the unit costs of homes. It should be possible for some employers to meet some of these costs from within their current expenditure by reordering priorities. However, most employers will require funding help from Central Government - through a continuation of the Training Support Programme which is 70% funded by Government with a 30%

contribution by local authorities - and targeting part of this specific grant on training for staff in children's homes.

10.38   Refurbishing children's homes is a matter of capital priorities. Improving them will cost extra money and they could be given higher priority within local authority capital programmes. It might be possible also for Central Government to assist this process by allowing local authorities to use 100% of accumulated capital receipts for any scheme of improvement to children's homes. There might also be higher guideline figures for social services within the block allocation.

10.39   There are some recommendations that will require action on resources by Central Government:

- Continuation of a Training Support Programme, with part of it targeted on staff in children's homes.

- Improvements in specialist health service support such as psychology to children's homes.

- Improvements in police vetting.

- Improved standard setting and monitoring, together with pump-priming some particular initiatives.

- A national awareness campaign.

Again, however, we believe that it may be more a matter of re-ordering priorities than new public expenditure. Our recommendations would cost a very small part of the total Department of Health budget but they would require Ministers to give a higher priority to children's homes within total expenditure on the Personal Social Services and the NHS.

Conclusions

10.42   We have identified the problem areas that we have found and we have proposed solutions to the problems. We have set out in paragraphs 10.22 and 10.26 the key aspects for employers and Government in bringing about change. Our detailed recommendations are collected together at the end of this Chapter. They need to be studied and acted upon. We hope that the Government will establish a Development Action Group of the kind we have proposed to oversee a programme of change. Although our proposals have resource implications, we do not believe that they are great given the scale of the Personal Social Services budget. Much could be achieved by reordering priorities for resources nationally and locally and with better local planning.

10.43   We would like to conclude on a note of optimism. We observe a change among many managers, professionals and politicians and in the public mood. In the two seminars we conducted there was considerable support for new approaches. Despite other pressures and resource constraints we have detected a growing sense that children's residential care has to be regarded as a special case, deserving of priority, resources and sustained management attention. We believe that there is a good chance that our recommendations will attract widespread support among staff, managers, employers and decision-makers. We hope so - for the sake of the children.

Norman Warner (Chairman)
Dick Clough
Adrian Gozzard
Jim Hughes
Florence Iles
Adrianne Jones
Richard Lansdown
Dudley Procter
Susan Thomas
Richard White

SUMMARY OF RECOMMENDATIONS

All of the recommendations made in our report are collected together in this summary under their chapter and subject headings.

Chapter 3: Recruitment of Staff

Improving the Recruitment Climate

Recommendation 1

The Department of Health should, within two years, fund a centrally run campaign to raise the public's awareness of children's residential care, and to promote the positive aspects of working in children's homes as a career.

Defining the Job and Postholder

Recommendation 2

Employers should only recruit staff after preparing a job description clearly related to the home's current statement of purpose and objectives; and a person specification for each post to be filled setting out clearly the competencies (ie, skills and personal attributes) and experience required to discharge satisfactorily the responsibilities in the job description.

Recommendation 3

Employers should use as a basis for job descriptions and person specifications an agreed up-to-date and publicly available statement of purpose and objectives for each home that makes clear the type and characteristics of the children in the home and the objectives of the care and treatment programmes it is providing.

Advertising

Recommendation 4

Employers should ensure that all vacancies are advertised - usually externally - and are open to competition; and that all heads of home posts should be advertised externally and nationally.

Advance Recruitment

Recommendation 5

The Local Authority Associations should establish a number of carefully monitored pilot projects for the advance recruitment of children's residential care staff against predicted vacancies and encourage the formation of consortia of employers in all sectors for this purpose.

Use of Commercial Agencies

Recommendation 6

Employers should appoint all heads of homes on direct employment contracts, and should not use agency staff as heads of homes.

Recommendation 7

Employers who wish to use agencies should satisfy themselves that they represent good value for money and do not have an adverse effect on the resources available for the care of children; and should require any agencies used to adopt selection and appointment procedures as rigorous as those for directly employed staff set out in this Report.

Chapter 4: Selecting Staff

Application Forms

Recommendation 8

Employers should require applicants for posts in all children's homes to complete application forms specifically designed for these posts and that collect core information relevant to the posts, as defined in the job descriptions and person specifications.

Recommendation 9

Employers should send applicants job descriptions, person specifications and full information about the home where they have applied for a post.

Written Exercises

> **Recommendation 10**
>
> Employers should use written exercises in the selection process (including shortlisting) to test the ability of candidates to think clearly and to express themselves.

Visits to Homes

> **Recommendation 11**
>
> Employers should require all shortlisted candidates to visit the home and meet staff and children in advance of the interview. Information about the interaction on visits between candidates and staff and children should be made available to those involved in deciding the appointment of candidates by a person involved in the appointment process.

Group Exercises

> **Recommendation 12**
>
> The Department of Health and the Local Authority Associations should establish a project to evaluate existing experience on group exercises and discussions and to develop ways of ensuring that these techniques are available to all employers with children's homes, particularly for the appointment of heads of homes.

> **Recommendation 13**
>
> Employers should use appropriate aptitude tests as part of the normal selection process for shortlisted candidates for heads of homes and other senior management posts in residential homes.

> **Recommendation 14**
>
> The Department of Health and the Local Authority Associations should commission work to evaluate currently available aptitude tests; and to devise more appropriate tests where necessary for use in the selection of staff for children's homes.

Recommendation 15

The Department of Health and Local Authority Associations should evaluate current personality tests; and consider commissioning the design of the most appropriate tests for posts in children's homes.

Preliminary Interviews

Recommendation 16

Employers should use preliminary interviews as a standard part of establishing a fuller picture of the character and attitudes of shortlisted candidates for <u>all</u> posts in children's homes.

References

Recommendation 17

Employers should require candidates when applying to provide a full employment history, including periods of unemployment, with dates (to the nearest month) and the names and addresses of past employers. Candidates should be free to provide the name of a referee in addition to an employer if they wish.

Recommendation 18

Employers should always approach an applicant's present employer; should tell applicants that they reserve the right to approach any previous employer (or line manager) about a shortlisted candidate's character and performance before interview; should seek written references on the basis that referees have the job description and person specification and are encouraged to comment frankly on shortlisted candidates' strengths and weaknesses in relation to those two documents; and where necessary should explore any aspects of references by telephone with a current or past employer.

Recommendation 19

Employers should keep a record of conversations with referees and pass the result to those responsible for making appointments; and they should retain records of disciplinary offences or concerns that enable them to be passed on to a potential employer when requested in connection with a job which involves working with children.

Shortlisting

> ### Recommendation 20
>
> Employers should ensure that, wherever possible, shortlists have at least three candidates; that shortlisting panels should include line managers and a person independent of the line management of a home; and a that the panel should have no more than three members balanced by in gender and, where appropriate, race.

Final Interviews

> ### Recommendation 21
>
> Employers should ensure that final interview panels consist of no more than three people balanced by gender and race as far as possible and appropriate; and should include an independent person as well as the line manager and person senior to the line manager - one of whom should be authorised to make the appointment.

> ### Recommendation 22
>
> Employers should ensure that final interview panels should have available to them and use all the information about candidates from earlier parts of the selection process; and that panels are free to explore areas of doubt and concern in order to discharge their overriding responsibility to make safe and competent appointments in children's homes.

> ### Recommendation 23
>
> Employers should only assign people to interview panels if they have had appropriate training, and should consider the use of external assessors when it is difficult to appoint a panel without an independent element.

Equal Opportunities Policies

> ### Recommendation 24
>
> Employers should be required to use a wider range of selection techniques (as set out in Table 4.2) for the appointment of care staff and heads of children's homes.

Chapter 5:   Appointment of Staff

The Designated Appointing Officer

Recommendation 25

Employers should only offer appointments after completing police checks; checks against Central Government lists (and any lists of approved practitioners that may be established in future); and verification of birth certificates and educational/professional qualifications; and should allow no unsupervised access to children before completion of all checks.

Recommendation 26

Employers should designate people at a level above the manager of the appointee as "designated appointing officers" who should be take final responsibility for all appointments; oversee all stages of the appointment process; and ensure that all checks are made.

Police Checks

Recommendation 27

Employers should not make appointments before completing police checks, but should confine requests to those candidates which they intend to appoint, rather than all shortlisted candidates; and local authorities should ensure liaison between Chief Constables and Directors of Social Services to reduce delays in conducting police checks for appointments to children's homes.

Recommendation 28

Police forces should continue to complete checks on staff applying for posts in children's homes through nominated officers in local authorities; should wherever possible provide written confirmation of the information given to nominated officers when the modernisation of the police computer system has been completed in 1995; and should complete checks within three weeks at the latest and within ten working days where there is no need to check outside the home force.

Recommendation 29

All police forces should check staff to work in voluntary and private homes through the nominated officers in local authorities or the National Council for Voluntary Child Care Organisations, and in accordance with a procedure acceptable to the police.

Recommendation 30

The Home Office should take steps to reduce the unacceptable delays in some police forces and promulgate examples of good practice; should consider introducing a 'fast track' system for requests for checks on staff appointed to work in children's homes; and in revising guidance should clarify what police information other than convictions should be made available to employers, and the form of that information.

Crown Prosecution Service Information

Recommendation 31

The Crown Prosecution Service should make available to the police information suggesting that individuals should not work with children, who in turn could inform employing authorities through the medium of police checks.

Central Government Lists and Inter-Agency Checks

Recommendation 32

The Department of Health should issue guidance, clarifying the categories of behaviour which should be notified to the Consultancy Service and the information which should be provided, and publicising the existence and value of the service.

Recommendation 33

Employers should be required by Regulation to consult the Department of Health's Consultancy Service and the Department for Education's List 99 in respect of any person they intend to appoint to a children's home.

National List of Approved Practitioners

Recommendation 34

The Government should consider the introduction of arrangements for giving a "licence to practise" to care staff working in children's homes and for withholding or withdrawing such licences when agreed conditions were not fulfilled.

Probationary Appointments

Recommendation 35

The Local Authority Associations should negotiate amendments to the National Terms and Conditions so that probationary periods of 12 months become standard practice for <u>all</u> new appointments to children's homes irrespective of whether a person comes from within the same employing authority or another local authority.

Recommendation 36

Employers should ensure that the performance of individuals is rigorously monitored and documented by the immediate line manager during probationary periods with formal assessments within the first six weeks, within six months, and a final appraisal at 12 months, with a certificate that the person has satisfactorily completed probation; and that assessments are seen by the designated appointing officer.

Traineeships

Recommendation 37

The Department of Health and Local Authority Associations should consider establishing a number of carefully monitored pilot projects whereby new entrants to work in children's residential care could be regarded as trainees working under supervision for a defined period as an alternative to the probationary system.

Applicants from within the European Community

Recommendation 38

The Department of Health and the Home Office should consider the implications of greater mobility of labour within the European Community for the checking of staff from other EC Countries who wish to work in children's homes in the United Kingdom.

Chapter 6: Managing Homes

Statement of Purpose and Objectives

Recommendation 39

Employers should approve, keep up-to-date and monitor a publicly available statement of purpose and objectives for each home - or in large homes each unit - covering the items specified in paragraph 6.7 as part of the obligations placed on them by the Children's Homes Regulations.

Management Structures and Principles

Recommendation 40

Employers should review the management structures within which their children's homes operate to assess their consistency with the principles set out in this report, ensuring where possible that the management of homes is not linked to the management of field social work because of potential conflicts of interest.

Recommendation 41

Employers should consider grouping smaller homes under a single manager, or with other related services where this is not feasible; should ensure wherever possible that the person to whom heads of homes report has experience of residential care; and should provide each home or unit with its own budget and the maximum delegated authority for heads of homes to redeploy resources within approved policies, work programmes and budgets.

Supervision

Recommendation 42

The Government should require employers to ensure that regular supervision of all staff by line managers takes place at least fortnightly and appropriate remedial or developmental action is agreed, recorded and taken as a result.

Recommendation 43

Employers should ensure that supervision is seen as the normal means by which staff are able to raise with their line manager any concerns about the welfare or treatment of a child; but that staff have access to advice about a child outside the line management chain and are able to raise any concerns through an independent staff support service.

Recommendation 44

Line managers should take the initiative in supervision sessions in raising developmental issues with staff and should ensure that Personal Development Contracts are used effectively to develop staff in ways consistent with a homes objectives.

Performance Appraisal

Recommendation 45

The Government should require employers to introduce within a year arrangements whereby all staff have their performance formally appraised annually by their line manager; and an employee's personal file should contain a record of the appraisal showing the level of performance achieved and the agreed training needs to be met within the next 12 months as part of the individual's Personal Development Contract.

Recommendation 46

Government and employers should ensure that training material on supervision and appraisal is available to all managers.

The Role of Governing Bodies and Elected Members

Recommendation 47

Governing bodies and elected members should approve the statement of purpose and objectives for homes; and review and modify them as necessary from time to time; allocate the necessary resources; monitor that the physical standards of the home and its quality of care are satisfactory by means that they have determined; and ensure that they receive a report on the overall performance of homes once a year.

Recommendation 48

Governing bodies and elected members should recognise that they have an over-riding responsibility for the welfare and protection of children in their care; should regard it as their duty to have fully investigated any evidence of malpractice or behaviour that puts children at risk of abuse and to take appropriate action to protect children; and as part of these responsibilities should continue to visit homes.

Recommendation 49

The Department of Health and the Local Authority Associations should prepare guidance for elected members of local authorities and governing bodies on the purpose of visits to children's homes, the information to be collected, the format of their reports and the systems for reporting back information; and the Government should regard such visits as approved duty for the payment of attendance allowances and expenses.

Independent Visits to Children's Homes

Recommendation 50

The Department of Health should establish several pilot projects extending the role of Panels of Independent Visitors established under the Children Act 1989 to enable Independent Visitors to visit children's homes; and should prepare national guidelines for the conduct of independent people visiting homes that clarify the parameters within which they are operating.

Complaints Procedures

Recommendation 51

Employers should provide children with easily understood guidance on how children can raise concerns and complaints and in particular how this may be done initially without the knowledge and involvement of the person complained of.

Recommendation 52

Employers should ensure that all children in residential care have access to a telephone helpline on which they can raise concerns without being overheard and have the support of their own advocates when pursuing serious complaints against staff.

Recommendation 53

Employers should accept that staff in residential homes for children should be able to raise significant concerns outside their normal line management when they consider the line manager has been unresponsive or is the subject of concern; they should enable staff to make use of complaints procedures established by legislation.

Recommendation 54

Employers should have published procedures that make it clear to staff how complaints will be taken up and investigated, by whom and within what timescale; should inform placing agencies and inspection/registration units of serious substantiated complaints; and should involve the police when conduct of an apparently criminal nature is alleged.

Contracts

Recommendation 55

When children are placed in residential care, the placing agency should have a clear written agreement (contract) with the home on the nature, duration, cost and anticipated outcomes of the care to be provided in accordance with the home's statement of purpose and objectives; should ensure contracts are consistent with national and local standards for inspection and registration; and should jointly review agreements/contracts at regular intervals, with the involvement of the child and parents.

Independent Inspection and Monitoring

Recommendation 56

Within any national guidance, local authorities responsible for the registration and inspection of children's homes should have published standards for homes and agreed arrangements for the frequency and nature of visits by inspection units and for the pursuit of unsatisfactory reports. Inspection units should share information with contracting agencies and those responsible for managing homes.

Recommendation 57

Employers responsible for homes should have clearly defined operating targets and performance criteria for monitoring performance in homes.

Chapter 7:   Staff Development, Training and Qualifications

A New Training Strategy for Residential Child Care

Recommendation 58

The Government, employers and qualification-awarding bodies should agree a new training strategy for staff in children's homes, with more emphasis on work-based training, and less on lengthy secondments to educational establishments; that uses a more formalised system of supervision and appraisal to identify staff development and training needs; that introduces a Personal Development Contract for all staff and managers in children's homes; and that secures more accreditation and portability of qualifications for supervised and assessed work-based training.

Recommendation 59

Employers should regard training as a major means of recruiting and retaining staff, and dealing with change in the home; should ensure staffing levels that enable staff to maximise supervised work-based training; should provide time, encouragement and financial assistance to enable suitable staff to obtain relevant training; and should ensure that their training programmes are structured and delivered in ways that maximise their portability through acceptability for recognition by qualification-awarding bodies

---

Recommendation 60

Employees should accept their responsibility to be supervised and appraised regularly and to contribute ideas for their personal development as part of their Personal Development Contract, including identifying opportunities for training and obtaining qualifications; and should take the initiative in raising with line managers their doubts about being able to cope with particular situations or young people with a view to securing appropriate guidance and training.

The Personal Development Contract

Recommendation 61

Employers should develop model Personal Development Contracts for all care staff and managers in Children's Homes and introduce a new system within two years.

Professional Qualifications

Recommendation 62

The Government should reconsider its current policy on qualifications for heads of homes; and should consider arranging the design and introduction of a new Diploma, focused more on the group care of children and young people at an equivalent level to the Diploma in Social Work as the preferred professional qualification for staff working in children's residential care.

Recommendation 63

This new Diploma should be designed on a modular basis, drawing on the relevant skills of professions other than social work; should minimise absence from the workplace for staff undertaking it; and should be obtainable over a period longer than two years.

Vocational Qualifications

Recommendation 64

The Government should take steps to ensure that the new system for recognising and awarding NVQs meets the training needs of children's homes staff in the ways we have described as quickly as possible.

Induction Training

Recommendation 65

Employers should provide structured induction training to all new employees in children's homes before they have unsupervised access to children, and use this period to set goals for the successful completion of the probationary period.

Management Training

Recommendation 66

Employers should ensure that all new heads of homes have undertaken appropriate management training no later than six months after appointment; and should review the management training needs of existing heads of homes.

Recommendation 67

The Local Authority Associations should commission work on the identification of the core elements of a management development programme for heads of children's homes, and if possible link this with the Management Charter Initiative.

Costs of Training

Recommendation 68

The Government and employers should accept that a better-trained workforce in children's homes is likely to require extra expenditure by them on training, supervision and replacement costs.

Recommendation 69

The Government should give clear financial recognition to the importance of training as a means of improving the quality of care in children's homes by continuing a targeted Training Support Programme for several years with a specific grant meeting part of the cost borne by employers; and should encourage joint training programmes for staff in all sectors in order to raise standards everywhere.

Chapter 8: Specialist Services and Support for Staff

Improving Specialist Support to Homes

Recommendation 70

The Government should issue new guidance to health and local education authorities on the services and support they are expected to provide without payment to those responsible for running children's homes and relate this to Regional Health Authority priorities and the need to work collaboratively with Social Services Departments in improving support to children's homes.

Recommendation 71

Within the next 12 months all employers should audit services in children's homes, distinguishing between the needs of staff and children and between individual and group work; should identify whether or not there are adequate arrangements for providing specialist support to children and staff and should plan how to rectify identified deficiencies in collaboration with their local health and education authorities.

Recommendation 72

Health authorities should ensure that adequate specialist services such as clinical psychology are available to meet the identified needs of children in residential care; and Local Education Authorities should take steps to meet more fully the identified educational needs of children in residential care, including the provision of educational psychology services.

Support for Staff

Recommendation 73

Employers should accept responsibility for funding any psychology services required primarily for the purposes of staff training, development and support and should arrange such services in consultation with the local health authority or, in the case of educational psychology services, with the local education authority following their audit of specialist services required by children's homes.

Recommendation 74

Employers should ensure easy access to independent Staff Care schemes for providing support to staff in children's homes that they can access independently of line management to discuss any concerns and receive advice and counselling.

Recommendation 75

All employers should have written staff grievance and disciplinary procedures that are consistent with local child protection and complaints procedures.

Care and Control Issues

Recommendation 76

The Government should issue full guidance for staff on the issues of control, restraint and physical contact with children in residential care; keep this up-to-date; and reinforce it by ensuring the provision of authoritative training ,material that allows staff to apply the guidance in real situations.

Suspension of Staff

Recommendation 77

Staff should only be suspended from duty where a preliminary inquiry and careful assessment by the line manager, taking into account the interests of children and other staff suggests that a complaint could lead to dismissal or prosecution; or where a child could be endangered without suspension.

Recommendation 78

Staff should be informed on appointment of the policy and procedures on discipline and suspension from duty; should be able to receive assistance from professional associations or trades unions in any investigations of their conduct or disciplinary proceedings; and on return to work after suspension should be fully supported by management and colleagues, with appropriate retraining if necessary.

Chapter 9: The Policy and Planning Framework for Children's Homes

Policy Framework and Guidance

Recommendation 79

The Government should give a clear lead on the importance, purpose and nature of residential care for children through the issue of well-informed guidance which should be kept up-to-date through the regular collection of information from employers and systematic monitoring of their activities by the Social Services Inspectorate; and should commission the preparation of a new Code of Employment Practice.

Standards and Enforcement

Recommendation 80

The Government should commission the preparation of a Code of Practice defining the national standards of residential care for different groups of children and young people, that should be followed by all employers and inspection and registration units.

Planning

Recommendation 81

The Government should commission the compilation of a National Directory of children's homes, to assist agencies when making out-of-area placements; and make arrangements to keep the Directory up-to-date.

Recommendation 82

The Government should require local authorities to produce needs-led children's services plans where necessary jointly with neighbouring authorities, and in consultation with the voluntary and private sectors, and education and health authorities.

Chapter 10: Our Findings and Proposals for Change

Recommendation 83

The Government should establish for three years a small independent Development Action Group, reporting direct to the Secretary of State for Health to monitor and facilitate a programme of change for children's homes agreed by the Government.

APPENDIX 1: THE MEMBERSHIP OF THE COMMITTEE OF INQUIRY

Chairman

Norman Warner   -   Former Director of Social Services, Kent County Council

Committee

Dick Clough MBE   -   General Secretary, Social Care Association

Adrian Gozzard   -   Group Personnel Director, Trustee Savings Bank Group

Jim Hughes   -   Professor of Technology and Business Studies, Strathclyde University. Formerly Director of Human Relations, Thorn EMI PLC.

Florence Iles   -   Principal Personnel Consultant, William M Mercer Fraser Ltd

Adrianne Jones CBE   -   Director of Social Services, Birmingham City Council

Richard Lansdown   -   Consultant Psychologist, Department of Psychological Medicine, The Hospital for Sick Children, Great Ormond Street, London

Dudley Procter   -   Chief Executive, Lincolnshire County Council

Susan Thomas   -   Chief Personnel Officer, London Borough of Lewisham

Richard White   -   Solicitor in Private Practice, White and Sherwin Solicitors

Secretary

Mark Davies   -   Department of Health

APPENDIX 2: PEOPLE AND ORGANISATIONS WHO ASSISTED THE COMMITTEE

Written Evidence

Some 70 organisations were invited to submit written evidence to the Committee, under a series of headings suggested by the terms of reference of the Inquiry: Recruitment and Selection of Staff; Qualifications and Experience; Equal Opportunities; Employment Contracts and Discipline; Management and Staffing Arrangements; Training, Support and Guidance for Staff and Management; Staff Complaints and Grievances; and Good Practice. The letters inviting evidence invited respondents also to give their views on any other relevant subject. We also received the views of people whom we had not approached directly.

We received written submissions from the following individuals and organisations:

Advice, Advocacy and Representation for Children (ASC)

Association of Chief Police Officers

Association of County Councils

Association of Directors of Social Services

Association of Metropolitan Authorities

Aycliffe, Centre for Children

Christopher Beedell

British Association for Adoption and Fostering (BAAF)

British Association of Social Workers (BASW)

British Paediatric Association

British Psychological Society

Central Council for Education and Training in Social Work (CCETSW)

Childline

Children's Legal Centre

Roger Clough, Cumbria Social Services Department

Community Services Volunteers

Dartington Social Research Unit, University of Bristol

Roy Grimwood, Redsands Children's Centre

Independent Representation for Children in Need (IRCHIN)

Institute of Personnel Management

International Graphoanalysis Society

Barbara Kahan

Staff Care Unit, Centre for Counselling Studies, Keele University

Law Society Local Government Group

Faculty of Health and Social Care, Leeds Polytechnic

Department of Continuing Adult Education, University of Leeds

Leicestershire Social Services Department

Allan Levy, QC

Local Government Management Board

London Boroughs Children's Regional Planning Committee

Department of Psychiatry, University of Manchester

Mill Grove

National and Local Government Officers Association (NALGO)

National Children's Bureau

National Children's Home

National Council of Voluntary Child Care Organisations (NCVCCO)

National Institute for Social work (NISW)

National Society for the Prevention of Cruelty to Children (NSPCC)

Newland Park Associates Ltd

The Royal Association for Disability and Rehabilitation (RADAR)

Royal National Institute for the Blind

Mr J G Rusling

St Piers School Lingfield

The National Deaf-Blind and Rubella Association (SENSE)

Sheila Shaw

Shepherd Moscow Training Associates Ltd

Social Care Association

Social Care Association, Birmingham Local Area Branch

Social Information Systems Ltd

Society of Chief Personnel Officers

Mrs R E J Spencer

Wagner Children's Charter Group

Oral Evidence

Rather than taking separate oral evidence from large numbers of individuals and organisations, we decided that it would be more useful to hold two seminars, bringing together a range of people to discuss particular issues. The first seminar covered issues around the framework within which individuals operate, in particular training; management arrangements; and quality control. It was attended as follows:

Nick Barlow	(British Psychological Society)
John Beer	(Surrey Social Services Department/Association of County Councils)
Malcolm Billinge	(British Psychological Society)
Dr Roger Bullock	(Dartington Social Research unit)
Roger Clough	(Chief Inspector, Cumbria Social Services)
Roy Grimwood	(Principal, Redsands Children's Centre)
Tony Hall	(Central Council for Education and Training in Social Work)
Dr Masud Hoghughi	(Aycliffe, Centre for Children)
Brian Jones	(Association of Metropolitan Authorities)
Barbara Kahan	(National Children's Bureau)
Des Kelly	(Social Care Association/National Institute for Social Work)
Dr Mike Lindsay	(Children's Rights Officer, Leicestershire Social Services)
Mary MacLeod	(Childline)
Ruth Nissim	(British Psychological Society)
Janet Ollier	(Project Co-ordinator, ASC - Advice, Advocacy and Representation for children)
Richard Taylor	(Local Government Management Board)
Jane Tunstill	(National Council for Voluntary Child Care Organisations)
Ian White	(Director of Social Services Oxfordshire/Association of Directors of Social Services)
Tom White	(National Children's Home)

Representatives from the Department of Health also attended.

The second seminar covered the issues of recruitment, selection and appointment of individuals, and was attended as follows:

Nick Barlow	(British Psychological Society)
Angela Baron	(Institute of Personnel Management)
Dr Barry Brown	(British Psychological Society)
Dr Roger Bullock	(Dartington Social Research Unit)
Stephen Campbell	(Association of County Councils)

Gillian Hindley	(Oldham Metropolitan Borough Council/Society of Chief Personnel Officers)
Barbara Kahan	(National Children's Bureau)
Des Kelly	(Social Care Association)
Pat Lindley	(Newland Park Associates Ltd)
Alwyn Rea	(Chief Personnel Officer, Gloucestershire County Council/Society of Chief Personnel Officers)
Sally Roach	(British Psychological Society)
Maurice Rumbold	(National Children's Home)
Robin SeQueira	(Director of Social Services, Dorset/Association of Directors of Social Services)
Sheila Shaw	
George Thomas	(National Council for Voluntary Child Care Organisations)
Vivian Walker	(Institute of Personnel Management)
Arnie Wickens	(Community Service Volunteers)
Peter Wilkinson	(Aycliffe, Centre for Children)

Representatives of the Department of Health and the Home Office also attended.

Government Departments

We took written and oral evidence from the Government Departments which would be concerned with implementing any recommendations: the Department of Health, the Home Office and the Department for Education. We obtained written evidence also from the Crown Prosecution Service.

We considered it important to visit other United Kingdom jurisdictions to learn of their experience. We met with officials from the Department of Health and Social Services in Northern Ireland; the Scottish Home and Health Department; and the Welsh Office. In the course of the visits we met with local authority managers, and visited children's homes, in the statutory and voluntary sectors.

Local Authorities

Committee members visited a number of local authorities in England. The authorities were chosen to exemplify the range of authorities by type (ie, county, metropolitan or London borough), size and geographical location. The local authorities visited were:

Dorset
Croydon
Hammersmith and Fulham
Lancashire
North Yorkshire
Oxfordshire
Southwark
Sheffield
Stockport
Wolverhampton

On most of these visits there were meetings with the Chief Executive and Chief Personnel Officer; meetings with the Director of Social Services and senior social services management; and visits to local authority children's homes and usually a private or voluntary home.

We are grateful for all the effort made in arranging these visits, for the helpfulness and openness of everyone we met, and for the opportunity to meet managers, staff and children. We recognise that visits to children's homes are very disruptive for staff, and would particularly like to thank all the homes we visited for making us welcome.

Europe

In order to gain a picture of practice in Europe, Committee members visited the Netherlands. There we met with Government officials; local government officers; officials of the independent organisations which provide children's residential services; and staff and children in homes. Once again we would like to thank those who gave their time to see us, in particular the Stichting Overleg Jeudvoorzienningen Nederland, the organisation which arranged the programme for us.

Others

Finally, we met with a number of other organisations and individuals who kindly agreed to assist us and to provide information. These meetings were helpful in providing information about specific areas of work for the Inquiry. These visits and meetings included Aycliffe Centre for Children; the Maudsley Hospital; Kent Constabulary; the National Association of Local Government Officers and the National Union of Public Employees; and the National Association of Young People in Care.

208

APPENDIX 3

**SURVEY OF LOCAL AUTHORITY AND INDEPENDENT
SECTOR CHILDREN'S HOMES**

OCTOBER 1992

Price Waterhouse

CONTENTS	Paragraph

212

EXECUTIVE SUMMARY

Background to the survey

1   This report presents the findings of a questionnaire-based survey carried out during the period March to July 1992 by Price Waterhouse on behalf of the Committee of Inquiry into the Recruitment and Selection of Staff in Children's Homes. The survey, designed to cover all children's homes in the local authority, private, voluntary and assisted community home sectors, aimed to provide a solid foundation of basic information, policies, practices and perspectives to assist the Committee in its deliberations.

2   The survey work was undertaken in two phases. During the first phase, full and detailed questionnaires were developed in a consultative process in which the input of Committee members was complemented by suggestions from a number of social services departments, voluntary organisations and representative bodies.

3   In recognition of the time and effort which would be required for completion of the detailed questionnaires, the Chair of the Committee wrote to directors of social services and chief executives and proprietors of voluntary, assisted and private sector organisations advising of the questionnaires' imminent distribution. In particular, it was stressed that the intention of the survey was to elicit information on current policy and practice, not to make presumptions about what good policy and practice should be. In addition, a help desk was set up at Price Waterhouse to provide guidance and support during the process of questionnaire completion. In the event, extensive use was made of this facility by a large number of homes and organisations

4   Returns were received within the required timescale from over three-quarters of local authorities (and analysis of late returns showed these to be representative of those included within the survey findings). However, because the proportion of returns from independent sector homes and organisations (while acceptable for a postal questionnaire) was less satisfactory, the Committee saw benefits in instigating a smaller, second phase of work designed to seek basic information from independent sector homes and organisations which had not responded to the survey.

5   In this second phase, to increase the likelihood of response, a more limited number of questions were asked, focusing on:

- beds and occupancy

- age of children

- number, and duration in current post, of persons in day to day charge.

6   Around 75 percent of known independent sector homes have thus provided basic or fuller information to assist the Committee so that the Committee's deliberations on issues affecting the independent sector are as strongly founded as for local authority homes.

213

7   The paragraphs which follow summarise the findings of the survey and are based upon information received during both phases of work.

Profile of children's homes and residents

8   Key facts emerging:

- There were an estimated 11,250 children in children's homes in England on 31 March 1992. Of these, an estimated 7,790 (69%) were in around 950 local authority homes, 2,065 (18%) in around 170 voluntary and assisted community homes and 1,550 (14%) in around 180 private sector homes. (The private sector figures may be a slight understatement as only those homes reported by local authorities could be included in the survey)

- There are on average nine children's homes per local authority

- The average number of beds per home is 11 for local authority and private sector homes, but nearly 16 for voluntary and assisted community homes

- Occupancy rate in all three sectors averages around 75 percent, but, is slightly higher in the independent sector than in local authority homes

- By far the largest reported client group in all three sectors is children with emotional/behavioural difficulties

- The average age of children in children's homes in all sectors is 14, though the range is very wide

- Around one third of children in local authority children's homes, one third in private homes and one quarter in voluntary/community assisted homes are reported to have been sexually abused

- Key trends:

  -    continuing emphasis in new homes on children with emotional/behavioural difficulties

  -    reduced numbers of homes and beds in local authorities and voluntary organisations.

Characteristics of care staff

9   Key facts emerging:

- Proportionately more agency staff are used in local authorities than in other sectors

- The average age of care officers, at 35, is higher in local authorities than in the other two sectors. However, the average age of officers in charge (39-40) is similar in all three sectors

- The proportion of officers in charge with traditional social work qualifications is higher in local authorities than in the other sectors

- In local authorities, care officers work more actual hours per week than officers in charge. In the other two sectors the position is reversed

- Vacancy and sickness rates are highest in local authorities.

Recruitment

10   Key facts emerging:

- External advertising is very much the norm for officer in charge and care officer recruitment

- Private sector use of the professional/social work press to attract officers in charge is low compared with the other sectors

- Local newspapers are more commonly used than national or professional press to attract care officers in all sectors

- Job descriptions and application forms are sent to enquirers in all sectors in the vast majority of cases, though person specifications less so

- Around one quarter of local authorities discourage or disallow pre-interview informal discussions, a significantly higher proportion than in other sectors. Such discouragement is particularly common in London Boroughs

- All sectors report difficulties in achieving appropriate ethnic mixes in staff groups

- Authorities are very concerned about the unattractive image held by residential work, and tend to view this as a serious impediment to effective recruitment.

Selection

11   Key facts emerging:

- Interview remains by far the most prominent selection method

- Panel sizes tend to be higher, in policy and practice, for officers in charge than for care officers, although the modal figure is three in both instances

- Achievement of a satisfactory ethnic mix on panels is viewed as elusive, particularly in local authorities (where the criteria may be more precise and rigorous)

- All sectors express the importance of exploring candidates' attitudes to control/punishment and equal opportunities issues in interviews

- Local authorities' perceptions of equal opportunities interviewing appear in some cases to lead to less exploration of personal issues and less secondary or spontaneous questioning

- Training for interviewers is markedly more pronounced in local authorities than in other sectors

- Consensus is the preferred selection method in interviews. However senior people tend to be authorised where necessary to make the decision or apply a veto

- There is minimal room for bypassing organisational selection procedures in any sector.

References and checks

12   Key facts emerging:

- Two references are usually required, but three is also quite common in voluntary and assisted community homes and the private sector

- References are obtained in writing, and sometimes complemented by telephone calls. No telephone only references are sought in any sector

- References are normally sought between short listing and interview, but some appointments are made subject to satisfactory references

- The length of time required for police checks means that people are acknowledged to be start jobs before the results of checks are received

- Inter-agency checks such as the DH Consultancy list are used, but less than might have been expected

- It is not consistent practice in any sector to alert other prospective employers about staff leaving about whom concerns exist

- References/checks for agency staff are frequently not made. It appears that this is often because it is known/assumed that this is handled by the agencies themselves.

Probation

13   Key facts emerging:

- Probationary periods are virtually always required in private sector homes and other single establishment organisations. Exclusions apply in various circumstances for local authority appointments

- The length of the probationary period is usually six months in all sectors, but there is wider variation in terms of shorter and longer periods in both voluntary/assisted community homes and the private sector

- The rate of probation failure is proportionately higher in the private sector than in voluntary/assisted community homes or local authorities

- Some respondents stressed the benefits of establishing probation as a continuous process of feedback and development rather than a snapshot judgement after six months.

Employment contracts and discipline

14   Key facts emerging:

- Most local authority employment contracts for residential staff are with single named homes, although there may be a trend towards more generic contracts

- Few authorities seek information on previous disciplinary offences either on application or in interview, although these practices are much more common in the private sector

- Dismissal rates are substantially lower in local authorities than in the other sectors

- Suspension is more frequent in local authorities than either final warnings or dismissals, but is not necessarily part of the disciplinary process

- Member approval for dismissals is required in 9 percent of authorities. However, Member overturning of officer decisions is rare.

Induction, training and supervision

15   Key facts emerging:

- Sixty percent of local authorities have statements of minimum training requirements for residential staff. This figure is lower than that in the private sector, but higher than in voluntary and assisted community homes

- Formal induction is provided in around 75 percent of authorities for officers in charge and over 80 percent of authorities for care officers

- The availability of training appears to demonstrate policy commitment to providing some relevant training for as many staff as possible

- Appraisal systems exist in 30 percent of authorities for officers in charge and in 18 percent for care officers. The figures are higher for the other sectors

- Formal supervision of care officers by officers in charge takes place fortnightly to monthly in nearly all cases.

Inspection and complaints

16   Key facts emerging:

- Line managers' monitoring is more frequent than formal inspections by registration and inspection units

- Visits at night are undertaken less by line managers (but more by inspection units) in local authorities than in the other sectors

- Arrangements for the investigation of complaints are extensive in all sectors

- The use of leaflets to inform children of complaints procedures is more common in local authorities than in the other sectors, at around two thirds and one half respectively

- Voluntary/assisted community homes and private sector homes are more confident than local authorities that they have adequate advocacy systems in place, and that children with communication difficulties are properly represented

- Most authorities have arrangements whereby care officers can make complaints to, and receive confidential counselling and support from, more senior staff outside the home and outside the line management structure.

Contracts between agencies

17   Key facts emerging:

- All local authorities place children in independent sector homes

- Forty percent of local authorities report having formal contracts with such homes. Of this 40 percent, two thirds note the following service specification elements to be in place: service aims and objectives, service inputs, care tasks, monitoring/evaluation arrangements and means of handling complaints

- Less frequently specified elements are: staff qualifications and training, service outputs and service quality standards

- Similar patterns are reported by voluntary/assisted community homes and the private sector.

BACKGROUND TO THE SURVEY

Survey origin and aims

18   A Committee under the Chairmanship of Mr Norman Warner was set up by the Secretary of State for Health to conduct an inquiry into recruitment, selection and other staffing and management issues in children's homes.

19   In February 1992, Price Waterhouse Management Consultants were commissioned to conduct a questionnaire-based survey designed to cover all children's homes in the local authority, private, voluntary and assisted community home sectors. The survey findings, included in this report, would aim to provide a solid foundation of basic statistics and information about policies, practices and perspectives which would assist the Committee in its deliberations.

Setting up the survey

20   Separate questionnaires were required for submission to:

- local authorities

- voluntary organisations and assisted community homes

- private sector homes.

21   The process of developing the questionnaires was fully consultative. The input of Committee members was complemented by feedback from a number of social services departments, voluntary organisations and representative bodies.

22   Names and addresses of private sector children's homes were obtained from local authorities. Although a small number of authorities did not return the information, the vast majority of private sector homes have been included in the survey.

23   Names and addresses of voluntary organisations and assisted community homes were already held by the Department of Health, so the survey covered all homes in these categories.

24   In recognition of the time and effort required for completion of the questionnaires, the Chair of the Committee wrote to directors of social services and chief executives and proprietors of voluntary, assisted and private sector organisations advising of the questionnaires' imminent distribution. In particular, it was stressed that the aim of the survey was to elicit information on current policy and practice, not to make presumptions about what good policy and practice should be. In addition, a help desk was set up at Price Waterhouse to provide guidance and support during the process of questionnaire completion. Extensive use was made of this facility by responding authorities and organisations during the survey period.

Response rate in two phases of the survey

25   Questionnaires were issued on 23 March to all sectors. However a number of private sector homes received their questionnaires later owing to delays in receiving information from local authorities on private sector homes in their area.

26   The final date for receipt of completed questionnaires was 7 May.

27   Completed questionnaires were returned by:

- 97 local authorities, representing 89 percent of the possible figure of 109

- 94 voluntary and assisted community homes, representing 56 percent of the possible figure of 169

- 61 private sector homes, representing 42 percent of the possible figure of 144.

28   The proportion of returns received from local authorities was thus high, particularly for a postal survey.

29   However, the proportion of returns received from the independent sector, while in many respects acceptable for a postal questionnaire, was less encouraging. Likely factors in the relatively low response are:

- the reduced time available for a number of private sector homes to complete the survey questionnaire for the reason noted in paragraph 25

- difficulties in answering many questions relating to formal policy and practice arrangements. Telephone calls received at the Price Waterhouse help desk, as well as comments made in individual responses, showed that a number of small private and assisted community home proprietors had difficulty in defining their relatively informal arrangements in the manner required.

30   For this reason, the Committee saw benefits in instigating a smaller, second phase of work designed to seek basic information from independent sector homes and organisations which had not returned survey questionnaires. Although the information to be sought in this follow up survey work would be substantially less than that sought in the full questionnaires, it would be sufficient to provide some indication of how far some of the main patterns emerging were broadly representative of the independent sector. The questions asked in the second phase of survey work focused on:

- beds available

- occupancy levels

- age of children

- duration in post of persons in day to day charge.

31   The forms were sent to identified non-responding independent sector homes and organisations on 23 June 1992, with a deadline five weeks later. It was also possible to send forms to additional private sector homes/organisations by then identified by local authorities. This follow up survey generated responses covering a further 31 homes in the voluntary/assisted community sector and 75 homes in the private sector. The combined response rate from both phases of the survey is therefore as summarised in the table below:

INQUIRY INTO THE RECRUITMENT AND SELECTION OF STAFF IN CHILDREN'S HOMES			
FINAL SURVEY RESPONSE RATE			
Sector	Possible returns	Actual returns	Percentage response
Local authorities (Initial survey only)	109	97	89%
Voluntary and assisted community homes	169	125	74%
Private sector homes	178	136	76%

Acknowledgement

32   The Committee of Inquiry and Price Waterhouse wish to acknowledge the great deal of time and energy dedicated to completion of the questionnaires, particularly within what is recognised to have been a tight deadline among competing pressures. In particular, the additional information, ideas and suggestions included within the completed questionnaires have complemented the statistical material in identifying a range of important issues for the Committee's attention.

Report format

33   This report presents the findings of survey, and is based upon information received during both phases of work. The format broadly follows the sequence of the survey questionnaires. The following sections therefore outline the findings in relation to:

● profile of children's homes and residents

● characteristics of care staff

● recruitment

● selection

- references and checks

- probation

- employment contracts and discipline

- induction, training and supervision

- inspection and complaints

- contracts between agencies.

34   Each section includes:

- a summary statement of key facts and issues emerging

- an overview of responses, including any particular points of comparison and contrast:

  -    between London Boroughs, County Councils and Metropolitan Boroughs and Districts

  -    between the different sectors

- illustration of respondents' views and experiences by examples and/or direct quotations where applicable

- any additional points of potential value to the Committee arising from the responses.

PROFILE OF CHILDREN'S HOMES AND RESIDENTS

THE KEY FACTS AND ISSUES

- There is an average of nine children's homes per local authority

- The average number of beds per home is 11 for local authorities and private sector homes, but nearly 16 for voluntary and assisted community homes

- Of over 11,000 children's homes on 31 March 1992, around 68% were in local authority homes, 18% in voluntary and assisted community homes and 14% in private sector homes

- Occupancy rate in all three sectors is around 75 per cent

- Children with emotional/behavioural difficulties are the largest reported client group in all three sectors

- The average age of children in children's homes in all sectors is 14, though the range is very wide

- Around one third of children in local authority children's homes, one third in private homes and one quarter in voluntary/community assisted homes are reported to have been sexually abused

- Key trends:

  - continuing emphasis in new homes on children with emotional/behavioral difficulties

  - reduced numbers of homes and beds in the local authority and voluntary sectors

---

Number of homes in authorities and voluntary organisations

35   These number of local authority-owned children's homes varies from 0 (Solihull, Lewisham, Bromley, City of London and Warwickshire) to 40 (Birmingham) and 57 (Lancashire). The average however is nine per authority, varying from 4.5 in London Boroughs to 13 in counties.

36   The only responding voluntary organisation to have more than 7 homes is Barnardos, with 24 (though it should be noted that no response had been received from National Children's Homes by the final deadline date). Over half the voluntary and assisted community homes related to organisations with one home only.

Size of homes

37   The average number of beds per home in the different sectors is as follows:

- for local authorities, 11 (varying from 9 in London Boroughs to nearly 12 in Counties)

- for private sector homes, 11

- for voluntary organisations and assisted community homes, nearly 16.

Numbers of children and occupancy rates

38   There were an estimated 11,250 children in children's homes in England on 31 March 1992. Of these, an estimated 7,790 (69%) are in around 950 local authority homes, 2,065 (18%) in around 170 voluntary and assisted community homes, and 1,550 (14%) in around 180 private sector homes. (The private sector figures may be a slight understatement as only those homes reported by local authorities could be included in the survey).

39   Occupancy rate in all three sectors is around 75 percent. For local authorities this may reflect unplanned under-use or a deliberate 'winding down' policy. For other sectors, one interpretation could be reduced demand for their facilities by local authorities. Occupancy rates three years ago were very similar in local authority and voluntary and assisted community homes, although the bed numbers were certainly larger (see paragraphs 46 and 47). However private sector homes responding to the survey indicated that their the occupancy rate was significantly higher three years ago (88 percent) than now (78 percent).

Single sex homes

40   Just over one third of authorities have one or more single sex establishments. The equivalent figures for the private sector and for voluntary and assisted community homes were lower, at around 10 percent and 20 percent respectively.

Client group of residents

41   In all three sectors the main client group is reported to be, by a considerable margin, children with emotional and/or behavioural difficulties. Indeed, responding private sector homes had no children in homes primarily providing services for children with physical disabilities or learning difficulties. However, whereas the number of children with learning difficulties was considerably greater than the number with

physical disabilities in local authority homes, in voluntary and assisted community homes the picture was reversed.

Sexual abuse

42   Most authorities felt able to provide estimates of the numbers of children in their homes who had been sexually abused (though some indicated that their estimates were probably on the low side). The average reported proportion was almost one-third.

43   By contrast, similar calculations in the two other sectors show the estimated proportion of sexually abused children to be:

- in private sector homes, also around one third

- in voluntary and assisted community homes, around one quarter.

Age of children

44   The average age of children in homes in all three sectors is around 14 (though slightly lower, at 13.5, in private sector homes). However, this mean figure masks significant variations. In particular, and even allowing for a margin of error in completing the questionnaires, a number of homes can and do accommodate very young children, including babies. Possible explanations might include:

- questionnaires completed in a 'snapshot' way might include young children placed overnight in a home as a necessary expedient rather than as a matter of good practice. This in turn might indicate inadequate numbers and/or types of foster parents in some authority areas

- a belief that residential placement does meet the needs of some very young children with particular difficulties in some circumstances. Further study would be required to examine how far this possible explanation might apply, and in what circumstances.

45   At the other end of the age scale, the survey indicates the presence of adults in children's homes in all sectors. Thus around one quarter of authorities have one or more persons aged 21 or over in their homes. A similar proportion of respondents from the other sectors, providing information in most cases on a single home, reported caring for people 21 or over. This may reflect the practical difficulty of finding suitable alternative accommodation for those children and young people who need support well into adulthood.

Trends in homes opening and closing

46   Local authorities' returns indicate that they owned around 15 percent more homes on 31 March 1989 than three years later. There is also significant variation between authority types. Whereas counties had about 10 percent more beds in 1989, London Boroughs had about 40 percent more beds, showing the decline in authority owned homes to be particularly pronounced in London. Moreover, a trend towards

smaller homes can be discerned, in that the average number of beds per local authority has dropped from nearly 12 to nearly 11 over the three year period.

47   It is not possible to ascertain, on the basis of this survey, the extent of a decrease or otherwise in homes or beds in the voluntary, assisted community or private sector. This is because the survey did not extend to those organisations or homes which have closed over the period. However, it may nevertheless be useful to note that:

*   those voluntary organisations and assisted community homes responding to the survey had around 5 percent more homes and 15 percent more beds three years ago, than as at 31 March 1992

*   nearly 40 percent of the private homes responding to the survey were not in existence three years ago.

48   Newly opened homes in all sectors appear to be mainly geared to children with emotional or behavioural difficulties, reflecting the pattern of existing homes.

Therapeutic methods and techniques

49   Respondents were asked to indicate therapeutic methods and techniques used in their homes. From a relatively small number of responses in all sectors, the most commonly occurring were:

*   behaviour modification and rewards systems

*   normalisation programmes

*   group work

*   art/music therapy

*   social skills work

*   preparation for independence

*   life story book work.

CHARACTERISTICS OF CARE STAFF

THE KEY FACTS AND ISSUES

* Proportionately more agency staff are used in local authorities than in other sectors

* The average age of care officers, at 35, is higher in local authorities than in the other two sectors. However, the average age of officers in charge (39-40) is similar in all three sectors

* The proportion of officers in charge with traditional social work qualifications is higher in local authorities than in the other sectors.

* In local authorities, care officers work more actual hours per week than officers in charge. In the other two sectors the position is reversed

---

Numbers of care staff

50   Responding local authorities reported a total of 9,900 care staff (including officers in charge and care officers) in their homes, suggesting that the complete national figure will be around 11,300. Similar calculations in the other sectors suggest that there are probably around 2,100 care staff working in voluntary/assisted community homes and 1,600 in known private sector homes.

Use of agency staff

51   In local authorities, over 10 percent of officers in charge and a similar proportion of care officers are from agencies. Use of agency staff is particularly pronounced in the London Boroughs, where 13 percent of officers in charge and 21 percent of care officers are from agencies. Authorities' comments and statistics show significant variation in policy and practice regarding agency staff. Some do not use agency staff at all, whereas others keep use to a minimum through reliance as far as possible on relief pools.

52   The comparative figures for the other sectors are:

* for voluntary and assisted community homes, around 5 percent of officers in charge and 8 percent of care officers are from agencies

- for private sector homes, agency staff account for around 3 percent of both officers in charge and care officers. (This relatively low figure may reflect the continuing family nature of many private sector homes).

Age

53   The average age of local authority officers in charge is 39. The average age of care officers, four years lower at 35, is perhaps greater than the general perception (echoed in some responses) of relatively young staff without life experience.

54   The comparative figures on age for the other sectors are:

- for voluntary and assisted community homes, around 40 for officers in charge and 33 for care officers

- for private sector homes, around 39 and 30 respectively.

55   There is therefore, on average, a greater age difference between officers in charge and care officers in voluntary and assisted community homes and in private homes than in local authorities. This is largely due to the higher average age of care officers in local authorities.

Qualifications

56   The proportions of qualified officers in charge and care officers in the different sectors are as set out below:

	Local authorities		Voluntary and assisted community homes		Private sector homes	
	OICs	COs	OICs	COs	OICs	COs
Percentage of staff with CQSW, CSS and/or Dip SW	41%	6%	38%	9%	30%	7%
Percentage of staff with other relevant qualifications	7%	14%	40%	23%	50-60%	30-40%

Note: Some inconsistencies in information supplied affects the reliability of the statistics for the private sector homes, so range figures are given for indicative purposes.

57   Key points relating to these figures are:

- The proportion of officers in charge with CQSW, CSS or Dip SW qualifications is higher in local authorities than in the other sectors, but not substantially so

- In both the voluntary and assisted community homes sector and private homes, the proportion of staff with other qualifications deemed by the respondents to be relevant is higher than the number with CQSW, CSS and/or Dip SW (in the case of the private homes sector, nearly double), and substantially higher than the equivalent figure for local authorities. Especially in the private sector, there may also be a broader view of what constitutes an "other relevant qualification"

- Analysis of comparative figures shows that the proportion of qualified officers in charge is similar in Metropolitan Boroughs/Districts, Counties and London Boroughs. However the proportion of qualified care officers is lower in London Boroughs (3.6 percent) than in the other two authority types.

Working hours

58   Average standard working hours per week are:

- for local authorities, just under 39 for both officers in charge and care officers, as compared with actual working hours of 42 and 46 respectively

- for voluntary and assisted community homes, over 40 for both officers in charge and care officers, as compared with actual working hours of 45 and 42 respectively. (These average figures are pulled up by a small number of organisations/homes where the figures are 50 or more)

- for private sector homes, 41.5 and 38 for officers and charge and care officers, as compared with actual working hours of 42 and 36 respectively.

59   Thus the local authority pattern whereby care officers work on average more hours in a week than officers in charge is reversed in the other sectors. The distinct local authority pattern may be explained, at least in part, by a greater reliance on (and/or a greater recording of) overtime than is the case in the other sectors.

Vacancy time

60   The proportion of vacancy time in local authorities (year ending 31 March 1992) is 7 percent for officer in charge posts and slightly less for care officer posts. These figures are around double the equivalent figures for the other sectors, possible explanations being:

- lengthier recruitment and selection procedures in local authorities

- local authority budget restrictions causing frozen posts

- difficulties in attracting staff to work in the local authority environment.

Length of time in post

61   Length of time in post for officers in charge and care officers is around 4 years for all sectors, the exceptions being:

- a relatively high figure (7 years) for officers in charge in voluntary and assisted community homes

- a relatively low figure (less than 2 years) for care officers in private homes. (This may be explained by the fact that around 40 percent of the private sector homes have been opened in the last three years.)

Sickness rates

62   Around 2 percent of days were lost through sickness in private homes in the year ending 31 March 1992. This was lower than in the other two sectors, most notably in local authorities where the care officer sickness rate was 5 percent. In addition, for both officers in charge and care officers the sickness rate in Metropolitan Boroughs/Districts is around twice that in Counties and London Boroughs.

RECRUITMENT

THE KEY FACTS AND ISSUES

- External advertising is very much the norm for officer in charge and care officer recruitment

- Private sector use of the professional/social work press to attract officers in charge is low compared with the other sectors

- Local newspapers are more commonly used than national or professional press to attract care officers in all sectors

- Job descriptions and application forms are sent to enquirers in all sectors in the vast majority of cases, though person specifications less so

- Around one quarter of local authorities discourage or disallow pre-interview informal discussions, a significantly higher proportion than in other sectors. Such discouragement is particularly common in London Boroughs

- All sectors report difficulties in achieving appropriate ethnic mixes in staff groups

---

Advertisements

63   External advertising is very much the norm for both officer in charge and care officer appointments. The figure does however dip a little for officers in charge of private sector homes (undertaken 'usually' or 'always' in 82 percent of cases), though not for their care officers. One factor here is, as also suggested in interpretation of the private sector response to an earlier question, the family-based nature of some smaller private sector children's homes. One home in this sector specifically referred to recruiting known people and not employing "strangers".

Recruitment media

64   For both local authorities and voluntary/assisted homes, more than 50 percent of respondents 'always' use the professional/social work press for officer in charge

recruitment. This is nearly double the equivalent private sector figure. Use of the professional/social work press is significantly greater in London Boroughs than in the other types of authority, for both officer in charge and care officer recruitment.

65   Local newspapers are more commonly used in all sectors than either the professional press or national newspapers to attract care officers. Local recruitment is seen as desirable by several private sector homes, and local authorities note that use of media other than local newspapers does not in practice prove cost-effective to recruit care officers. The exception again is London Boroughs, where there is less use of local newspapers than of the professional/social work press.

Information sent to enquirers

66   The large majority of authorities report always sending job descriptions out with information to enquirers. The figures, while slightly less, are also very high for the other sectors.

67   Use of application forms is 100 percent in local authorities, and around 90 percent for the other sectors, perhaps indicating the increasingly formal nature of private sector recruitment practices. Person specifications are distributed less frequently, in around 50 percent of cases for all three sectors.

Informal discussions prior to interview

68   Around one quarter of local authorities discourage, or actually disallow, informal pre-interview discussions. This figure drops to around 8 percent for voluntary and assisted community homes and even further for private sector homes, where prospective officers in charge are actively required or encouraged to attend informal interviews in all cases.

69   The one quarter of local authorities discouraging or disallowing informal pre-interview discussions contains significant variations, particularly between London Borough and Counties, where the figures are 44 percent and 0 percent respectively.

Gender and ethnic mix within staff groups

70   More than half local authorities acknowledge having no policies in place to ensure gender and ethnic mix within staff groups. This is in contrast to the other sectors where a considerably higher proportion of organisations/homes state such policies to be in place. Possible explanations are:

- the relative ease of establishing policies in small organisations, and especially single self-managed homes

- authorities' stricter criteria on interpreting the question.

71   In practice, private sector homes report greater success in implementing gender mix policies than do the other sectors. Nevertheless, in each of the three sectors around one quarter of respondents report clear failure in achieving an appropriate ethnic mix within staff groups. Analysis of local authority variations however shows that a far smaller proportion of London Boroughs report such failure (8 percent) than Metropolitan Boroughs/Districts (48 percent).

Additional comments from respondents

72   A number of respondents in all sectors report recruitment difficulties arising from the unattractive image of residential social work. Factors perceived as contributing to this unattractive image include poor pay, limited training and career development opportunities, insufficient recognition of and compensation for anti-social hours, inadequate supervision and support arrangements, and, as one voluntary organisation put it, "the association of residential child care with poorly paid women's work". Recruitment difficulties are then accentuated and perpetuated by retention difficulties as staff who do become qualified move into fieldwork positions.

73   To alleviate recruitment difficulties, some authorities report local initiatives such as career grade progression, integration of field and residential grades and the promise of training. Although such measures appear to have helped to some extent, the reality remains that, to quote one authority respondent, "one is forced to employ the best on the day rather than be too selective".

SELECTION

THE KEY FACTS AND ISSUES

- Interview remains by far the most frequent selection method, and is often the only one used

- Panel sizes tend to be higher, in policy and practice, for officers in charge than for care officers, although the modal figure is three in both instances

- Achievement of a satisfactory ethnic mix on panels is viewed as elusive, particularly in local authorities (where the criteria may be more precise and rigorous)

- All sectors express the importance of exploring candidates' attitudes to control/punishment and equal opportunities issues in interviews

- Local authorities' perceptions of equal opportunities interviewing appear in some cases to lead to less exploration of personal issues and less secondary or spontaneous questioning

- Training for interviewers is markedly more pronounced in local authorities than in other sectors

- Consensus is the preferred selection method in interviews. However senior people tend to be authorised where necessary to

---

Selection techniques

74   Interviews remain by far the most frequent selection method, used in 100 percent of cases in all sectors for all appointments (with a slight dip for care officers in private sector homes).

75   Group interviews/discussions are the most frequently used of other techniques listed in the questionnaire, which include candidate presentations, skills assessments and personality assessments. All the listed techniques are used more frequently in officer in charge than in care officer appointments.

76   These other techniques are also used more frequently in private sector appointments than in the other sectors, demonstrating either a greater flexibility in

selection methods or perhaps a looser interpretation of the question. One private sector home comments that "being such a small organisation, our procedures (rely upon) good sense, gut reactions and sharing the decision making".

Size of the interview panels

77   As a matter of both policy and practice, there is a tendency in all sectors for officer in charge interviews to be conducted by larger panels than is the case for care officer interviews. This tendency is indicated below:

	Local authorities		Voluntary and assisted community homes		Private sector homes	
	OICs	COs	OICs	COs	OICs	COs
Cases in which policy requires panel size of 4 or more	23%	15%	57%	20%	48%	41%
Cases in which panel size in practice averages 4 or more	25%	11%	52%	17%	52%	34%

78   The table shows the lower frequency of large panels in local authorities than in the other sectors. However, in all sectors the most frequently occurring panel size was found to be three.

Membership of interview panels

79   The most frequently occurring member of interview panels is the prospective appointee's line manager, followed by person(s) senior to that manager.

80   Other points of particular relevance to emerge from analysis of the detailed statistics are:

- the presence of elected Members on one third of all officer in charge appointment panels in Counties and Metropolitan Boroughs/Districts, a significantly higher proportion than in London Boroughs (4 percent).

- the higher use of external consultants (eg child care consultant, psychiatrist) in the other sectors than in local authorities, where no respondent reported such use

- the tendency in all sectors to include personnel officers 'always' or 'usually' in around one third of officer in charge appointments, though less so for care officer appointments.

Gender and ethnic mix of panels

81   In respect of gender/ethnic mix of panels:

- around three fifths of all respondents feel an appropriate gender mix is achieved in panels. However the overall local authority figure includes a higher proportion of London Boroughs reporting a suitable mix (71 percent) when compared with Counties (52 percent) and Metropolitan Boroughs/Districts (48 percent).

- local authorities express less achievement of ethnic panel mixes than do respondents in the other sectors. Thus, whereas around one third of authorities state they achieve an appropriate mix, the proportion in the other sectors is in each case around a half. Again, London Boroughs perceive more success in achieving an appropriate mix (63 percent) than do Metropolitan Boroughs/Districts (20 percent) or Counties (17 percent).

Interview questions

82   Of the options listed in the questionnaires, attitude to control and punishment emerges as the most frequent interview question area, occurring in the large majority of responses in all sectors.

83   The second most frequently occurring question area lies in attitudes to equal opportunities issues. The figures, for both officers in charge and care officers, suggest that this area is 'always' or 'usually' explored in around three quarters of cases for local authorities and the private sector, though slightly less so in voluntary and assisted community homes. The local authority overall figure contains variations in that exploration of this area is markedly more common in London Boroughs than in the other types of authority.

84   Probably in adherence to their equal opportunities policies and as a matter of perceived good practice, local authorities' exploration of other specified question areas (notably significant childhood events and the stability of candidates' personal relationships) is minimal. This is in contrast to private sector responses, suggesting that private sector homes do not see equal opportunities practices as a barrier to probing into more personal areas.

85   What one authority respondent terms the "search for balance" between achieving equal opportunities principles and providing more probing, tailored interviews is an area in which that respondent requests particular advice from the Committee. Certainly several local authority respondents feel that tight authority procedures often prevent tailoring and flexibility necessary for effective selection.

237

86   Agreed and fixed questions tend to be determined in advance in all sectors, for care officer appointments not much less than for officer in charge appointments. However, although secondary or spontaneous questions are very frequent, they are used less often in local authority interviews than in those in the other sectors. This may reflect the existence in some local authorities of a stricter perception of the role and meaning of equal opportunities-sensitive interviewing structure and processes.

Interview/selection training

87   Training is generally provided for elected Members who sit on interview panels. Training for officers is markedly more frequent in local authorities than in the other sectors. It is provided 'always' or 'usually' in over 80 percent of responding authorities, compared with equivalent figures of around one third in the other sectors.

Decision-making

88   Whether aspiration or reality, responses in all sectors show a strong tendency to selection by consensus. Two thirds of local authorities state this as the method, compared to even higher proportions in the other sectors. The designated appointing officer is the decision maker in around one quarter of authorities (including 12 percent of Metropolitan Borough/Districts and 31 percent of Counties), though in a lesser proportion of cases in the other sectors.

89   Nevertheless in all sectors the power of veto is prominent, and generally held by the most senior panel member. Indications are that, where consensus is not achieved, the most senior panel member and designated appointing officer (probably the same person in most instances) has his/her say either in making the decision or in applying a veto.

90   However, it should be noted that in all sectors the power of veto is also said to be held by others either instead of or as well as the most senior person on the panel. Notably, around one third of the responses in all sectors named elected Members (or governing/council members) and/or the candidate's prospective line manager as having the power of veto.

91   In addition, it is extremely rare for officers in charge to have the authority to by pass organisational procedures, especially in selecting prospective employees (as opposed to agency staff). This may be indicative of increasing reliance on, and tightness of, formal selection processes.

92   Finally, use of external assistance in any part of the recruitment processes is rare in all sectors.

REFERENCES AND CHECKS

THE KEY FACTS AND ISSUES

- Two references are usually required, but three is also quite common in the voluntary and assisted community homes and private sector

- References are obtained in writing, and sometimes complemented by telephone calls. No telephone only references are sought in any sector

- References are normally sought between short listing and interview, but some appointments are made subject to satisfactory references

- The length of time required for police checks means that people sometimes start jobs before the results of checks are received

- Inter-agency checks such as the DH Consultancy list are used, but less than might have been expected

- It is not consistent practice in any sector to alert other prospective employers about staff leaving about whom concerns exist

- References/checks for agency staff are frequently not made. It appears that this is often because it is known/assumed that this is handled by the agencies themselves.

Number of references sought

93   The most frequently occurring number of references required is two in all sectors, almost invariably including one from the current or most recent employer. However, it is nevertheless quite common practice for voluntary and assisted community homes and the private sector to seek three references, especially for officers in charge.

Means of obtaining references

94   No authority, organisation or home in any sector sought references only by phone. The use of both letter and phone was as follows:

- for local authorities, in about 15 percent of cases for both officers in charge and care officers

- for voluntary organisations and assisted community homes, in about one fifth of cases for officer in charge appointments and one quarter for care officers

- for private sector homes, in a more substantial two fifths of cases for officers in charge and nearly one third for care officers.

Timing of references

95   Around one tenth of voluntary/assisted community and private sector organisations/homes seek references before shortlisting, although this is the practice in no responding local authority.

96   The norm in all sectors is for references to be sought between short listing and interview although the local authority figure contains stark distinction between Counties (all of which seek references at this point) and London Boroughs (a relatively low 42 percent). However, in around one quarter of local authorities (notably in London Boroughs) and voluntary and assisted community homes, references are sought after interview. This practice is more pronounced in the private sector, where post-interview references are sought:

- for officers in charge in nearly two fifths of cases

- for care officers in over one half of cases.

97   Thus, the extent to which appointments are made before the receipt of references varies from just over one tenth of officer in charge appointments in local authorities to over one third of care officer appointments in private sector homes.

98   Nevertheless, several organisations in different sectors note certain safeguards:

- the appointment remains subject to receipt of satisfactory references

- in circumstances where people actually start jobs before references are received, employment may be (and comments indicate sometimes is) terminated if references subsequently received prove unsatisfactory.

Police checks

99   In local authorities, police checks are undertaken in all circumstances. However, police checks are not undertaken in around one tenth of responding voluntary/assisted community and private sector homes. Private sector homes in particular commented upon difficulties in obtaining access to the information they need.

100   The proportion of people starting work before receipt of the results of the police checks appears to be higher for voluntary and assisted community homes and the private sector than for local authorities (where the figure is around 4 percent). One voluntary

organisation noted however that staff starting work before receipt of police checks are not allowed to work unsupervised until satisfactory information is received.

101   More than half of all respondents state more than four weeks as the average time for completion of police checks. Within authorities, this difficulty is particularly acute in London Boroughs, where delay of more than four weeks occurs in over 75 percent of cases. A number of respondents express great frustration at this, noting that in many cases potentially good recruits are therefore lost. This is why some appoint before receipt of police checks; as one local authority respondent put it, "Delaying would cause organisational chaos".

Use of informal inter-authority checks

102   Patterns relating to the use of informal inter-agency checks are:

- a tendency, in just over half of cases, to use the Department of Health consultancy list in local authorities and voluntary assisted community homes, but less so (under one third of cases) in the private sector

- some use in each sector (though heavily outweighed by non-users) of the DES list 99

- rare use of informal telephone calls in all sectors except private homes, who 'always' or 'usually' employ this method in around two fifths of cases.

103   In addition, comments by respondents from the different sectors point to the development of other (often home grown) checking mechanisms such as the maintenance of files within the authority/ organisation/home. These include circulars/letters distributed by other agencies.

104   Concerns about the adequacy of information exchange on potentially unsuitable candidates will be accentuated by the fact that only around half responding authorities (and a slightly higher proportion of respondents from the other sectors) claim 'always' or 'usually' to alert other potential employers about staff leaving their employment about whom there may be concerns. Therefore those agencies maintaining their own files will have at best a partial database.

References/checks for agency staff

105   Around 15 percent of local authority respondents said they made no background checks for agency staff. The figure was slightly lower in the private sector, but higher (at around 25 percent) in the voluntary and assisted community sectors. However, several respondents noted that they required agencies to undertake the prior checks. Two voluntary organisations noted greater difficulties with obtaining suitable references and checks for staff from overseas.

PROBATION

KEY FACTS AND ISSUES

- Probationary periods are virtually always required in private sector homes and other single establishment organisations. Exclusions apply in various circumstances for local authority appointments

- The length of the probationary period is usually six months in all sectors, but there is wider variation in terms of shorter and longer periods in both voluntary/assisted community homes and the private sector

- The rate of probation failure is proportionately higher in the private sector than in voluntary/assisted community homes or local authorities

- Some respondents stressed the benefits of establishing probation as a continuous process of feedback and development rather than a

---

Probationary requirements for new staff

106   Probationary periods are virtually always required in private sector homes and other single establishment organisations. In local authorities the picture is more complex, probation not being required in circumstances where for example the appointment is:

- within the authority (21 percent of authorities)

- from another authority but to a related post (18 percent of authorities)

- from another authority to an unrelated post (14 percent of authorities).

Length of probation

107   The length of the probationary period is six months in over four fifths of local authorities, the largest other response being three months which occurs in around 6 percent of authorities including 15 percent of Metropolitan Boroughs/Districts.

108   A little over half the respondents in each of the other sectors similarly note six months as the length of probation. This creates a more variable picture than in local authorities, in that:

243

- over one fifth of respondents in both the voluntary and assisted community homes and the private homes sector have probationary periods (usually three months) which are less than six months. These are usually of three months duration

- around 15 percent of respondents in the voluntary and assisted community homes sector, and 3 percent in the private sector, have 12 month probationary periods, a response given by no local authority.

109 Around four-fifths of respondents in each sector confirmed the existence of a formal appraisal at the end of the probationary period.

Failing probation

110 In local authorities, it is very rare for officers in charge to fail probation. In only three percent of authorities has this occurred in the last three years, and even then has applied to only one officer in charge in each of the authorities concerned.

111 Local authority care officers failed probation more frequently during the period than officers in charge, although it must be borne in mind that care officers do of course comprise a far higher group. However, the numbers remain small:

- In 70 percent of authorities, no care officers have failed probation

- In 27 percent of authorities, between one and three care officers have failed probation

- In the remaining 3 percent of authorities, more than five care officers have failed probation.

112 The actual number of staff who have failed probation in the voluntary and assisted community homes sector is statistically very similar to that in local authorities. However, since the average number of homes per respondent in this group is far lower than is the case with local authorities (two and nine respectively), the number of failures expressed as a proportion of staff is of course far higher.

113 The number of staff who have failed probation is highest of all in the private sector. This statistic is all the more striking as numbers provided by private sector respondents relate only to one home. The statistics show that:

- around one eighth of private sector homes report one or more probation failures of officers in charge over the last three years

- over three fifths of private sector homes report probationary failure for over one or more care officers; 7 percent report failure for five or more.

114   Tentative explanations might include:

- the practice, more wide scale in the private sector than in the other two sectors, of seeking references after interview, perhaps leading to a greater need for post-appointment weeding out

- less formal procedures in private sector organisations, making it easier in practice to fail staff and terminate employment

Probation as a 'no surprise' process

115   A small number of respondents, particularly in local authorities, pointed to the importance of handling probation as more of a continuous 'no surprises' process of feedback and development, rather than a snapshot final judgement. For example, one authority commented specifically on its practice of holding probationary assessments after 10, 16 and 22 weeks before the final probation report after 26 weeks.

EMPLOYMENT CONTRACTS AND DISCIPLINE

THE KEY FACTS AND ISSUES

- Most local authority employment contracts for residential staff are with single named homes, although there may be a trend towards more generic contracts

- Few authorities seek information on previous disciplinary offences either in application or in interview, although these practices are much more common in the private sector

- Dismissal rates are substantially lower in local authorities than in the other sectors

- Suspension is more frequent in local authorities than either final warnings or dismissals, but is not necessarily part of the formal disciplinary process

---

Workbase

116   Two thirds of local authority employment contracts are with a single home, although nearly a quarter specify for placement anywhere within the authority. Contracts with named single homes are most prominent in Counties; a contract for placement anywhere within a large geographical area would presumably affect the attraction of residential work in many counties. Some respondents however note that contracts increasingly specify placement anywhere, presumably as a practical response to the rapidly changing type and amount of residential care provided within authorities.

117   A higher proportion of employment contracts in the other sectors are with single homes, reflecting the predominant single establishment structure of these groups.

Information on recruits' disciplinary history

118   A number of respondents express concern at authorities' failure to elicit information on candidate's disciplinary history, either at application or interview stage. Indeed, 85 percent of authorities 'never' seek this information at application stage and nearly two-thirds 'never' ask at interview.

119   This information is sought a little, but not substantially, more by voluntary and assisted community homes. However the pattern is different for private sector homes, which 'always' seek this information on application in 44 percent of cases and in interview in 52 percent of cases.

Use of disciplinary procedures

120   One authority respondent points out the challenge of helping staff "to deal with difficult behaviour against a background of 'do not's". Another stresses that staff on probation or short term contracts would not require dismissal under disciplinary procedures. Bearing these points in mind, prevalence of the use of disciplinary procedures in the different sectors over the last three years is set out in the table below:

	Subject to any part of disciplinary procedure			Given formal final warning			Dismissed		
	Local authorities	Voluntary/ asst'd community homes	Private homes	Local authorities	Voluntary/ asst'd community homes	Private homes	Local authorities	Voluntary/ asst'd community homes	Private homes
Proportion of respondents reporting 0-2% of staff	24%	38%	66%	82%	83%	78%	82%	70%	68%
Proportion of respondents reporting >2-5% of staff	38%	19%	8%	16%	4%	0%	16%	17%	13%
Proportion of respondents reporting >5-8% of staff	20%	10%	8%	0%	9%	13%	2%	0%	3%
Proportion of respondents reporting >8% of staff	18%	33%	18%	2%	4%	9%	0%	13%	16%

121   Two key points to emerge from this table are:

- comparison of the responses from the different sectors shows that relatively low proportions of staff have been subject to any part of the disciplinary procedures in the private sector. By contrast, relatively high proportions have been subject to formal final warning. This contrast may suggest an earlier, less 'hierarchical' use of formal final warnings in private homes than in the other sectors

- dismissal rates in local authorities are substantially lower than in other sectors. Tentative explanations might be the relatively formal, final and lengthy nature of this procedure in local authorities and the existence of various means whereby it is not reached or carried out.

Use of suspension

122   Analysis of the prevalence of suspension in local authorities over the last three years shows it to be more frequently used than final formal warnings or dismissals. Eight percent or more staff have been suspended in over 6 percent of local authorities, whereas only 2 percent of local authorities have given formal warnings to 8 percent or more of staff, and none have dismissed such a proportion of staff.

123   This may indicate the use of suspension in local authorities as a 'no prejudice' mechanism outside formal disciplinary procedures. One authority respondent comments specifically that suspension does not "prejudice the outcome" but is used "to enable an investigation to take place". Another respondent indicates extreme difficulties when allogations made by children about staff are subject to lengthy police enquiries resulting in no prosecution.

Retirement or resignation during disciplinary proceedings

124   To examine means by which disciplinary proceedings might in practice be avoided, the questionnaires asked respondents how many staff involved in disciplinary proceedings had resigned or retired before the completion of proceedings over the 1989 to 1992 period. In all sectors the numbers were very low indeed.

Dismissal decisions

126   In over half local authorities, the Director of Social Services has the power to dismiss. With the agreement of the Personnel Department, he/she can dismiss in a further third of cases. This leaves about 9 percent of authorities in which Member approval is required, a figure which is highest in London Boroughs (13 percent).

127   The evidence suggests that Members overturn dismissal decisions only during the course of appeals (and even then in no authority more than once during the last three years).

INDUCTION, TRAINING AND SUPERVISION

THE KEY FACTS AND ISSUES

- Sixty percent of local authorities have statements of minimum training requirements for residential staff. This figure is lower than that in the private sector, but higher than in voluntary and assisted community homes.

- Formal induction is provided in around 75 percent of authorities for officers in charge and in over 80 percent of authorities for care officers

- The availability of training appears to demonstrate policy commitment to providing some relevant training for as many staff as possible

- Appraisal systems exist in 30 percent of local authorities for officers in charge and in 18 percent for care officers. The figures are higher for the other sectors

- Formal supervision of care officers by officers in charge takes place fortnightly to monthly in nearly all cases

---

Minimum training requirements

128   Around 60 percent of local authorities have a statement of minimum training requirements for officers in charge, and 13 percent for care officers. For both staff groups such statements are most common in County authorities.

129   A higher proportion of private sector organisations, but a smaller proportion of voluntary/assisted community homes, have such statements in place when compared with local authorities' figures.

Formal induction

130   Formal induction is provided in around three quarters of authorities for officers in charge, and in over four fifths of authorities for care officers. Comparison of these figures with the other sectors shows that, by some margin, the most frequently occurring and most lengthy induction is provided in the private sector. (It should however be added that there could be some discrepancy over what constitutes induction.)

131   The lesser frequency for officers in charge of formal induction than for care officers may reflect the ease of on-site induction by more senior people for care officers.

132   In the large majority of cases in all sectors, induction commences within the first two weeks in post.

133   Respondents were asked about the content of induction. Induction programmes in all sectors include, in at least 75 percent of cases in each sector:

- time with managers senior to the officer in charge. (This was naturally less applicable to care officers)

- guidance on departmental child care policy and procedures

- full guide to the home's aims, structure and methods

- requirements of the 1989 Children Act.

134 Guidance on handling violent behaviour, while less frequently provided, nevertheless takes place during induction in two thirds of cases in all sectors. Interestingly, it is more common for care officers than officers in charge to receive such guidance, perhaps reflecting the greater experience and qualification base of officers in charge.

135 'Time in other establishments' was for all sectors the least frequently occurring induction component among the possibilities listed in the questionnaire. Single home organisations are clearly not in a position to provide such a programme, at least within their own organisation. However this does not apply in local authorities, whose relatively low use of this induction component may reflect practical considerations such as difficulties in providing cover.

Training eligibility and provision

136 A small number of authorities report or imply the existence of many staff who lack the training or experience to move residential care, as one respondent put it, "from child-minding to an active therapeutic service". Nevertheless the large majority of staff in all sectors are eligible to receive assistance for training. This applies especially to staff (whether qualified or not) seeking training which, while relevant, does not lead to qualifications. In addition, extensive eligibility for 'relevant' (rather than qualification) training probably reflects policies that spread training resources thinly across larger numbers of staff rather than concentrate on relatively expensive secondments for smaller numbers of staff.

137 However, authorities' additional comments suggest that the issue is not eligibility but funding, not only for the training itself but also for cover in the work environment. This cover becomes especially important if residential staff are trained as teams, which is seen as helpful in promoting team building and cohesion.

138 Implementation of 'spread thinly' policies is also indicated by take up of assistance for training in the year ending 31 March 1992, as indicated in the table below:

	Local authorities		Voluntary and assisted community homes		Private sector homes	
	OICs	COs	OICs	COs	OICs	COs
Proportion of cases in which 30 percent or more staff received assistance towards professional qualifications (year ending 31/3/92)	12%	5%	9%	21%	12%	23%
Proportion of cases in which 30 percent or more staff received assistance for relevant training, but not leading to qualifications (year ending 31/3/92)	80%	79%	65%	75%	52%	49%

139   The table appears to demonstrate the commitment, particularly in local authorities, to providing some relevant training for as many staff as possible. Nevertheless, one local authority respondent draws attention to the dependence of successful in house training upon a positive climate, made difficult at a time of residential care reduction and consequent staff anxiety.

Supervision

140   Formal appraisal systems exist as a component of supervision processes in 30 percent of authorities for officers in charge and in 18 percent of authorities for care officers. This summary statistic however contains significant variation between authority types, especially between Metropolitan Boroughs/Districts (where the figures are 8 percent for officers in charge and 4 percent for care officers) and Counties (54 percent and 32 percent respectively).

141   Over half the organisations or homes in the other sectors have appraisal systems for both officer in charge and care officers. However the involvement of people other than line managers in appraising staff in these sectors is less common than in local authorities.

142   Formal supervision of care officers by officers in charge takes place fortnightly to monthly in nearly all cases. Although interpretation of formal supervision may vary between sectors, it is useful to note that, for voluntary and assisted community homes, formal supervision takes place around weekly or more in nearly one quarter of cases, and, for the private sector, in nearly one half of cases.

143   Frequency of supervision may not, however, be the key. One authority respondent refers to "the vicious circle in which staff require supervision by more senior practitioners who are not trained to provide it".

144   Specialist advice is available, at least to some extent, to homes in the large majority of authorities (particularly Counties) whether or not the homes have a specialist therapeutic role. Figures for the other sectors show similarly high levels of such advice, particularly from psychotherapists for homes with specialist therapeutic roles.

145   Ninety-two percent of authorities report visits of elected members to their homes, although well over half of these visits are less than monthly. To the extent that comparisons can be drawn with the role of lay/governing bodies in the voluntary and assisted community homes sector, it may be useful to note that the regularity of their visits is greater, ie monthly or more in over three quarters of cases.

146   Such visits appears to be supported by clear and formal mechanisms for feedback to more senior officers in most cases.

INSPECTION AND COMPLAINTS

THE KEY FACTS AND ISSUES

- Monitoring by line managers is, not surprisingly more frequent than formal inspections by units

- Visits at night are undertaken less by line managers, (but more by inspection units), in local authorities than in the other sectors

- Arrangements for the investigation of complaints are extensive in all sectors

- The use of leaflets to inform children of complaints procedures is more common in local authorities than in the other sectors.

- Voluntary/assisted community homes and private sector homes are more confident than local authorities that they have adequate advocacy systems in place, and that children with communication difficulties are properly represented

- Most authorities have arrangements whereby care officers can make complaints to, and receive confidential counselling and support from, more senior staff outside the home and outside the line management structure.

Inspections

147   Local authorities demonstrate, both in policy and practice, what might be an expected distinction between the respective roles of line managers and inspection units. Thus, whereas inspection unit inspections are normally (or will be) carried out six monthly, line managers' monitoring is carried out more frequently.

148   However, less than one quarter of authorities reported mechanisms or checks to ensure that policy requirements regarding inspection are actually carried out. This may be one implication of an 'arms length' relationship of inspection units to the department.

149   These questions may be less applicable to, or at least require different interpretation in, the other sectors. Nevertheless, around half or more respondents from voluntary/assisted community homes and private sector homes reported formal inspections by line managers and/or an internal inspection unit taking place quarterly or more frequently.

150   The table below shows the proportionate frequency of different types of inspectorial visits in the different sectors:

	Local authorities		Voluntary and assisted community homes		Private sector homes	
	Line Managers	Inspection Unit	Line Managers	Inspection Unit	Line Managers	Inspection Unit
Proportion of respondents reporting night inspection visits	56%	81%	62%	45%	76%	49%
Proportion of respondents reporting unannounced inspection visits	90%	88%	100%	67%	77%	64%
Proportion of respondents reporting pre-arranged visits	90%	87%	88%	63%	85%	81%

151   One particular point to emerge from the statistics is the greater proportion of night visits by line managers which take place in voluntary/assisted community homes and private sector homes than in local authorities. This is balanced however by the lesser night visit frequency of the inspection units in these sectors. (Again, however, care needs to be taken as the meaning of an internal inspection unit may be less prescribed in assisted community and private sector homes).

Prevalence of arrangements for the investigation of complaints

152   Formal arrangements for the investigation of complaints made by staff, the children and children's families/representatives are common in all three sectors, and especially in local authorities.

153   Almost all local authorities also have in place arrangements whereby complaints for investigation can be made by members of the public or their representatives. This is less pronounced in the voluntary/assisted community homes sector and in the private sector, but the proportions with such arrangements are in both cases around two-thirds.

Complaints by children

154   Almost all local authorities have arrangements whereby children can make complaints outside the line management of the home. In 84 percent of cases this can be done privately, eg by the use of freephone facilities, tear-off slips to the Director, or direct access to the Chief Inspector or Children's Rights Officer. However, one authority drew

attention to the implications of such facilities, noting a "difficulty in respecting residents' rights without debilitating staff".

155   The proportion of homes in the other sectors with such practices is broadly similar.

156   In nearly two-thirds of authorities, and most notably in Counties, children are made aware of complaints procedures through the use of leaflets either before or on arrival. In the other sectors the proportions are lower, this practice taking place in around 50 percent of cases.

157   In around one quarter of authorities, verbal methods are used to inform children of complaints procedures, usually before or on arrival in the home. As would be expected given the relatively higher absence of leaflets in the other sectors, their use of verbal methods is higher than in local authorities.

Use of advocates

158   When asked whether systems are in place whereby children can have advocates of their choice external to the social services department, 23 percent responded with a clear 'Yes' and 17 percent with a clear 'No'. Sixty one percent of authorities responded to 'To some extent', and several comments indicated that such systems tend to be at development stages and are not yet felt to be complete or satisfactory. Some authorities have forged relationships with voluntary organisations to support advocacy arrangements.

159   Voluntary and assisted community homes and private sector homes both gave a higher proportion (over a third in each case) of clear 'Yes' responses. This may indicate relative ease in establishing such systems in single home organisations or, as stated earlier, a tendency to apply less strict criteria in responding.

Representation of children with communication difficulties

160   Forty percent of all local authorities (including 50 percent of London Boroughs) state that policies are in place to ensure the proper representation of children with communication difficulties, and two thirds monitor adherence to such policies. Responses in both the other sectors are higher.

Complaints by, and support for, care officers

161   In a little over two thirds of authorities, care officers have guidance on circumstances in which they should make a formal compliant. Again, in both voluntary/assisted community homes and the private sector the proportion giving this response is higher.

162   The proportion of local authorities in which care officers can make complaints to more senior staff outside the home and outside the line management structure is 80 percent and 65 percent respectively. In addition, care officers in local authorities have access to private and confidential counselling support outside the line management structure in around two thirds of authorities (including in 72 percent of London Boroughs).

163   Other sectors are less amenable to analysis in these respects, since the large majority are single home establishments. Nevertheless, the very high proportion of private sector homes which make arrangements for care officers to have such confidential advice and support, at 85 percent, is worthy of note.

CONTRACTS BETWEEN AGENCIES

THE KEY FACTS AND ISSUES

- All local authorities place children in independent sector homes

- Forty percent of local authorities report contracts to be in place with such homes. Of this 40 percent, two thirds note the following service specification elements to be in place: service aims and objectives, service inputs, care tasks, monitoring/evaluation arrangements and means of handling complaints

- Less frequently specified elements are: staff qualifications and training, service outputs and service quality standards

- Similar patterns are reported by voluntary/assisted community homes and the private sector.

Use of independent sector homes

164   All local authorities make placements in independent sector homes. This includes the use of consortia arrangements to provide care for children with special needs, eg the London regional establishments. In 40 percent of cases formal contracts are in place, though markedly more so in London Boroughs (54 percent) than in Metropolitan Boroughs/Districts (24 percent). Some other authorities report setting up contracts on an as/when required basis, particularly where the level of demand for a particular service is not anticipated to be high.

165   Just under half the voluntary and assisted community homes report formal contracts with social services departments to be 'always' or 'usually' in place; for private sector homes the equivalent proportion is nearly two thirds. One voluntary organisation noted the national advantage to voluntary and private sector homes of 'block' rather than case by case contracts, although local authority reluctance to block contract was understood.

166   One authority points to the potential use of service specification as the basis for "developing partnership relationships with external organisations attempting to fill this gap in the market". In addition, some authorities retain anxieties about the capacity of some private and voluntary sector providers to stick with some of the more disturbed children, and for that reason are particularly keen to define and agree placement termination criteria and arrangements.

Service specification elements

167   Over two thirds of authorities which use contracts 'always' or 'usually' have the following service specification elements in place:

- aims and objectives of the services

- service inputs (staffing facilities etc)

- care tasks and style

- monitoring/evaluation arrangements

- means of handling complaints.

168   Less frequently specified elements (but still contained in one third to one half of authorities using contracts) are:

- staff qualifications and training provided

- service outputs

- service quality standards.

169   Broadly similar patterns of service specification content can be discerned upon analysis of responses from voluntary/assisted community and private sector homes. Indeed, there appears to be a growing tendency for larger voluntary organisations to take the initiative in developing partnership agreements with local authorities, with such agreements incorporating service specification elements such as those above. This appears to be generally productive, although one authority noted that "there is sometimes conflict around the question of 'whose contract?'" where contracts developed by both agencies are not easily compatible.

APPENDIX 4: BIBLIOGRAPHY

This Bibliography lists only those publications which are referred to in the text of the Report.

General

DEPARTMENT OF HEALTH. (1991): *"The Children Act 1989: Guidance and Regulations Volume 4 - Residential Care"*. HMSO, London.

DEPARTMENT OF HEALTH. (1991): *"Children in Care of Local Authorities Year ending 31 March 1990"*. Government Statistical Service.

Chapter 1

WAGNER, G. (1987): *"Residential Care - A Positive Choice"*. HMSO, London.

UTTING, W. (1991): *"Children in the Public Care. A Review of Residential Child Care"*. HMSO, London.

SOCIAL SERVICES INSPECTORATE - WALES and SOCIAL INFORMATION SYSTEMS LTD. (1992): *"Accommodating Children. A Review of Children's Homes in Wales"*. Welsh Office.

HOWE, E. (1992): *"The Quality of Care. A Report of the Residential Staffs Inquiry"*. Local Government Management Board.

KAHAN, B and LEVY, A. (1991): *"The Pindown Experience and the Protection of Children. Report of the Staffordshire child care inquiry"*. Staffordshire County Council.

WILLIAMS, G and MACREADIE, J. (1992): *"Ty Mawr Community Home Inquiry"*. Gwent County Council.

HUGHES, W H. (1985): *"Report of the Committee of Inquiry into Children's Homes and Hostels"*. HMSO, Belfast.

Chapter 2

BERRIDGE, D. (1985): *"Children's Homes"*. Basil Blackwell.

CURTIS COMMITTEE (1946): *"Report of the Care of Children Committee"*. Cmd. 6922.

WILLIAMS COMMITTEE (1967): *"Caring for People: Staffing Residential Homes"*. Allan and Unwin.

BEEDELL, C. (1970): *"Residential Life with Children"*. Routledge and Keegan Paul.

LONDON BOROUGHS REGIONAL CHILDREN'S PLANNING COMMITTEE (1991): *"A Strategy for Residential Child Care in London 1991-2000"*. LBRCPC, London.

KNAPP, M and SMITH, J (1985): *The Costs of Residential Child Care: Explaining Variations in the Public Sector"*. Policy and Politics, Vol. 13, No. 2.

MOSS, M. (1990): *"Abuse in the Care System: A Pilot Study by the National Association of Young People in Care"*. NAYPIC, London.

WESTCOTT, H. (1991): *"Institutional Abuse of Children - From Research to policy: A Review"*. NSPCC, London.

CLIFFE, D and BERRIDGE, D. (1991): *"Closing Children's Homes - An end to residential Child Care?"*. National Children's Bureau, London.

RUTTER, M, QUINTON, D and LIDDLE, C. (1983): *"Parenting in Two Generations: Looking Backwrads and Looking Forwards"*, in N.MADGE (ed.), Families at Risk. Heinneman.

Chapter 4

BHALLA, P and RIDDLE, P. (1992): *"Psychometric Tests and Racial Equality"*. Commission for Racial Equality, London.

ARAJI, S and FINKELHORN, D. (1985): *"Explanations of paedophilia: a review of empirical research"*. Bulletin of the American Academy of Psychiatry and Law, 13, 17-37.

BLINKHORN, S and JOHNSON, C. (1991): *"Personality Tests: the Great Debate. The Case"*. Personality Management.

GRANLEES, J, HENDERSON, P, BROWN, K and TURNER, I F. (Undated): *"Report to the DHSS on Child Abuse in Institutions: The utility and efficiency of psychological tests in personnel selection of child care staff"*. The Queen's University of Belfast.

HADDOCK, M D and MCQUEEN, W. (1983): *"Assessing Employee Potential for Abuse"*. Journal of Clinical Psychology, 39, 1021-1029.

MILNER, J and WIMBERLY, R. (1979): *"An inventory for the identification of child abusers"*. Journal of Clinical Psychology 35, 95-100.

MILNER, J and WIMBERLY, R. (1980): *"Prediction and explanation of child abuse"*. Journal of Clinical Psychology, 36, 875-884.

SAVILLE, P, NYFIELD, G, SIK, G and HACKSTON, J. (1991): *"Enhancing the Person-Job Match Through Personality Assessment"*. Paper presented at the Annual Conference of the American Psychological Association, San Francisco.

WILSON, R and LESLIE, J. (1987): *"Assessing the Propensity for Child Sexual Abuse of Applicants for Posts in Residential Care: A review of the literature"*. University of Ulster.

Chapter 5

THE HOME OFFICE. (1991): *"The National Collection of Criminal Records. Report of An Efficiency Scrutiny"*. Home Office.

PARKER, R. (1990): *"Safeguarding Standards"*. National Institute for Social Work.

Chapter 6

SOCIAL SERVICES INSPECTORATE. (1991): *"The Right to Complain. Practice Guidance on Complaints Procedures in social services Departments"*. HMSO, London.

Chapter 7

BARR, H> (1987): *"Perspectives on Training for Residential Work"* (CCETSW Study 8). The Central Council for Education and Training in Social Work.

Printed in the UK for HMSO Dd 0295537 12/92 C40 3937 12521